ALWAYS A DISTANT ANCHORAGE

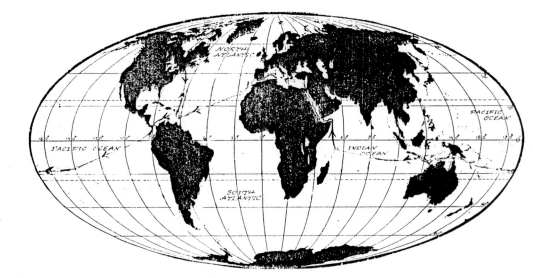

BOOKS BY HAL ROTH

Pathway in the Sky
Two on a Big Ocean
After 50,000 Miles
Two Against Cape Horn
The Longest Race
Always a Distant Anchorage

Always
A Distant Anchorage

by HAL ROTH

PHOTOGRAPHS BY THE AUTHOR

MAPS BY DALE SWENSSON

W · W · NORTON & COMPANY

New York   London

134

Published simultaneously in Canada by Penguin Books Canada Ltd,
2801 John Street, Markham, Ontario L3R 1B4
Printed in the United States of America.

The text of this book is composed in Bembo,
with display type set in Bembo.
Composition by ComCom.
Manufacturing by the Murray Printing Company.
Book design by Jacques Chazaud.

First Edition

Library of Congress Cataloging in Publication Data

Roth, Hal.
Always a distant anchorage / by Hal Roth; photographs by the author; maps by Dale
Swensson.—1st ed.
p.   cm.
1. Whisper (Yacht)   2. Roth, Hal—Journeys.   3. Voyage around the
world—1981–   1. Title.
G440.W616R67 1988
910.4′1—dc19   88-29219

ISBN 0-393-03312-0

W. W. Norton & Company, Inc., 500 Fifth Avenue, New York, N. Y. 10110
W. W. Norton & Company Ltd., 37 Great Russell Street, London WC1B 3NU

1 2 3 4 5 6 7 8 9 0

To Margaret

the best mate
a man ever had

Contents

. . . .

Maps

. . . .

Photographs

. . . .

NOTE: Every country in the world (including Canada and Mexico) except the United States uses the metric system for weights and measurements. Since this book is about a world voyage, I have used the metric system throughout except in a few places. Here are some handy equivalents:

LENGTH:

1 inch = 25.4 millimeters or 2.54 centimeters
1 foot = 304.8 millimeters or 30.48 centimeters or .3048 meters
1 yard = .914 meter
1 meter = 3.28 feet
1 meter = 100 centimeters = 1,000 millimeters

VOLUME:

1 quart = .946 liter
1 gallon = 3.785 liters
1 liter = 1.057 quarts = .264 gallons

AREA:

1 square foot = 929 square centimeters or .0929 square meters
1 square yard = .836 square meter
1 square meter = 1.196 square yards or 10.76 square feet

WEIGHT:

1 ounce (avoirdupois) = 28.35 grams
1 pound = 453.59 grams = .453 kilograms
100 grams = 3.527 ounces
1 kilogram = 2.2 pounds
1 long ton = 2,240 pounds = 1.016 metric tons = 1,018 kilograms
1 metric ton = 2,204.7 pounds
1 gallon of fresh water (3.785 liters) weighs 8.33 pounds or 3.77 kilograms (and occupies 231 cubic inches).
1 gallon of salt water (3.785 liters) weighs 8.556 pounds or 3.875 kilograms.
1 liter of fresh water weighs 1 kilo or 2.2 pounds.
1 liter of salt water weighs 1.02 kilos or 2.26 pounds.

ALWAYS A DISTANT ANCHORAGE

Looking back at Mt. Desert Island, Maine

. . . .

CHAPTER ONE

Toward Bermuda

*I*t was a cool day in late July when Margaret and I sailed from Somes Sound in Maine toward Bermuda. I pulled on a wool sweater and nudged the tiller with my thigh, while Margaret coiled up a line and heaved it into a locker. A trifling wind scarcely filled our biggest sails, yet the breeze pushed us slowly to the south-southeast as the mountainous coastline of Maine's Mt. Desert area opened out and began to recede behind us. By midnight the wind had collapsed completely, so we left a bright light burning and turned in on a tranquil Atlantic.

At dawn we were poking along in light southerlies, wondering what had happened to the easterlies so eloquently described by the weatherman. From time to time we saw fishing boats—mostly draggers—heading to and from the banks south of us. During the afternoon we watched a handsome blue and white cruise ship, *Caribe* of Bremen, all flags flying, steam eastward. Suddenly the big vessel came to a stop, paused, and then headed off to the northwest, a thoroughly mystifying performance. Had someone on the bridge made a mistake? Was James Bond on board?

We sailed on a wonderful magic carpet named *Whisper,* a 10.7-meter black-hulled fiberglass cutter designed by John Brandlmayr and built by the Spencer Boat Works in Vancouver, Canada. The yacht measured 8.5 meters on the waterline, had a beam of 2.90 meters, and, when fully laden for a long voyage, displaced about 7.20 tons, roughly a ton and three-quarters over her designed weight of 5.45 metric tons. In this condition she drew 1.80 meters.

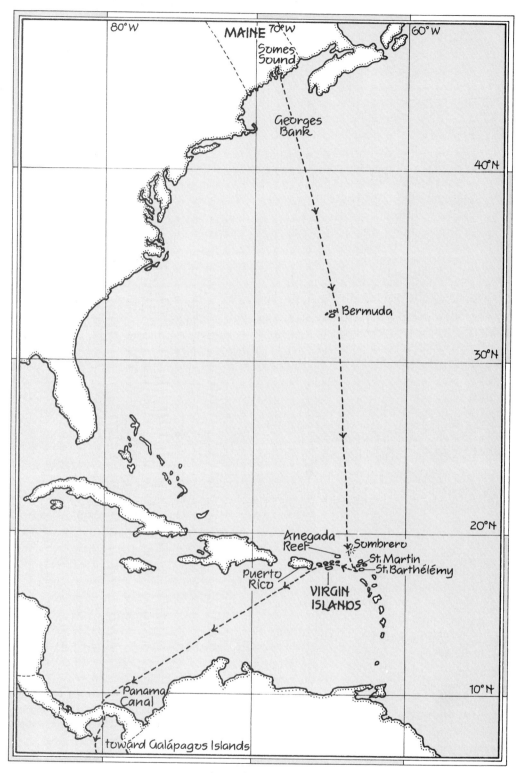

1. Maine to Panama

If you're old-fashioned and think in feet, *Whisper* measured 35 feet long and 28 feet on the waterline. Her beam was 9.5 feet, her draft was 5.9 feet, and she weighed about 12,000 pounds empty.

Over the years we worked out many structural modifications, generally to make the yacht more watertight, to simplify her handling and maintenance, and to make her more pleasant to live on. We added a little sail area (she totaled 62 square meters, or 663 square feet) to help her light air performance, and broke her foretriangle area into a more easily managed staysail and jib. Just before the voyage I made a new and very streamlined rudder, and we added a folding propeller for the one-cylinder, eleven-horsepower auxiliary diesel engine. *Whisper* sailed well, she was fun to live on, and Margaret and I were quite attached to our little floating home.

It was late on the second night while I was watching four fishing boats that I suddenly saw searchlights in the sky. "I've gone mad," I muttered to myself. "Completely bonkers." I splashed water into my sleepy eyes. But I kept looking. All at once I realized that I was seeing the northern lights, which appeared as enormous streaks of silvery paint that a giant hand seemed to have brushed vertically up and down on the arctic side of the midnight sky. It was magic. I had never seen the aurora borealis before, and the strange flickering lights were a stupendous sight, much larger and grander and more mysterious than I had imagined.

By the end of the third day the southerly wind had freshened precisely from the direction of where we wanted to go. (The Chileans have a saying: "The wind always blows from the bow of the ship.") Tacking would have done little to have improved our position. Besides, there were patches of whitish fog in the air, so north of Georges Bank we hove to for a rest. *Whisper*'s daily runs of forty, fifty-two, and thirty miles on our first three days were simply terrible. We were near the boundary of the cold Labrador current and the warm Gulf Stream, however, so we looked for a weather change, hopefully for the better. When the shift finally came, though, it was surprisingly decisive.

[From the log] July 27th. 1510. Never have I seen such a contrast in a few hours. First we were heeled over with wind and seas from the southwest. Then no wind at all, an up-and-down mixed-up swell, and the start of a northwest wind. The face of the ocean was covered with heaped-up small seas. Pyramids jumping up, holes between swells, and suddenly little erupting waterfalls. While I was kneeling on deck dealing with some lines, a rogue wavelet quietly hopped on board behind me and surprised me by suddenly filling my boots with cold water.

The yacht was jumping all over the place, and soon we began to dip first one deck, then the other. The crazy seas filled the cockpit several times,

and small waves—flying everywhere—even gushed through the Dorade
ventilators. The ocean was a mass of bubbling overfalls. The noise was
astonishing. Certainly we were in shoal water.

Fishing draggers worked in the distance, and thousands of screaming sea
birds flitted about near us. Obviously we were in prime fishing waters. Too
bad that I am the world's worst fisherman and at that moment had no appetite
at all. Finally I knew what the banks fishermen meant when they said that
even the codfish got seasick.

All this commotion lasted only a short time. A few miles to the south
the seas smoothed out and the fair northwest wind strengthened. The mad
scene on Georges Bank was over. Soon we had the running rig up, were on
course for Bermuda, and were laughing and peeling off the woolens under
our oilskins because it had become warm, even hot. And like all zany sailors,
I was busy calculating how many more days it would take to make our
landfall, based on a few fragments of fair winds. Sure enough, a little after
midnight the breeze was back in the south and fitful and erratic. Finally, on
July 30th the wind got up to twenty knots and then veered to the west-
southwest, where it stayed for a day and gave us 116 miles in the right
direction. That night *Whisper*'s wake was a glowing trail of greenish fire.
At last we were making good time.

Margaret and I stood watch and watch, and we slept a lot during the
daytime. We generally saw one or two ships every twenty-four hours. Once
at midnight we passed close to a large vessel that was mysteriously stopped
and showed two vertical red not-under-command lights.

We sailed across masses of yellow gulfweed, daffodil bright against the
hard blue of the warm ocean. Some of the clusters of the sun-colored plants
were the size of a man's head; others had collected into accumulations as long
as the yacht and made gentle swishing noises when we passed over them. The
batches of gulfweed are kept afloat by berrylike air sacs, and the close-packed
branches are home for tiny shrimps and crabs and strange pea-sized creatures.
Each clump of the golden gulfweed seemed a separate star in an ocean
universe.

The water temperature increased to twenty-seven degrees Celsius or
eighty degrees Fahrenheit. We scrimmaged with a nervous west wind that
gradually veered to the north and then east with compensating sail changes
and logged runs of 131 and 96 miles. Two white-tailed tropicbirds with
rasping, high-pitched calls, rapid wing flaps, and long, swordlike tail feathers
circled round and round before noon one day. These birds nested on Bermuda, which began to announce itself on the broadcast band of the radio.
August 1st (some said August 15th) was the beginning of the hurricane season,
and we were anxious to find a secure harbor. We continued with a good deal
of sail drill in squally weather and little by little began to see flying fish and
bright blue skies.

Before dawn on August 3rd we hove-to near several cruise ships that were standing off Bermuda waiting to make a grand entrance after the passengers' breakfast. *Whisper* was in soundings, and the hard purplish blue of the deep ocean had become the light bubbly green of shallow water. The weather continued unsettled, with rain and clear weather standing watch and watch.

A little after first light the cruise ships got under way and soon disappeared into rain showers. At 0825 Margaret worked out a position and passed me a course for Northeast Breaker buoy, which appeared on schedule at 0920. We still had to sail around the reefs east of Bermuda, but now we recognized landmarks and steered from buoy to buoy before we hardened up to beat into St. George via the narrow entry of Town Cut, which is always exciting to tack through into the smooth water of Bermuda's easternmost harbor.

Foolishly (and we really knew better), we had failed to flake down our anchor chain properly when we left Maine, and the rolling sea passage had tumbled the piled-up chain into a horror of tangles. I pulled and tugged from on deck, but the chain was jammed. We finally dropped a second anchor and line. Margaret then sorted out the mess in the chain locker while I hauled all the galvanized iron links on deck. We vowed never again to sail with the chain piled in a conelike heap.

We stayed in Bermuda for two and a half months and found it a surprising place for an island with only twenty-one square miles of land. The low, coral-bound, hook-shaped island is fifteen miles long, roughly one mile wide, and is surrounded by dozens of small bays, sounds, and beaches. The 58,000 residents of this British crown colony live mainly on tourism and offshore banking, and the island was fairly bursting with vitality and fashionable living. Luxury hotels peered down at us from many of the choice hilltops, and here and there we saw stunning homes that belonged to an international circle of English-speaking people—some extremely wealthy—who generally kept low profiles and were out of sight to the casual tourist. Since everything except the weather and the local lobsters and fish was imported, the living costs were high.

Bermuda's climate was warm and inviting, her gardens and flowering trees luxuriant, and swimming and sailing were big pastimes. There were splendid restaurants and nightclubs with famous performers. Behind the tourist facade, however, hovered a complex social and business structure that seemed remarkable for such a small island. Although the black population (70 percent) was well looked after, a few key white families controlled much of the island's commerce. I felt that I was visiting a well-oiled corporation instead of an island nation. "How long can the oligarchy continue?" I wondered.

Margaret and I found the island orderly and the people extremely friendly. After a few days in St. George we began to sail around Bermuda

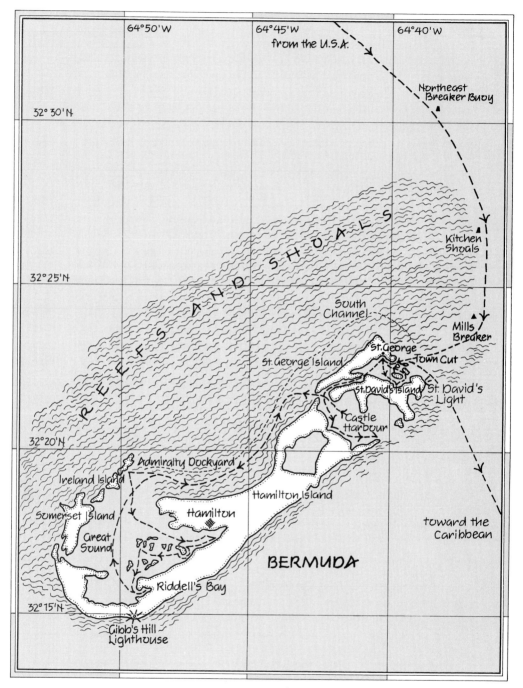

2. Bermuda

and eventually visited every part of the island and somehow managed to log 149 miles. There were three hurricane alerts during our stay. We passed the first at the old Admiralty Dockyard, where we tied to enormous bollards with a forest of lines. One of the Bermuda tugs pulled in behind us, and her crew quickly lashed the squat, big ship tender to the hurricane bollards with four-inch-diameter hawsers passed back and forth. After the tug was secure, her captain strolled over to inspect our lines.

"Hey, mon," he said. "Why you tied up with dem little strings? Let me give you something you *needs!*" The captain sent his crew over with spare two-inch hawsers that we barely managed to secure around our winches and cleats.

We spent the next two hurricane alerts in Riddell's Bay near Gibb's Hill lighthouse, where we were lent a colossal mooring—an old, big ship's anchor and chain that must have weighed at least two tons. With a length of new twelve-millimeter chain shackled to the dinner-plate-sized thirty-six-millimeter links, we felt very secure, especially since we were inside a landlocked harbor. In spite of a lot of talk, however, none of the cyclones materialized, although there was a big scare one night when the U.S. Navy announced that a huge storm—code-named Emily—was about to blast the island. The authorities closed the schools, shopkeepers boarded up windows, and everyone bit his fingernails. The radio stations chanted warnings all night, and Bermudians were told to collect emergency food supplies and to have flashlights ready in case the power system broke down. In the resulting run on the stores, three-dollar flashlights were soon bid up to ten and twelve dollars. Unfortunately, the twelve-dollar flashlight buyers were unable to buy batteries because they had all been sold.

"What bastards there are in this world," shrieked one customer, who clutched his useless twelve-dollar flashlight in the Riddell's Bay supermarket. "I'se been ripped off ah-ginn."

Margaret and I stripped off *Whisper's* sails, unrove the halyards, sank the dinghy, and moved all the deck gear below into the cabin. In an hour the yacht was as sleek as a seal. A big U.S. television network had flown in a camera team "to record the devastation," but the storm never came, and the sheepish forecasters pretended not to hear the insults hurled their way. Flashlights were back to three dollars.

The old Bermudians who lived near St. David's light at the east end of the island laughed at the forecasters with their weather satellites, clacking teletypewriters, and computer printouts. The white-haired boatmen and fishermen did *their* hurricane predicting with shark liver oil, which they bottled and hung in special places. When bad weather threatened, the shark oil—evidently sensitive to low barometric pressure—became cloudy. Various intriguing opaque patterns then appeared in the oil, and the locals claimed that they could predict the size, force, and direction of an approaching storm by reading the patterns in the oil. All this smacked of witchcraft, folklore, and gypsy tea rooms, but the record of the shark oil watchers was fully as good as that of the professional weathermen (who gnashed their teeth at the mention of shark oil).

"Dem navy guys is confusing theirselves with all dem machines," the locals would say. "Wot de captain he need is de shark oil."

Of course most of the yachtsmen bought bottles of shark oil and made friends with the old-timers from St. David's. Every morning the first item of conversation was, "Hey, mon. How's de shark oil?"

Our neighbors in Riddell's Bay were Bobby and Penny Doe and their two daughters, who lived on a fifty-eight-foot three-master named *Christian Venturer*. The yacht was big and roomy, and though only four years old (and locally built of Airex, fiberglass, and epoxy), she had the feel of a traditional fishing craft with long lean lines, lots of sheer, and masses of rigging wires. The Does caught their fresh water from rain and made electricity from a generator that was powered by a big, slow-turning propeller driven by the wind. When you saw *Christian Venturer* from a distance, your eyes always went to that rotating propeller. . . .

Bobby was short, powerfully built, and a seaman through and through. He had entered his vessel in a Tall Ships race and had crisscrossed the Atlantic at least three times—once with a crew of cadets, once with his wife Penny,

View north across Riddell Bay, Bermuda

and once by himself. Bobby was the most successful commercial fisherman in Bermuda and had worked out a scheme to catch large groupers—those dark fish with enormous girth whose filets and steaks are worshiped by gourmets. Bobby's catches were reserved by a deluxe restaurant, which paid him the incredible price of $7.70 a kilo for the whole fish, gutted. Bobby fished alone from a small, high-speed fiberglass runabout with a 120-horse-power diesel outdrive. In the mornings he would put on his baseball cap, take a bottle of water, and race out to the edge of the offshore banks. He fished with wire lines at tremendous depths—as much as one thousand meters down, he said—and retrieved his thin wires on reels driven by an automobile engine starter.

"Are the other fishermen jealous of your success?" I asked him.

"You bet," said Bobby. "None of them know how I do it, but they're all watching me and trying to learn my secrets."

He used frozen squid and mean-looking hooks about twenty-eight or thirty millimeters across, suitably offset and sharpened (together with some-thing else I am sworn not to disclose). One day I helped Bobby and Penny and one of their daughters unload his boat. We put sixteen of the zeppelin-shaped groupers (each about seventy-five centimeters to one meter long, weighing 16 to 18 kilos) into the Does' little car. (Some fishermen watching us stamped their feet with excitement at the sight.) We then drove to the restaurant, where we unloaded the 275 kilos of fish into a cold room. I let out a whistle when Bobby showed me a check for $2,100.

"I hope the fish last," I said.

"So do I," said Bobby. "What do you think is paying for *Christian Venturer?*"

Bobby was deeply religious. He never swore, he abhorred alcohol, and he said he was a born-again Christian. He often talked about church, Jesus Christ, and helping people. In fact, he was so direct and outspoken that I sometimes felt a little nervous. Whenever we all ate together on his vessel, Bobby would have everyone at the table join hands while he said a prayer to bless the food and the people about to eat. At first I thought the hand-holding was a little too much. In retrospect, however, the holding of hands for few moments gave us all a pleasant link and a sense of oneness for the evening, and now, much later, I recall our meals together with pleasure.

When Bobby swam, he could stay underwater for one to two minutes, which seemed like an eternity to me. On the day he put a new chain on *Whisper*'s hurricane mooring, I tried to help him. Bobby dived to twenty-one feet and calmly set to work with a hammer and chisel. All I could manage was to dive down, hand him a tool, and surface at once, gasping and spluttering.

Bobby was convinced that enormous unknown creatures lurked in the depths off the Bermuda reefs. "Some mornings when I'm after the groupers, something grabs my bait and pulls harder and harder to a very high tension and then suddenly lets go." Bobby took my arm and demonstrated with a steady, direct pull that abruptly stopped. "When I get my gear back, my big hooks are as straight as spears and my poor monel line is all twisted and kinked and looped and ruined.

"Other times there's a series of heavy and light jerks, each lasting ten to fifteen seconds," he said. "Completely different from the first kind of pulls." Bobby took my arm and demonstrated the heavy and light jerks.

"There's a third monster down there," said Bobby. "This one sends up a quick, heavy jerk. A pause. Then a quick, heavy jerk and a pause. And so on. Almost like Morse code." Again I got an arm demonstration.

"After storms I've found weird things on the remote beaches," he said. "Remains with thick leathery skin unlike anything in the books of the fishing institute here in Bermuda. Believe me, there's a whole world of unreal creatures down there. Giant squid? Two-meter lobsters? Clams the size of a dishpan? Three-eyed fish? I don't know. But whatever is down there, they're big and powerful. The sea may be calm at times, but it's full of mystery."

. . . .

CHAPTER TWO

South in the Atlantic

*W*e sailed south from Bermuda on October 17th, and headed for St. Martin in the Caribbean, nine hundred miles away. In the beginning the winds from the north blew briskly. The sea swell was lumpy, our stomachs were fluttery, and we rushed along with small sails. On the third day, however, the breeze fell away and soon we rolled gently on a quiet Atlantic.

During the afternoon we watched—with some apprehension—gigantic cumulonimbus clouds rise up around us on all sides. We looked at mile-high thunderheads, whose billowing cheeks gleamed purple, white, or gray depending on the angle of the sun. We knew that the air in these clouds was shooting up and down at elevator speeds. Sheet lightning flickered here and there, and we heard rumbles of distant thunder. But no wind came, and we continued to roll easily until the following afternoon, when squally weather and twenty-five-to-thirty-knot easterly winds blew up for several days. Then came more calms.

On tranquil nights when the moon was down and the clouds mostly gone, the stars were spectacular. I know of no more peaceful experience than to sit on deck far out at sea and to look at the heavens. First I rattle off the dozen or fifteen stars that I can identify. Then I try to recall the name of a new star that I am trying to learn. My knowledge quickly runs out, however, and I can only gasp at the hundreds more up there. My favorite group is the Pleiades, that little cluster of stars in the constellation Taurus, just above Aldebaran on a line going up from Orion's belt. There are six (or seven) stars in the Pleiades, which is also known as the Seven Sisters, named by the Greeks for the seven daughters of Atlas and Pleione. It's easy to count six stars, and sometimes I think I can see seven. With binoculars you can pick out many more, although at sea it's a shaky, eye-straining business to use field glasses on stars.

According to the one-volume *Columbia Encyclopedia* that we carry on *Whisper,* the Pleiades are 325 to 350 light years away, a figure far beyond my mental calipers. It's hard to realize that these stars are so far distant that a twinkle of light that started from them in the middle of the seventeenth century (say 1650) and has been streaking toward us at *186,000 miles a second* is just now reaching us.

We kept hoping to find the northern edge of the easterly trade wind with its steady breeze. But the winds blew fitfully, and we lived with squalls, heavy rains, and more towering clouds. The sheet lightning was almost as regular as the roll of the ship. We timed these small flashes, which seemed to go off every seven seconds or so.

Since leaving Bermuda, we had seen five ships and two yachts. No doubt the yachts were part of the October procession from the northeastern coast of the United States to the Virgin Islands. Often these pleasure vessels take the Intracoastal Waterway to Morehead City, North Carolina, before heading east and then south in the Atlantic.

One day when the sea was smooth I went up the mast to fix something. I happened to glance down and saw three big dorados near the stern. Two were green and one was blue. You would think that blue and green fish would merge into vague shadows on a bluish sea. From my high perch on the mast, however, the quivering greens and electric blues seemed ribbons of accented light that floated on a sea of glass. I saw a watercolor box of heavenly greens and blues that made my heart sing. The three fish swam along slowly, their bodies like unfused dynamite, until something startled them and they streaked away. I can still remember those greens and blues. . . .

A big problem in the northern Caribbean is Horseshoe Reef, which adjoins Anegada Island sixty-seven miles west-northwest of St. Martin. A ship's longitude is critical because the west-setting north equatorial current tends to push everything toward the reef, which has snared hundreds of vessels since the days of the Spanish. With Anegada in mind, I decided to make our landfall on Sombrero, an isolated pinnacle rock forty-three miles east of the reef. This course avoided the reef and gave us an eighteen-mile navigation light in case of a night arrival.

As we slatted and drifted along, the lightning displays continued. Not large ones, but localized sheet lightning from a single cumulonimbus cloud system. Sometimes we had seven or eight small electrical displays around us. One night I thought I was in a light bulb testing factory because every few seconds a distant flicker of lightning knifed across the sky. The quality of the light was eerie and made the sea look strange. Was somebody up there angry?

Late on the evening of October 25th we picked up a southeast breeze that freshened to fourteen knots and continued on and off for two days and drove us along for the last 220 miles. When we sighted the rocky islet marked by Sombrero light we saw two supertankers slowly cruising back and forth, keeping station a few miles off. We later found out that these very large crude carriers (VLCCs) were loaded with part of an oil glut, and it was cheaper to keep the massive vessels marking time at sea than to move the oil ashore. It was incredible to watch these three-hundred-meter-long oil storage tanks motoring back and forth while speculators in New York and London and God knows where else dickered with one another over prices and destinations. Certainly we were looking at a bizarre chapter in the maritime history of the world.

By noon of October 27th we could see the seven-mile-long blue and green ribbon of St. Martin on our port bow. That evening we anchored on the south coast in Groot Baai, a mile-wide harbor with marvelously clear water over a bottom of mostly white sand. The bay was open to the south, and a light swell came in that made the coasters, fishing boats, and yachts (we counted sixty) roll and pitch a little. We had a good time swimming in the crystal water and scrubbing off the goose barnacles that had grown around *Whisper*'s waterline near the stern. The main settlement ashore was Philipsburg, a Dutch town that bustled with tourist shops.

Landfall, St. Barthélémy

After two days we sailed fifteen miles southeast to the French island of
St. Barthélémy. This small island, known for its wines and spirits at perhaps
the lowest prices in the world, seemed to glow in the sun. The people we
met were hospitable, with a bit of French charm, and we saw flowers
everywhere. The main harbor of tiny Gustavia was crowded with thirty-five
yachts, with another ten anchored outside. Margaret pulled out a 1966
National Geographic article that showed a photograph of Carleton Mitchell's
thirty-eight-foot yawl *Finisterre* alone in the harbor. "Just look at that
picture," she said. "Obviously we were born fifty years too late." Now in
Gustavia everyone needed bow and stern anchors or an anchor and a line
ashore to keep from swinging. Some yachts were too close to one another
and banged together. Privacy was lost, and tempers sometimes exploded.
Some of the magic was gone.

Gustavia was in the midst of a building boom, and I counted fifty
housing permits on the town hall bulletin board. While I was examining the
notices, a man asked me if I was a carpenter (I was carrying a piece of

Tho-pa-ga entering Gustavia, St. Barthélémy

plywood I had just bought). "There is plenty of work," he said. "Good pay too. You can start this afternoon."

During our stay a French schooner about thirty meters long named *Tho-pa-ga,* registered in Panama, arrived from Guadeloupe. The wooden vessel had an enormous cargo that included *fourteen* small cars on deck. The local stevedores quickly took off the cars, using a small crane, and then began to unload tractor tires, bags of cement, lumber, plastic pipe, and a great pile of boxes and crates. All this cargo on the wharf seemed to make little difference to the vessel's Plimsoll lines, which suggested that she still had plenty of stuff on board for the next stop. *Tho-pa-ga* had a slow-turning diesel, but she also had an enormous gaff rig with particularly lofty main and fore topmasts. While examining her rig with my binoculars, I was surprised to discover that her spars were made from large-diameter aluminum pipes painted brown. She was certainly an impressive cargo carrier.

Every day before noon four sleek, sixty-foot catamarans loaded with tourists from St. Martin came skimming into Gustavia Harbor. Each of the high-speed Peter Spronk catamarans took thirty people, who paid thirty dollars apiece for the day. Only beer and soft drinks were served on board. The tourists then had lunch—at their own expense—somewhere on St. Barthélémy and sailed back to Philipsburg in the late afternoon. The tourists loved the sail, and the restaurant owners loved the tourists. We heard that the costs of these catamarans were recovered in a single year (no meals, no reservations, no correspondence, no agents, no checks—cash only, please). No wonder the smiles of the bronzed captains and attractive stewardesses seemed so genuine. Certainly this charter business was a sweet arrangement.

On November 6th we sailed to the British Virgin Islands, an easy overnight run of 116 miles with the easterly trade wind behind us. We cleared customs at Road Town and began a leisurely inspection of the various harbors and anchorages on Tortola and the nearby small islands. The water was clear and warm, the sun constant, and the wind steady. White sails were everywhere, almost like snowflakes on the sea.

The main nautical business was bareboat chartering. In theory, a person who rented a yacht for a week or two was supposed to be an experienced small boat captain, but in practice the companies chartered to almost anyone with money. The companies salved their consciences by giving the customers a short lecture on the rules of the road. This meant that you would find novices at the wheels of forty- and fifty-foot vessels with all sails up in winds that sometimes blew at thirty-five knots. Right-of-way situations became nightmares. After a few near misses, all humor vanished, and we soon learned to regard any crossing situation with a bareboat charter yacht as big trouble.

The charterers' anchoring techniques weren't much better. The vacation captains tended to anchor on top of you and to put out an extra-long anchor line of seven or eight times the depth of the water (this had been drummed

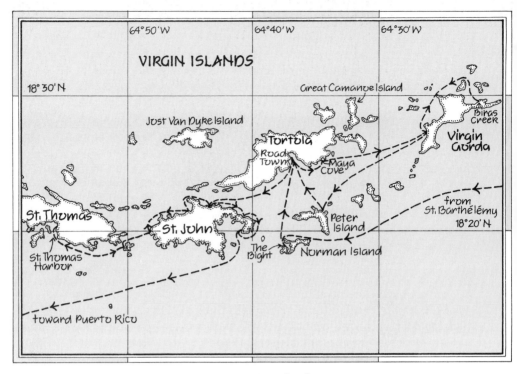

3. Virgin Islands

into them by the companies). The charterers then motored off somewhere in their dinghies and left their nifty plastic-and-chrome floating apartments (with engines running to charge the batteries and refrigeration) to drift down on you, complete with fumes and noise. The next bareboat charterer to come along would invariably anchor close to the first—often *between* you and the other boat—*to be friendly,* and so on.

By an unfortunate choice, our initial anchorage in the British Virgins was at a place called The Bight, on Norman Island. We sailed in and anchored in the early afternoon. It was a gorgeous place with not a soul in sight. An hour later a bareboat charterer motored in and anchored next to us. Then another, and another, until there were twenty yachts in a tight little knot in a corner of the large bay. It seemed a shame to spoil such a nice anchorage with the noise and smell of engines, the flames and smoke from barbecues at the sterns, and the booming music from competing stereo systems that shrieked across the water.

In the middle of the night a light wind came up. I heard a strange noise, so I got out of my bunk and climbed on deck. I saw a nearby boat renter rowing a line in my direction. When he got over *Whisper*'s anchor chain he stood up in his dinghy and began to lift up an anchor.

"What are you doing?" I suddenly asked in a loud voice that startled the man.

"Oh!" he said, surprised to see someone watching him. "There's some wind now and I'm a little nervous. I see that you're nicely anchored with chain and seem to know what you're doing. I thought I would drop my second anchor across yours. Then we will all be tied together."

"That's not a bad idea," I replied, "but that's not quite how it's done." I suggested that he row off in another direction.

(In fairness I must add that a few bareboat charterers had plenty of experience and impeccable skills; yet most were novices and best avoided. In truth, much of their so-called sailing was simply motoring between deluxe restaurants.)

The old hands in the Virgins often anchored in small, out-of-the-way coves and nooks. These were often lovely little spots, calm and clear, behind a reef. Sometimes you needed two anchors to keep from swinging too close to the coral. Often the swimming and snorkeling were superb, and occasionally you might find a lobster. Most of these places were red-lined on the charts issued by the bareboat charter companies, which meant that boat renters were not allowed to enter these dangerous areas. Usually the red-lined anchorages were perfectly good, however, but perhaps had a tricky entrance that required pilotage from aloft when the sun was high so you could see the coral.

In the U.S. Virgin Islands we saw more yachts—of every size, of every design, both new and old, from North America and Europe, with a few from South Africa and even Japan. In the big harbor of St. Thomas there were some three hundred yachts, along with half a dozen cruise ships whose passengers came for a day of duty-free shopping. Ashore, St. Thomas was a tourist circus. The only things lacking were dancing elephants and cowboys on horseback. Where, oh where were those peaceful West Indian towns of yesteryear? We thought back to a sailing trip twenty years earlier when we had estimated the *entire* Caribbean pleasure boat population to have been about two hundred. Now there were at least two thousand yachts in the U.S. and British Virgin Islands alone.

St. Thomas had some ugly social problems, and everyone warned us not to walk around at night. In Pueblo, the largest supermarket, four armed guards patrolled the aisles, and while we were in town one of the guards shot and killed a thief. There was a great outcry that somehow tried to justify the behavior of the dead man, but the guard had repeatedly warned the thief not to run off with the store's goods.

On Tortola we found a bit of reverse discrimination. Jitney rides cost two dollars for whites, one dollar for blacks. At the native open-air market in Road Town there were two price scales, one for each race (you could save money by hiring a black to shop for you if you were buying a lot).

Vegetables were often sold "by the heap," and the sellers in the market stalls displayed little piles of beans or okra or peppers. One Saturday morning I started to hand a man twenty-five cents for a heap of beans marked with a "25¢" sign. The seller whisked the sign away. "Oops," he said. "Dat's de black price. De white price is fifty cents."

But small things aside, the native markets were pathetic compared with a generation ago when farming was important, both for the central market (for cash) and for individual families (for food). Now many Tortola men preferred to drive taxis rather than farm, and plenty of good land lay idle. Much of the British Virgins' food was imported from the United States, and the food costs, even for the locals, were quite unreal.

One day while we were anchored in Biras Creek in Virgin Gorda, a nice-looking wooden Herreshoff Mobjack ketch sailed in and anchored near us. *Candlewin* was forty-seven feet long and had been built by her owner, a Canadian from Vancouver Island named Greg Janes, who was sailing with his wife and five-year-old daughter. When we invited the Janes over for coffee one morning, I noticed that Mrs. Janes rowed the dinghy and that Greg climbed aboard *Whisper* with difficulty. Something seemed wrong with his right shoulder, but I didn't say anything. We eventually learned that in Road Town a week earlier, two black thieves had come aboard the anchored yacht at midnight. Greg had rushed on deck with a heavy bilge pump handle and

Sailing friends Bill and Ellen Goodloe from the yacht *Black Watch*

struck at one of the intruders. When that happened the second man pulled out a .22-caliber revolver and shot Greg in the chest.

Fortunately Greg had enough presence of mind to shout to his wife: "Load the shotgun and bring it on deck!"

"He's gonna git the shotgun!" yelled the man with the revolver. "We got to go." The gunman helped his injured partner into their small boat, and the men disappeared into the night.

Back on the yacht there was blood all over Greg and on the deck, and much confusion before Mrs. Janes got some help and called the police. Her husband was taken to the hospital, where, luckily, his wound was found to be slight. The next day there was no mention of the incident in the newspapers or on the radio. "Perhaps it never happened," said Mrs. Janes cynically. "Perhaps it's like those eternally optimistic weather forecasts in the Bahamas. One wouldn't want to upset the tourist business in paradise."

But it's unfair to dwell on negative things. Ninety-nine percent of the people were law-abiding and orderly and lived in peace on their tropical islands. The local governments tried hard. As visitors, we learned to concentrate on the pretty bays and smooth, scrub-covered hills rather than on the junked cars and ragged housing. We spent delightful weeks on Tortola in tiny Maya Cove, a few miles east of Road Town. We anchored out near the reef, where we had a constant breeze and a good view of the sailing scene and the small islands to the south. I spent the mornings writing. Margaret dealt with letters or walked into East End to buy a few groceries. In the afternoons we worked on *Whisper,* visited friends, and swam. Many passing yachts stopped in the cove, and we visited old sailing friends (Bo Holmquist from Brazil; Ed Boden, last seen in Rarotonga). We made new friends, including the novelist Stephen Becker and yachting journalist Fritz Seyfarth.

We got acquainted with a dynamic, red-haired English artist named Roger Burnett, who lived on a ferrocement yacht of surprising quality that he had built himself, quickly and cheaply. Roger thought the British Virgins were heaven on earth, and he never stopped praising them to anyone who would listen. He had done an artist's sketchbook of the islands that was published locally and had sold quite well. He painted Virgin Island scenes and exhibited his work at both Maya Cove and in Road Town. Roger had volunteered to teach an art class at the island penitentiary, and his efforts with the prisoners were commended by everyone. The government ministers admired Roger's work and gave him a work permit, a hard-to-get item for foreigners (it seemed a paradox that an Englishman was a foreigner in the independent British Virgins). Roger's wife drowned in a tragic swimming mishap while we were there, but the red-haired artist carried on bravely ("What else can I do?"), and he rushed around at his usual pace on a dozen projects, from decorating his new gallery in Road Town to designing a new issue of postage stamps for the government.

Hurricane Hole, east end of St. John, U.S. Virgins

Our last anchorage in the Virgins was a deserted cove at the sparsely settled east end of St. John. We visited a quiet couple named Mike and Angela Ebner who were building a forty-two-foot traditional wooden schooner. Mike had been at work on the project for six years, but the vessel was only one-third done. His tiny wife had lost all hope. "Will I ever see the schooner in the water?" she moaned. "Is it going to take another twelve years to finish her? I can't stand to think of it." Mike was a perfectionist and demanded a piano-top finish even on interior parts that would be covered as construction progressed.

All we could do was to invite the Ebners aboard *Whisper* for a meal and to urge Mike to get afloat and not to be so fussy. The Ebners enjoyed the visit, and their eyes flitted from *Whisper*'s sailing books to the chart table, and from the polished brass lamps to Margaret cooking in the galley. At least our little floating home gave these land-based dreamers a whiff of the sea.

. . . .

CHAPTER THREE

Hello Pacific

*A*fter a winter in the Virgin Islands we headed for the southeast corner of the big island of Puerto Rico. We sailed to a man-made harbor with a little marina and boatyard that was part of a grandiose condominium-hotel complex called Palmas del Mar. The development was on a large piece of first-class ocean waterfront and not only included recreational boating, but had deluxe apartments, individual homes, golf courses, tennis courts, swimming pools, fancy restaurants, and so on.

The giant project was well designed (red tile roofs, buildings with a Mediterranean flair) and pleasantly landscaped (green hills, rows of shimmering palm trees, bougainvillea), but unfortunately had already been through several financial shakeouts. More shock waves appeared imminent. The whole place appeared to be falling apart because the buildings and grounds had never been properly completed. Apparently there was no money for gardeners to keep up the extensive landscaping and lawns. Some of the buildings and walls needed repairs and painting, and several pieces of nicely executed art work (a mosaic fountain, for instance) were falling into ruin. Yet I met a Spanish investor who claimed that he and his associates had just bought the marina and boatyard (rumored price: $10 million). While we were there, however, the French restaurant at the marina folded, and the head of the boatyard was cutting prices to attract customers.

Dutch and Italian investors were said to have paid $2 million for the weed-covered islets in the little harbor. Full-page advertisements glorifying

Palmas del Mar were running in the *Wall Street Journal.* The air reeked with exaggerations, hype, and boosterism. Meanwhile the hotel staffs were unhappy over low wages and threatened to strike. A famous Latin jazz pianist played in the lobby of the empty five-star hotel. Outside, the parking lot was a sea of mud. Rumors and gossip flew faster than the local birds, and a general feeling of mystery and intrigue was augmented by the sounds of strange languages from Swedish and German and Brazilian couples who wandered around in dark glasses and zippy sport clothes. A novelist would have loved the scene.

We had gone to the cut-rate boatyard to take *Whisper* out of the water for painting. She was plucked from the sea to the land by a giant four-wheeled Travelift, a huge, crab-like lifting machine that straddled the yacht in a special berth and raised her into the air by means of two enormous nylon slings that were passed underneath the hull. Once the yacht was out of the water and airborne, the Travelift drove *Whisper* to a convenient place on land where she was propped up with wooden shores. The Travelift operator then eased the slings and drove off, which left the vessel high and dry and ready for underwater repairs and painting. We were about halfway through our work when we heard a rumor (another rumor?) that a bank was about to seize the Travelift for nonpayment of something. The loss of the Travelift would have meant that we would be trapped on land.

During the day big Mercedes-Benz cars often pulled up alongside us while silent men in suits sat smoking cigars behind closed windows and watched us as we sanded and painted. Who were these men? Why didn't they get out of their air-conditioned automobiles and ask questions or take photographs or *do* something? Their white faces got to me.

In addition to the Travelift and the spectator problems, there was a story going around that the big yacht to our right was involved in drug smuggling and under surveillance by the authorities. Would we get involved?

"This place is full of crazies," said Margaret, madly rolling on bottom paint. "Let's finish up and get out of here before the Travelift disappears or one of these nuts in the cars knocks over *Whisper.* Or—worse yet—we might wind up in jail because of the drug boat."

While we stirred our paint we talked to a slim ex–U.S. Marine named Harry Menger, who was hard at work cocooning an old forty-eight-foot wooden ketch blocked up to our left. The yacht was a 1930-era classic hull with gentle overhangs and a pleasant sheer, and had been built by a famous yard with the best of everything. She had an excellent rig, good sails, a beautiful interior of solid mahogany, and a nice engine and electrical system. The yacht sailed well and her owner loved her. What was wrong was that the hull was full of rotten planks, half of the frames were cracked and broken, and many of the fastenings were corroded. The vessel leaked badly and was liable to open up and sink at any moment.

Boatbuilder Menger had worked out a technique of enshrouding these old vessels in a cocoon of thin strips of wood held together with epoxy glue. Harry would take a leaky forty- or fifty-footer out of the water, let her dry out, and do whatever structural beefing-up was necessary. Then he would crisscross the hull with three or four layers of 6-inch-wide, ⅛-inch-thick western red cedar. Each layer ran in a different direction, and each was glued and stapled to the wood underneath. The embrace of the cocoon strengthened the old hulls marvelously, stopped all leaks, and gave the old war horses another generation of life. The owners, delighted to be free from constant worry and pumping (and lying about how much), were in ecstasy.

We finally finished painting *Whisper,* and she was lowered into the water. A few days later we sailed for Panama. Never have I been so pleased to get away from the land and its complications to the simple peacefulness of the ocean. Every time I had walked around Palmas del Mar, salesmen had zeroed in on me and tried to sell me a vacation apartment, a house lot, or a golf club membership. When I said that I was simply a poor sailor working on his boat and wearing my customary old clothes, the salesmen smiled knowingly. I was a rich man who was slumming. Otherwise why would I be at Palmas del Mar? I tried the dodge of saying "No hablo inglés," but the salesmen opened up in Spanish because they were bilingual. . . .

The run to Panama was easy, for the most part, with the strong trade wind and west-setting current behind us. The distance was one thousand miles, and we hurried downwind with small sails. On the third day I was surprised to see the sky filled with long, heavy, cigar-shaped clouds that pointed north and south, almost at right angles to the low-level trade wind. A few hours later some evil-looking squalls with nuclear dimensions began to surround us. I had no wish to get flattened by atomic whirlwinds, so we yanked down the mainsail and set the trysail in its place.

We carried only two reefs in *Whisper*'s mainsail. For the next reduction we took down the mainsail entirely. In its place I hoisted a special small sail whose heavy material and construction were much better suited to severe strains than the lighter cloth of the mainsail. Our eleven-square-meter trysail was easy to handle in fresh winds because we set it loose-footed and didn't use the heavy main boom at all (which was then safely down and lashed to the permanent boom gallows). We carried the trysail in a bag at the foot of the mast with the sail slides bent on to a second mast track, and it took only five minutes or so to unbag and hoist the sail. The trysail steadied the yacht, reduced rolling, contributed drive, and was marvelously reassuring on a horrible black night when the wind shrieked and the rain lashed at our faces. Fortunately the squalls lasted only a few hours, and by the next morning we were back to normal sailing.

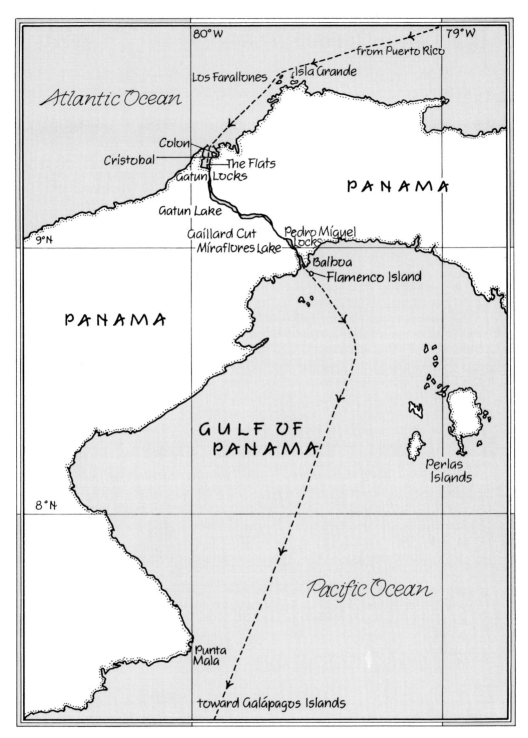

4. Panama Canal

One night a wave erupted through an open portlight and poured down on me while I was asleep in my berth. I was soaked and more than a little angry. Margaret was sympathetic, but she started laughing and couldn't stop, which of course made me angrier, until I too began to laugh. . . .

We had seen only five ships since Puerto Rico and expected more traffic as we neared the Panama Canal. Only the *Esso Kure,* however, a small Japanese tanker, slipped past us at dusk on June 26th. That afternoon we had begun to see the hills and coastal mountains of Central America through a hazy murk. We passed near a big, ugly-looking floating log almost as long as our hull. The wind was light and dying, and at nine degrees north latitude the heat of the sun poured down on the helmsman. The trysail and strong Caribbean winds seemed a long time ago. It took us hours to pass Ilha Grande and Los Farallones, two small islets thirty miles northeast of the canal, because of the well-known *east-* running current where the continent jogs to the southwest. That night we anchored inside the Panama Canal complex at a place for small vessels called The Flats.

The following morning we moved to the yacht club at Cristobal, and I got busy with the admeasurer and the paperwork. I spent the day filling out forms and paying a few charges. Meanwhile, Margaret made out a shopping list and went off to Colón, where she had the bad luck to get robbed. We had been warned that Colón was completely lawless, so Margaret left her watch and purse on *Whisper* and carried only a few bills that she tucked inside one shoe. During the morning she went to a bakery and asked for a pound of butter. Just as she pulled a bill from her shoe to pay the clerk, a thief rushed in from the street, snatched her money and the butter, ran out the door, and was gone. "The so-and-so even got my butter," she muttered.

On July 1st, at 0600, we fired up *Whisper's* one-cylinder Farymann diesel, and with a pleasant pilot named Leonardo Robinson (Robby) giving directions, we steamed south toward the Gatun Locks. For the required line handlers, we had recruited people from other yachts—our old friends Al and Beth Liggett, and a Japanese sailor named Tatsuya Asano. *Whisper* had six people on board.

In spite of all we'd heard about the canal, we weren't quite prepared for the nonstop parade of big ships. Forty-two ships flying seventeen different flags went through the canal on the day we crossed, and five of the vessels were over eight hundred feet long. It was exciting to see the powerful electric locomotives guide the ships into position, the huge lock gates swing shut like enormous bank vault doors, and the water swirl and boil as twenty-six million gallons filled the lock and floated the ships upward. During the morning we went in and out of three locks that lifted *Whisper* eighty-five feet. We tied alongside big tugboats that were going our way, which made the lockage easy.

Locking through, Panama Canal

A little before lunchtime we powered out on the wide expanse of Gatun Lake. We had a fair wind, so while the pilot was below having a sandwich we shut off the engine and hoisted a big green and white spinnaker. Robby got a little upset at the sudden silence, but when I said that we could do seven knots under sail versus five knots under power, the noise and fumes would stop, and he would get home earlier, he went back to his sandwich. Robby soon got into the spirit of sailing, and it wasn't long before he was steering while our hotshot crew of five adjusted the various strings of the spinnaker.

It was a marvelous sunny day, and we flew along on the smooth water, laughing and joking. Margaret was a little touchy about having been robbed, so naturally we kidded her. "Hey, Margaret. Lend me five dollars." Or "Hey, Margaret. Let me look in your shoe." Or "Hey, Margaret. I want plenty of butter on my sandwich."

We sailed across the twenty-three and a half miles of Gatun Lake past tall green islands and alongside great stretches of tropical jungle. At one place the pilot pointed out a five-foot alligator sunning himself on the shore. Late in the afternoon we entered the eight-mile Gaillard cut, where the canal slices through the continental divide. This is the area that required massive excavations and where so many workers lost their lives in the early days. Above us we saw a small monument to honor those heroic workmen. We all felt in awe of their efforts, which had given mankind such a wonderful waterway. What man can accomplish when he really tries is remarkable.

It was late in the day when we got to the Pedro Miguel Locks. As we entered, the canal line handlers threw down heaving lines to which we attached our lines, one from each quarter. Soon we were snug in the middle and were lowered 31 feet to Miraflores Lake. Then as the tropical night fell softly around us and shuttered the delicate twilight, we slipped into the Miraflores Locks together with the 497-foot *Boris Zhemchuzhin* from Russia and were locked down to the level of the Pacific. We were through!

Three generations of Americans have worked hard to perfect the administrative, engineering, and public health standards of the Panama Canal, one of the marvels of the world since it opened in 1914. Up to 1977, when the United States announced that it was giving the canal to Panama, America had spent about $3 billion, two-thirds of which was recovered by tolls. Since 1977, however, when Panama started to assume control (full authority in the year 2000), the standards have been going down. Some observers believe that the Panamanians consider the canal to be a political device and a potential money-maker rather than a nonprofit necessity for world commerce. Certainly the motivation levels and the examples set by the Americans have not been followed.

"The garbage was always collected daily, and the grasses and weeds were kept trimmed," *Whisper*'s admeasurer, Rick Williams, an American born in Panama, told me. "Now, because of gnats and flies, we are getting strange fevers for which there are no cures." Williams predicted that health problems will ultimately cause more difficulties than simple bad administration.

Many key engineering people had left, and there were few replacements. I was told that not long before our visit five Panamanian electricians had been electrocuted because nobody had thought to shut off the power. One hundred twenty-five new diesel-powered forklift trucks—a departing gift of the United States when Panama took over the docks—were ruined when all their tanks were filled with gasoline. The once-neat areas of clipped grass at Cristobal had become dumping grounds for ruined shipping containers.

Instead of the quick unloading of container ships that the Americans had prided themselves on, the Panamanians had already slipped to making the container ships wait three days, and so on. The canal itself was still operated by the United States, yet you couldn't help but wonder what would happen to the great locks when they came under the control of Panama. We spoke to veteran Panamanian employees who worried about the loss of U.S. sovereignty.

The dismal Panamanian offices that I went to in Cristobal were staffed by pathetic, untrained clerks, while work in the nearby American offices was quick and efficient. The American employees have always been well paid (some say too well paid), but the workers claim that they labor far from their homes in the United States, live in a hellish climate, and that the few extra benefits are trifling.

The big priority has always been to get more ships through the canal. In 1939, for example, there were 7,479 transits, compared with the 15,000 of today. Not only has the number of transits doubled, but the individual ships are much larger than those of two generations ago.

With the decline in yacht club memberships as Americans leave, the facilities of the club at each end of the canal have become poorer. This means that transits are difficult, because small vessels have always depended heavily on the yacht clubs for docking and services. The problem is not only that the yacht clubs are in marginal condition, but the number of transient vessels has increased enormously. Once there were a few dozen pleasure yachts a year; now there are hundreds. The service demands of large numbers of guest boats at the two overburdened yacht clubs make for an unsound practice, one that's unfair to both the yacht clubs and the transients.

Yachts need a proper haven where captains can deal with paperwork, crew changes, supplies, mail, fuel, food, and medical problems. The vessels may need repairs or bottom painting. All of these concerns are important because the next port may be thousands of miles away. Small-ship owners are quite willing to pay for these services, but nothing adequate exists.

The authorities should build a small marina and boatyard at each end of the canal and advertise the rates and conditions. Three-quarters of the paperwork and the antiquated measurement scheme could be eliminated. The yachts and fishing boats could travel through the canal in small groups, perhaps with a single pilot. This scheme could reduce the handling problems and costs, both for the small vessels and for the canal company. With something like a thousand small ships going through the Panama Canal each year, the yacht havens could provide first-class services and security and still make a profit for the canal, besides reducing the administrative and pilotage load. A simple, coordinated handling system would be convenient and save time, money, and anguish for everyone.

The canal is an important sea link and certainly one of the wonders of the modern world. Just now, with overall control changing, it's a good time for improvements and simplifications. Perhaps I have underestimated the abilities of the Panamanians. Perhaps after a few mistakes and a little seasoning, the administrators, the planning people, the engineers, and the medical staff will master the challenges of this miraculous waterway. I hope so. Otherwise the Cape Horn route may have a future.

. . . .

CHAPTER FOUR

Three Weeks at Sea

O n July 10th we lay anchored at Flamenco Island near the Pacific entrance to the canal. There was no wind. Not a puff. Nothing. A blanket of suffocating heat pressed down from above. The fishermen slept along the shore, and the sea gulls were too weary to argue. In the distance we heard passing ships, whose engines made grumbling sounds like the clearing of hundreds of old men's throats.

We had a full load of food and water, and our outbound clearance sat on the cabin table, but we hadn't gone anywhere because we had been whistling for a wind for three days. I was sure the sphinxlike calms of the Bay of Panama had trapped us for good. Weren't these the same waters where the sixteenth-century Spanish ships had rotted apart while the crews had prayed for wind?

"When Chile and Peru were first discovered, the voyage southward to Chile often took a year, for the wind was always foul," according to historian Clements Markham. "The vessels crept along the coast from headland to headland, and generally anchored at night. When the pilot, Pastene, went from Callao to Valparaiso in 1547 . . . he made what was thought a rapid passage. He was a Genoese of long experience, and was considered the ablest seaman in the South Sea. The voyage took him a little over eight months."[1]

When a zephyr from the north finally rippled the water around us, it took us only a twinkling to winch up *Whisper*'s anchor. We quickly poled out our largest sails and headed southeast toward the Perlas Islands. On the

Pacific side of the canal the tidal range is about five meters, and a strong ebb helped us leave the land and anchored ships behind. The sketchy wind was too light for the steering vane to work, so Margaret and I took turns at the tiller.

The sun was a great flaming ball at *Whisper*'s masthead. We soon broke out the golf umbrella to give the helmsman some relief and anxiously waited for sunset. By late afternoon the wind was northwest at ten knots. It was too late in the day to find an anchorage in the Perlas Islands, so we changed course to the southwest toward Cabo Mala. *Whisper* was now steering herself nicely. To our right in the distance I could see long lines of laden ships in the north-south shipping lanes. "What a spot for a German submarine forty years ago," I said to myself in an overblown moment of fantasy. By 1800 the wind had picked up to an incredible seventeen knots. Marvelous! Maybe we could get out of the Bay of Panama. We reefed the main, changed headsails, and charged through the night with a beam wind. By dawn we could just make out the hazy finger of Punta Mala, the western extremity of the bay.

We headed south to seek the trade wind. In 1938, during his second circumnavigation, it took Harry Pigeon *thirty* days to find this elusive wind. No wonder he complained about "the vast doldrum off the coast of Panama and Central America."[2]

An old book of sailing directions says: "The passage to the westward during the rainy season is a tedious affair. It often occurs that twenty miles of westing are not made in a week, and it is only by the industrious use of every squall and slant of wind that the passage can be made."

Ocean Passages for the World, published by the British Admiralty, laments less and is more practical: "Whether bound N or S from Panama push to the S and gain the South-east Trade; by so doing the doldrums and vexatious winds will not only be avoided but there will be the additional advantage of salubrious weather."

We poked along southward for the next four days parallel to the west coast of Colombia about 150 miles offshore. We had light westerlies, calms, and plenty of rain. At noon on July 15th we were forty-eight miles north of Punta Galera near the Colombia-Ecuador border at 1°37'N. when I decided to tack to the west and head for the Galápagos. In truth I was a little worried about the drug trade and the fishing boats from Colombia that we had begun to see around us.*

---

* This turned out to be a mistake. I could have tacked away from the fishing boats and when clear tacked southward again. I should have plugged down the coast to the equator or even one degree south, which would have made the succeeding days much easier. This route was later confirmed by Forest Nelson and Bud Devine, longtime residents of the Galápagos and both expert sailors. "Get south to the trade wind," they choroused.

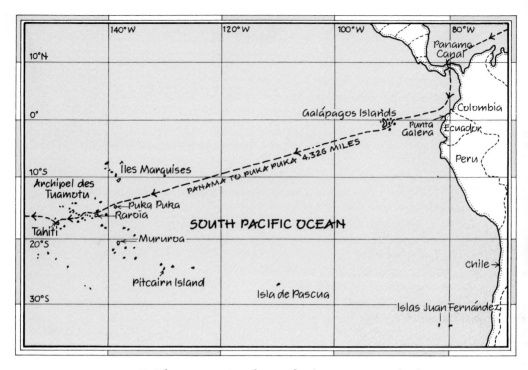

Map labels:
140°W, 120°W, 100°W, 80°W
10°N, 0°, 10°S, 20°S, 30°S
Panama Canal
Columbia
Galápagos Islands
Punta Galena
Ecuador
Peru
Îles Marquises
Archipel des Tuamotu
PANAMA TO PUKA PUKA 4,326 MILES
Puka Puka
Raroia
Tahiti
SOUTH PACIFIC OCEAN
Mururoa
Chile
Pitcairn Island
Isla de Pascua
Islas Juan Fernández

5. The eastern South Pacific (Panama to Tahiti)

For the next week we were hard on the wind from the south-southwest—from twelve to twenty-two knots—banging along trying to make a course a little south of west, with the handicap of a northwest-setting current of a knot or so. Even though we were on the equator with the sun almost overhead, at night the weather was chilly. We had to break out sweaters and jackets to keep from shivering. The explanation, of course, is that we had crossed into the cool water of the Humboldt Current.

As we slammed to windward day after day, I learned the value of foot and leech lines on headsails—particularly on old stretched sails—to prevent edge flutter and drumming. Lee Van Gemert of Hood Sails of Marblehead had shown us these lines on new sails, and the scheme worked so well that we decided to put the lines on our old sails.

We made a giant three-foot needle from a metal clothes hanger by straightening it, pounding one end flat, and drilling a small hole through the flat. Next we took the needle and pulled a length of nylon twine inside the edge tabling of the leech of a sail. We then used the twine to pull through a three- or four-millimeter-diameter braided Dacron line that we secured at the head of the sail. In effect, we made a sort of drawstring along one edge. We did the same on the foot of the sail and sewed the line to the tack. Then, with the sail hoisted and full of wind, we could tighten one or both of the lines by pulling a little at the clew of the sail where the lines came out of the tablings. It seemed best to secure these little lines to the clew grommet with a round turn and two half hitches, a most useful knot because it can be tied under tension. The drawstrings transformed a noisy, hard-flapping, shaky old sail into a silent, hard-pulling workhorse.

We thought *Whisper* was tight and impervious to all leaks, but a few days on the wind and a few thousand (million?) gallons of water over the foredeck always show up any weaknesses. Water began to trickle through our Canpa front hatch, so we hove-to and replaced the old hard gasket with a spare. The leak continued until we finally stopped again and gingerly removed the plastic acrylic itself and rebedded it. Success! The leak had been between the frame and the glass.

By July 19th we were near the Galápagos, but getting set north all the time. We tacked to the southeast—away from our target, which seemed crazy—to get a little southing. Where, oh where was the southeast trade wind? By the end of the following day the wind had backed to the south and then south-southeast. We tacked accordingly. Two days later on a calm sea we saw land ahead and gradually sorted out the islands. A squadron of blue-footed boobies flew out to inspect us ("Bobbies in uniform," Margaret called them), and we always had a circling frigate bird or two in sight. Academy Bay was too far to make by nightfall, so we stopped at the Plaza Islands off Santa Cruz, a rolly anchorage in the squally southeast weather.

The next morning we sailed the remaining seventeen miles to Academy Bay. From Panama the trip had taken a little over eleven days. Figured from noon positions, we had covered 1,320 miles and averaged 116 miles per day, which included calms and tacking.

On an earlier voyage we had spent two months in the Galápagos when the islands had been a popular yachting destination. I remember so well counting twenty-five yachts from all over the world in the little harbor at Academy Bay, which was now almost empty. At that time there were perhaps another thirty-five or forty private vessels spread through the dozen islands of the archipelago. On that trip we had sailed to all the islands and stopped at most of the anchorages, where we saw an astonishing variety of birds plus a few strange animals. Once a mockingbird landed on my hand, and we had a close look at the nesting and daily life of red- and blue-footed boobies, flightless cormorants, frigate birds, albatrosses, hawks, swallowtail gulls, flamingos, land and sea iguanas, and so on. Even small penguins, believe it or not.

Now, however, foreign yachts were banned from sailing through the islands, anchoring, and looking at the wildlife. The ostensible reason was wildlife conservation (supposedly pressed for by overzealous naturalists), but the edict seemed designed more to protect the monopoly of government-run Ecuadoran cruise ships. (The stratagems of Latin American politics are incomprehensible to a gringo: how small-boat sailors could have decreased cruise ship traffic is a mystery best left to the Ecuadorans.) It is possible to apply for a special permit to visit the islands, but the rules for foreign vessels are so cumbersome and costly that those who have tried it don't recommend it. (Among other things, you have to take a naturalist along on board.)

Official decree number 812 of the Ministry of National Defense (article eight) says in part: "Small vessels of up to six crew members navigating toward the South Pacific islands are permitted to make landfall . . . for . . . refueling, taking on food supplies, and water. . . . The maximum period that a vessel may be docked . . . is 72 hours."

So for better or worse, most yachtsmen have simply bypassed the islands. The merchants have lost the business of several hundred small vessels a year, and the communities have lost the intellectual stimulation from the visits of a thousand or more sailors from a dozen foreign countries.

When we anchored in Academy Bay, a most reluctant and sullen navy port captain levied landing charges of fifty-one dollars and gave us permission to stay for only forty-eight hours (extended to seventy-two hours after intervention by a friend). The port captain made it plain that we were not welcome, although his clerk (full of smiles and hope) immediately asked for rock tapes, T-shirts, dress shorts, cigarettes, and whisky. What was galling for an American visitor was that the Ecuadoran navy lived on U.S. hand-outs—ranging from old U.S. naval vessels to American rifles, sidearms (whose embossed holsters plainly said "U.S. Army"), and even fatigue uniforms.

What we wanted was a run ashore, a few nights in a quiet anchorage, and an opportunity to top up our water tanks and buy fresh stores. We were delighted to see our friend Forest Nelson again and to meet his son, Jack. Forest treated us to a meal and then challenged me to a game of chess (I lost). Our old friend Gus Angermeyer came out to *Whisper* for a visit. He spent an entire evening talking nonstop about a book that he'd written on his family and the adventures of the five Angermeyer brothers who had left Nazi Germany and settled in the Galápagos before World War II. Gus gave us 160 liters of good water, a precious item in the islands. The next morning we walked along the shore of Isla Santa Cruz to the home of Bud Devine for a visit. Back at the village we almost sank our dinghy with an enormous load of fruit. Big, juicy oranges—as sweet as you could want—cost two cents each. I bought half of an enormous stalk of bananas and about killed myself carrying it through the village to the dinghy.

We sailed for French Polynesia on July 26th. We spent the first day getting clear of the Galápagos, in particular the black volcanic mass of Isla Isabella, which we passed on an inky night under low clouds. Once away from the islands we relaxed a bit and settled down for a long passage. The sea was smooth, too smooth to be real, and the wind blew steadily from the southeast at twelve to fifteen knots. Our course was west-southwest, which meant that the apparent wind was close to the port beam. This allowed us to reach along with eased sheets on our normal fore-and-aft rig. We clapped a four-part tackle on the middle of the main boom to keep it quiet and to pull the mainsail down a bit and give it some shape.

At night the weather was still cool. We wore sweaters, and I needed a sheet over me when I slept. On the second day Margaret woke me to report "a grayish-black whale as long as *Whisper*," but when I looked out it was gone. On the third afternoon a frigate bird picked up our trailing fishing lure. I heard a noise and saw the bird in the air struggling with the hooks and line. Before I could stop the yacht, the bird was in the water and splashing behind at five knots. I hove-to immediately and hauled in the line and bird and poured half a pint of seawater from the bird's insides. But he—it was a male because of his red throat pouch—was dead, probably of shock when he hit the water. A moment before, the bird had been a thing of beauty. Now it was only a formless hulk of ragged black feathers, tough muscles, and an ungainly drooping head. I tossed the bird into the sea and threw the evil fishing lure into a cockpit locker. The episode was depressing and put us into a blue funk for several days.

We often saw tiny storm petrels dancing along the tops of the waves, and for a week we had chunky, white-breasted Audubon shearwaters around us. Sometimes a dozen porpoises dashed alongside for half an hour or so, twisting and turning and diving in groups of two or three. When the trade wind freshened, we tucked a reef or two in the mainsail to keep from rounding up. If the wind moved to the east we switched to the running rig and poled out a headsail to port. Then we eased the mainsail and held the main boom steady with a preventer line to the stem. The four-part tackle between the rail and the main boom pulled the mainsail down nicely and kept it from sawing itself to bits on the lee rigging.

Our best run was 160 miles in twenty-four hours, which included a 15 percent boost from the south equatorial current. The strength of this river in the ocean was erratic, however. One day we gained 24 miles; the next day the current set us back 1 mile. During the first week we logged an increase of roughly 20 miles a day. The second week the current dropped to about 4 miles a day, and during the last two weeks we showed none at all or a minus flow. On July 15 we were set back 15 miles.

Since Panama, we had seen no other vessels, so when Margaret checked around the horizon at 2230 on the twelfth night she was amazed to discover the white masthead light of another yacht directly in our path. Just ahead was a sloop twelve or thirteen meters long with a white mast, white cabin and decks, and a dark hull. We saw the silhouette of a radar antenna on the mast, and a dinghy lay capsized on the foredeck. The sloop was jogging along at about two knots under a single headsail. I blew our horn and got an immediate flash of running lights. We soon pulled past because we were sailing at five or six knots. The course of the other yacht was slightly more northerly, and I guessed that she was headed for the Îles Marquises, generally called the Marquesas. If our friend in the night pulled down his mainsail every evening, he must have taken a long time to get there. We watched the masthead light for a long time until it disappeared astern.

We began to study the pilot books and charts for French Polynesia. One of our goals was to visit the Archipel des Tuamotu, the tips of a drowned mountain range far out in the Pacific. The Dangerous Archipelago, as it is called, consists of seventy-eight atolls spread out in a vast oval whose long dimension extends southeast-northwest for 950 miles, from fourteen degrees south to twenty-three degrees south. The oval is about 300 miles wide, so the atoll group encompasses some 285,000 square miles of the east-central Pacific. The southern islands were off limits because of the French nuclear testing at Mururoa Atoll. The northernmost atolls—Takaroa, Ahé, and Manihi—were well known to transpacific voyagers sailing between the Marquesas islands and Tahiti. We hoped to visit some of the lesser-known atolls and shaped our course toward Puka Puka, the easternmost island of the Tuamotus. Puka Puka had no entrance to its lagoon and we didn't plan to stop, but this little dot in the ocean would serve as a guidepost to the islands farther west.

Once among the low atolls we would need to move carefully. There were no aids to navigation, and a landfall at night would mean a wreck and a total loss. A good way to travel was to leave an atoll at a carefully worked out time—perhaps the previous afternoon—so that we would arrive at the next island in daylight, preferably in the early morning. This would give us all day to find the pass, and time enough to wait for slack water or a flooding tidal stream so that we could enter the lagoon in good light for coral pilotage. It is usually impossible to anchor outside an atoll because the water plummets to great depths.

A Polynesian captain once counseled us to pass an atoll on its northern side if possible. The southern boundaries often have wide, imprecise reefs that extend toward the trade wind. The coral on the north and northwest sides is more defined, usually with islets and coconut palms. Of course we couldn't sail close to an atoll at night, but we could pass near one in the late afternoon to confirm our position. We could then continue slowly toward a second, maybe thirty miles away, and arrive the following morning.

"If something goes wrong with your navigation and you are unsure of yourself in the night, the best plan is to reverse your compass course under easy sail until daylight," another captain, the late Connie Hitchcock, a dear old friend from San Francisco, had once told me.

From the top of the mast under perfect conditions, the absolute sighting limit of a low atoll with coconut palms is ten miles, but five or six miles

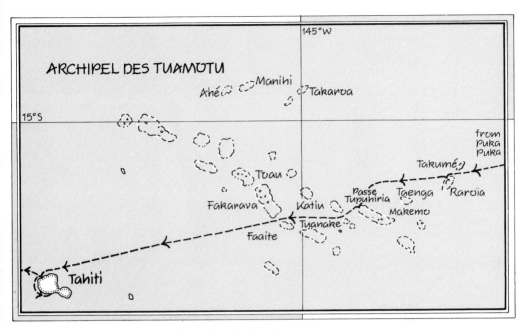

6. Archipel des Tuamotu

is more realistic. There is the additional hazard of strange currents that set vessels in unexpected directions, and it is almost impossible to hear breakers pounding on a reef to leeward. On the positive side, you often sail in smooth water because the atolls provide a lee. The wind is generally steady from the southeast or east; storms and westerlies are rare. You shoot the same stars every evening and morning, and they get to be old friends. Once you reach the sheltered part of a lagoon you can stay until you're rested. A sailor can even wait for a suitable phase of the moon because a little light at night gives one a bit more confidence.

On long ocean passages the days merge into one another and pass quickly. One day becomes two; two grow into four; a week slips by, then a second, and soon a third. Time becomes blurred and of no value. . . . In the morning you do a few small jobs and then walk around the decks to check for chafe aloft. There are the morning and noon sextant sights and the working up of the noon position. Lunch may be thick soup with a bit of cheese and crackers and a glass of wine. A nap in the afternoon to prepare for the night, some reading, and then maybe a change to a larger headsail if the breeze is lighter. You study the chart to see how far you've come and how many days are left. At sunset you look in vain for the green flash. (I have never seen it, although I have watched the tropical sunset hundreds of times.) The evening news crackles on the radio, but all the troubles seem far away. You switch off the distant voices, climb up three steps, and stand in the hatchway with your elbows on the coachroof. It's nice to just look at the stars and the sea and the vast darkness. Everything is so peaceful and easy

First sighting of Puka-Puka

as the yacht rolls smoothly from side to side. The water rushes past—
embracing the hull for a moment—and the mast scribes its arc against the
sky. The log makes a steady clicking sound, and a startled bird cries across
the night. You get so close to nature and the sea that any other life seems
impossible . . . and irrelevant . . . and meaningless.

You have found a secret life, full of hidden things and quiet meanings.
The magic is all around you, and the guts of existence seem to be at your
fingertips. *There is no more.* It's impossible to write about this secret bond—
the code you've broken—or to share it with others because the private
messages between you and nature and the sea are too personal, too delicate,
too lovely. . . .

Since we would need precise navigation in the islands ahead, we began
to get tuned up with star sights. Every evening—clouds permitting—we shot
the glowing beacons of Rigel Kent, Vega, and Arcturus. At dawn it was
Capella, Sirius, and Canopus. Margaret and I took turns with the sextant and
calculations.

By the evening of the twenty-first day we had logged 4,301 miles from
Panama. We were only 25 miles from Puka Puka, so we hove-to for the
night. At 0900 the next morning we saw a line of shimmering green in the

distance. The wind was light from the north, and we slowly glided up to the small atoll, whose yellowish-green coconut palms seemed very tall and very close together. We looked at white sand beaches on the northern side and at a few old buildings among the trees. The village lay at the western extremity, and we saw the church and some houses. I thought of anchoring off the village, but a half mile from shore we got no bottom at 100 fathoms on the echo sounder. Margaret studied the chart. "No wonder!" she exclaimed. "The water is 847 fathoms deep!"

The next four days were essentially windless. We averaged less than fifty miles a day, while the sails banged and slatted. In fact, one night the sea was so calm that we could see the image of Jupiter clearly reflected in the water. Finally, on August 20th, north of Fakahina, we got a touch of wind from the south. This was a big night for us because we were approaching Takumé and Raroïa and planned to pass between the islands after dawn. If our latitude was wrong we could be in big trouble. We put up the fore-and-aft rig—so we could reverse course if necessary—and continued cautiously. We wondered what was ahead.

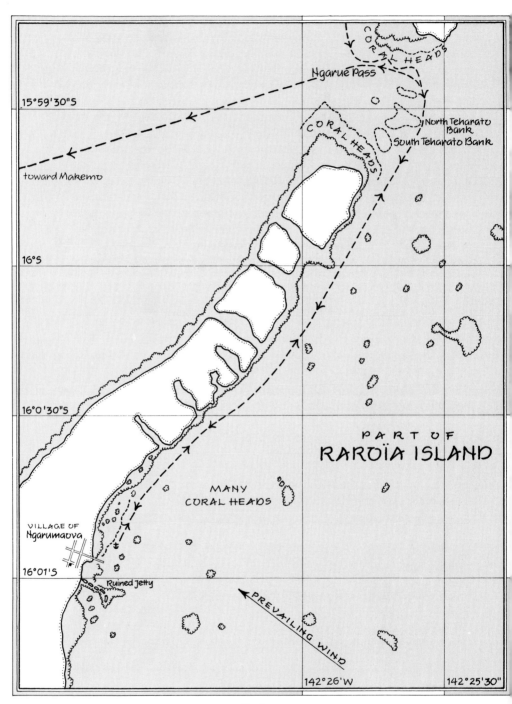

15°59'30"S

Ngarue Pass

CORAL HEADS

CORAL HEADS

North Teharato Bank

South Teharato Bank

toward Makemo

16°S

16°0'30"S

PART OF
RAROÏA ISLAND

MANY
CORAL HEADS

VILLAGE OF
Ngarumaova

16°01'S

Ruined Jetty

PREVAILING WIND

142°26'W

142°25'30"

7. Raroïa

. . . .

CHAPTER FIVE

The Happy Island

I was as nervous as a chicken who has just seen the shadow of the fox in the coop. At 0620 we sighted clumps of palm trees to starboard. I presumed this was Takumé. A little later we saw the reefs of Raroïa to port. An empty five-mile-wide strait lay between the islands. Our navigation seemed to be OK, so we carried on.

Two hours later we were in the lee of Raroïa and chuckling with glee as we reached along in smooth water with a dozen masked boobies flying around us. We sailed rapidly and passed islet after islet, some green with coconut palms, squat hardwoods, and coarse-leaved pandanus trees. Pleasant scents drifted out to us. We could hear the boom of waves on the reefs to the southeast. Several of the islets were nesting sites for birds, and we saw hundreds of white wings circling round and round. The water was a deep purplish-blue right up to the pink-colored reef. Occasionally we caught glimpses of marvelous shades of turquoise water inside the lagoon. By ten o'clock we were on the northwest side of the atoll.

From up the mast I looked ahead for signs of the pass into the lagoon. Sure enough, there it was. A long plume of white water that raced out of the lagoon at right angles to the reef for a half mile and marked the opening like a chalk mark. We reduced sail and jogged back and forth to wait for slack water.

We had been unable to get the French chart for the entrance. The best we could do was a crude sketch made from the description in the Admiralty pilot book. I had roughed out something initially, and Margaret had improved my drawing, but from the descriptive words it was unclear whether there were three separate passes next to one another or a single pass with three parts. I hoped we could get someone from the village to act as a pilot, so we sailed a little south, opposite the settlement. The village was on the lagoon side of the atoll, however, and not visible from the sea because of the coconut palms. We sailed back to the pass. Suddenly we saw an outboard-powered boat from the village with three or four men, several with goggles and spear guns. Before we could ask about assistance, the boat flashed past and with smiles and waves was gone. So much for pilotage.

By 1130 the turbulence and noise of the outpouring water had eased somewhat. The white water was gone, and now we looked at a disturbed ribbon of blue tumbling into the ocean. I hoisted a number two genoa, clamped the sketch chart between my teeth, climbed to the top of the mast, and motioned to Margaret to head in. With the sun high and a little to the north I could see into the thin water quite well, especially with my Polaroid sunglasses. Our problem was that the pass was narrow, strange to us, full of little whirlpools and eddies, and a fifteen-knot headwind was blowing out. We got halfway in, tacked once, and were going ahead slowly when *Whisper* got caught by the main stream of outflowing water. A giant hand seemed to push gently against us, and a minute later we were back out in the ocean. I had gotten a good look at the pass, however, which seemed clear on the north side.

We dropped the number two genoa, put up the larger number one for more drive, and headed in for a second try. Since I now had an idea of the pass, I stayed on deck and dealt with the headsail sheets when Margaret tacked. (We certainly could have used a third person at this moment. One to steer, one for the headsail sheets, and a lookout aloft.) Heading south into the southeast wind, we got sailing well on the port tack and speeded up to five or six knots before we hit the outflowing water. We had enough steam up to get even with the outer part of the land, which here was about a quarter of a mile wide. When we got to the dangerous middle part of the pass we tacked to the east. Although we were gaining ground, the contrary water was pushing us north. We watched the pink coral along the edge of the land to our right getting closer and closer and the color of the water growing lighter. We tacked again and picked up speed. Now the force of the opposing water was less, and in a twinkling we were through the pass, out of much of the current and tidal stream, and into the light green waters of the lagoon.*

---

* Someone might ask why we didn't use our engine. Because (1) we have much more power and control with our sails, (2) the sails won't quit at a vital moment, and (3) it's more fun and challenging to sail.

Ahead we saw half a dozen big patches of coral, most marked with crude beacons. Margaret turned southwest toward the village and eased the sheets, while I hurried up the mast to con the yacht from aloft. Sailing along parallel to the land was easy, and I was able to shout down steering instructions when we got too near a coral head.

The village was about two miles from the pass and thickly planted with coconut palms. We were surprised to see two yachts, one Swiss and one Spanish, at anchor. At 1300 our chain rattled out in seven fathoms, we handed the mainsail, and swung head to wind above turquoise water over white sand. Marvelous!

Raroïa (pronounced ra-roe-ee-a with no accents) is an oval-shaped atoll twenty-two miles long and seven miles wide. The island's greatest claim to fame occurred in 1947 when Thor Heyerdahl's raft *Kon-Tiki* fetched up on the eastern reef after the trip from Peru. Bengt Danielsson, the anthropologist on the raft, later spent a year on Raroïa and wrote an excellent small book about the life of the islanders.[3] Danielsson told of two hundred people and a thriving village; thirty years later, however, we found just fifty Tuamotuans. "Many have gone to Papeete for the bright lights," said an elder. Though the size of the village had declined, there was still plenty going on.

The islanders earned money by selling copra, the dried meat of brown coconuts, which is used in soap and cosmetics. When the price of copra was high (often supported by the French government), the villagers spent lots of

Fisherman, Tuamotus

money aboard the trading ship that came once a month. But whether the Tuamotuans had cash or not, they always had plenty of fish from the sea and the sweet milk from fresh green coconuts. On a bit of land only a few miles square and surrounded by the vast ocean, the people lived very close to the sea. Indeed they seemed part of the sea, sort of half fish and half human.

The Polynesians are the most hospitable people in the world, and when you describe them it's hard to avoid the words "happy" and "joyous." Above all else these people love to sing and dance and talk and just be with you. They are extremely courteous and are forever bringing gifts simply for the pleasure of giving. On our first day ashore we met half of the people in the village. On the next day we met the other half. We were given shell necklaces, pearl shells, fish, and drinking nuts. We visited the mayor, the local sculptor, the best fisherman, and the fastest copra cutter. We played with the children. We met Bernard, Etienne, Peni, Remy, and Lucie. . . .

On some of the thatched roofs we were astonished to see solar panels that charged twelve-volt batteries which in turn powered cassette players and a few lights. There was a general election in French Polynesia, and we heard all about the complicated politics ("Vote for Gaston Flosse, the people's choice" said the posters).

The villagers liked to come aboard *Whisper*. Someone always had a guitar or ukulele, and soon the yacht was filled with rollicking Tahitian music. Polynesian guitar playing is incredible; the musician uses only three or four chords but builds brilliance and variety by rapid and syncopated strumming and sudden endings. The music is infectious, and soon everyone is clapping and laughing; it's impossible to keep your feet still.

I went fishing with the men, who gleefully speared parrot fish that I could scarcely see. The men dived for pearl shells, pried them open with a knife, and presented us with the contents, which had little squares of tasty meat something like northern scallops. We walked among the small houses, cool under the palms. We swam from lovely beaches.

On Sunday mornings we went to the tidy century-old church together with the entire village. The men appeared in trousers and their best shirts. The women wore nice cotton frocks and had their waist-length black hair carefully combed and rolled up or simply combed long or worn in long braids. We marveled at the strong and harmonious voices that boomed out the hymns with such gusto and devotion. Unlike so many gloomy church services that appear to concentrate on sin and how we are guilty, etc., the service at the little Raroïa church was sober and dignified, yet pleasant and upbeat. Although I didn't understand a single sentence in the Tahitian prayer book, I came away from the church thoroughly refreshed. I felt that during this hour on Sunday morning all the people of the village were somehow brought together and united anew.

Margaret and I were invited to stay on Raroïa forever.

Yet every paradise has its problems. Flies and mosquitoes were a bother, coral cuts wouldn't heal, we couldn't fish because we couldn't recognize the poison fish, the diet grew monotonous, and boredom was a factor. There was no doctor, no store, no electricity, and no library. Schooling for the children was difficult, and fresh water had to be caught from rain. The islanders spoke Tuamotuan-Tahitian; their knowledge of French was limited. If there was any alcohol in sight the men drank it to the last drop; yet the Polynesians

Peni and ukulele, Raroïa

have little tolerance for alcohol and get very drunk. The lagoon anchorages were satisfactory during the normal trade wind, but if it blew up you were often on a lee shore with miles of open water in front of your vessel. Your ground tackle had to be good; yet the coral heads made proper anchoring difficult.

Like most civilizations, Raroïa was a mixture of light and dark, sweet and sour, blue against yellow. On balance I felt a great attraction for the island and the people. When the sun floated over the gently waving palm fronds, I heard someone laughing in the distance, and the limpid water lapped on the white sand, all my sensible resistance collapsed and my heart fairly broke. . . .

The Swiss yacht that we had seen when we had sailed in was *Le Maripier IV,* a shiny new blue-hulled Swan 57. On the morning of her departure, we rowed over for a visit and met the charming owner, Bertrand Maus, his captain, and his four guests. The voyage was the dream trip of a wealthy man, and all aboard were having the time of their lives. We heard from Bertrand that the captain of the other yacht in the anchorage had injured his back and was in a poor way. That afternoon we rowed across to the Spanish yacht, *Abuelo III,* to introduce ourselves and to see if we could help.

Lagoon and beach, Tuamotus

Juan Ribas hailed from Vigo in northwest Spain and was sailing around the world with his young American wife Nena and an infant daughter named Luisa. When we met him he was flat on his back. We saw a deeply tanned man who looked to be in his late forties and was as slim as a piece of celery. One day when Juan was ashore he had given a man a hand with some heavy lifting. A few hours later he was in terrible pain from a slipped disc in his back. He had lain flat on the starboard bunk in *Abuelo*'s saloon for two weeks, had moved too soon, and had reinjured himself. When we met him he had been flat on his back *for an additional four weeks,* in traction part of the time as advised by a Mexican doctor via radio. Juan complained of no feeling in his toes, which I thought was a bad sign.

Every Sunday at church the local people said special prayers for the Spanish captain. What he really needed, however, was expert medical attention. Juan's soft brown eyes were bright, and his teeth flashed when he smiled, but his spirits were flagging. He speculated on ending his days on Raroïa. "Not a bad place to go," he joked bravely, "but I'm not ready for the long box yet."

During the following days we visited *Abuelo* many times to cheer up Juan and his young wife. Nena was busy looking after Juan and the baby, cooking on board, keeping the yacht clean, and going ashore for water. Juan and I discussed a route to Tahiti via the atolls of Katiu and Toau. We both had similar plans, but I couldn't see how he could possibly handle his vessel. Nena could deal with the sails and anchors. She did not know celestial navigation, and Juan was too unsteady to use a sextant.

One day on *Whisper* we had a visit from the mayor of the village, who brought us pearl shells and shell necklaces. Margaret made coffee, and we had a long talk in very marginal French. The mayor told us that once there had been a thousand people on Raroïa. At that time the main village was across the lagoon on the east side of the atoll. In 1927 a number of villagers had died from a fever. Now there were only about fifty people—eleven families—all of whom lived at Ngarumaova on the west side where *Whisper* was anchored. We heard about a small project for cultured pearls, and we discussed the designs of outrigger canoes.

The mayor was intrigued with my questions. Perhaps entertained would be a better word, because few people took an interest in the history of Raroïa.

During our visit we kept hearing snippets of talk about gold. In the 1500s or 1600s or 1700s—the locals were not too precise with dates—a Spanish galleon carrying gold was wrecked on the eastern reef near the site of the old village. The Tuamotuans—or Paumotuans as the people were then called—took in the six or seven sailors who made it alive to shore. One of them was a Captain Flores, a man with red hair. Since there was no communication or trade between Raroïa and anywhere else, the survivors had no choice but to stay. The Spaniards salvaged part of their yellow cargo and buried it on the west side of the atoll. During the next few months, according to the story, Flores then killed his countrymen one by one so he alone would control the gold.

During his stay on Raroïa, Flores took several Paumotuan wives. With his number one wife he began a family that has descended in a direct line to the present day. Flores' people in today's village—some with a trace of red hair—even have an old treasure map on a piece of parchment which they keep rolled in a bamboo tube and hidden. (The family is well off, the elders say, and they are reserving the gold for the future.) One of the men in the family claimed to have dived forty-five meters to the shark-guarded wreck of his great-etc. grandfather and to have brought up a bar of gold. The diver showed it to a passing yacht captain who took it to be carbon-dated, but of course the captain and the gold were never seen again. A woman told Nena Ribas about a small, coral-encrusted box that had washed up on a beach. Inside were old gold coins. The woman said that she had seen the box and coins herself. Where is the box now? The woman didn't know.

When the *Kon-Tiki* raft appeared in 1947, the island people knew the six men were *after the gold*. Why else would they have chosen Raroïa? When anthropologist Bengt Danielsson came several years later and dug a few holes looking for artifacts and remnants (as scientists do), he too was *after the gold*. When Juan Ribas arrived in *Abuelo III* and the mayor learned that the ship and captain were Spanish, the mayor's first anxious questions were: "Are you a Flores? Are you *after the gold?*"

This story sounds like a sequel to *Treasure Island* that I suspect Robert Louis Stevenson would never have approved. (Could Flores have been Long John Silver, or was it the other way round?) Yet there could be a glint of truth, because Spanish ships did sail Pacific waters, and many were wrecked. *If* the ship existed. *If* she had gold. *If* her location were known. *If* the cargo could be salvaged at this late date. . . . The whole topic was based upon the haziest veneer of hand-me-down speculation, the strangling restraints of language barriers, and a reluctance on the part of the islanders to even discuss the subject. The mere mention of gold immediately brought grave looks, head shaking, and wrinkled foreheads to the islanders, who began to nod at one another with knowing glances. Just what value the gold would have had on Raroïa was a moot question anyway. A few new outboard motors, a colossal feast, a big drinking party, terrible hangovers, and finally a deep sleep.

Margaret and I had a long talk about Juan Ribas, his back problems, his family, and how he was in effect marooned in the Tuamotus with no hope of medical treatment. We rowed over to *Abuelo*. "Listen, Juan," I said. "You're in a poor way. We've got to do something. Margaret and I have a plan. Makemo is eighty miles away and has an airstrip. I suggest that we put Margaret on board *Abuelo* as captain while I take *Whisper* by myself. Both yachts can sail together, but if we get separated, each vessel will have a navigator. At Makemo you can get an airplane for Tahiti and medical attention. *Abuelo* can be left at Makemo or be taken to Tahiti by Margaret and me, using the air shuttle. Nena and the child can either go to Tahiti with you or stay on *Abuelo*."

Juan took a little time to think about our offer before he finally rejected it. "I don't want *Whisper* sailing into these hazardous passes without someone up the mast to watch for coral," he said. After more talk we decided to sail both yachts with their regular crews to Tahiti via Katiu, 115 miles to the west-southwest. *Whisper* would do the navigation and lead *Abuelo*. The course was direct without any intervening islands, and there was an anchorage in Katiu's pass where Juan could rest before we continued. This scheme would get *Abuelo* and the Ribas family to Tahiti with only one stop, which Juan thought he could manage.

The Spanish captain got up, and—smiling grimly—began to move around. He was extremely weak, and I didn't think there was any way that he could sail. Nevertheless, Margaret and I helped get *Abuelo* ready for sea. Nena scurried about doing a dozen jobs. Juan, full of powerful painkillers and somewhat dazed by it all, hobbled around the decks. I was terrified that he might re-injure himself again. With his slim figure and salt-and-pepper beard, Juan looked as if he had been plucked from one of those gloomy paintings of the Spanish Renaissance.

Polynesian departures are a disaster because everyone starts crying, and the crying gets worse and worse. At 0545 on the last day of August, *Whisper* and *Abuelo* headed out. Even at that hour half the village was up to wave goodbye and to dart out with last-minute gifts of fish and coconuts. We led, and *Abuelo* followed. We soon discovered that the Spanish yacht was hopelessly slow in light airs. She was built like an icebreaker and laden with diving gear and a whole catalog of broken-down electronic equipment plus a large, three-bladed fixed propeller. We made a drastic sail reduction on *Whisper* to stay even with the green ketch.

The twelve-knot trade wind gradually got lighter, and by noon of the second day we had made only sixty miles and had drifted a little south. From the masthead I could see the northwest coast of Makemo. Katiu's pass was still thirty-five miles to the west, too far to make before dark. Ten miles off a thirty-eight-mile-long reef was no place to be drifting at night with a wounded friend, so I started *Whisper*'s little diesel engine and steamed toward the pass at the west end of Makemo, the opposite end of the atoll from the village and airstrip. *Abuelo* followed, and we entered Passe Tupuhiria— fortunately at slack water—and anchored in the lagoon.

Juan was exhausted. That night the trade wind returned in force and set up a nasty chop on the lee side of the thirty-two-mile lagoon where we were anchored. The yachts needed second anchors, and by daylight the various chains and warps were wrapped round and round the coral heads beneath us. I wanted to sail with the fair wind. Juan was in poor condition, however, and had to have rest, so we stayed another day and did some re-anchoring and straightening out of warps and chains. I learned the value of keeping nylon warps above coral by using several small floats tied along the line.

On September 3rd Juan felt better and was smiling bravely. We had been nervously watching enormous quantities of water shooting in and out of the pass. At full ebb the pass looked like a horizontal waterfall of surging white water. Ten? Twelve? Fifteen knots? Who knows? We gauged slack water to be at 1100, pulled up the four anchors, and slipped out. Our plan was to sail past the islands of Katiu and Tuanake before dark, and then to head slowly westward so that we would see the islands of Faaite and Fakarava a little after daylight for safe passage between them. The trade wind blew the two yachts westward. In the lee of the various atolls the water was easy and smooth. Margaret and I navigated with great care. *Abuelo*'s masthead light faithfully followed *Whisper*.

Venus and Sirius still flickered in the dawn sky when we picked up the coconut palms on the north coast of Faaite. An hour later we could see an occasional flash of white water on the south reef of Fakarava. Soon we were safely past the two atolls and clear of the Tuamotus and their terrible reefs. The big island of Tahiti was 250 miles ahead on a clear course of 245° magnetic. *Abuelo* could easily find Tahiti by sailing a compass course. We shook out our reefs and sped westward. Goodbye *Abuelo*. Goodbye Tuamotus.

(Juan soon reached Tahiti, where he got medical advice and recovered. Juan and Nena continue to be good friends.)

CHAPTER *SIX*

. . . .

A Splendid Place

*T*he thirty-two-mile-long island of Tahiti is a stunning place to approach from the sea. From a distance it's high, cloudswept, and indistinct. A few hours later you begin to pick out one- and two-thousand-meter mountains whose impossibly steep walls are split into vertical slashes of light and shadow. Closer still, the distant gray turns to green: first the thinnest brushstroke of lime, then a smear of emerald, now a thumbprint of apple. Near the shore everything starts to shimmer with stronger and stronger greens, and from top to bottom the island vibrates with heavenly shades of tropical foliage dappled with black and silver and white and gold.

As we sailed closer, miraculous perfumes drifted out from the land. The ship rose on a swell, and all at once we saw the narrow coastal plain with a patchwork of dark forests and grassy slopes climbing beyond. Suddenly an insect crawled above the reef. With the binoculars the fly became an automobile, a squat Renault, which zipped along the coastal road. Now the spire of a reddish church poked above the reef. Smoke from a fire in someone's field meandered skyward, an inverted cone of gray. The northernmost headland sharpened into view, and we saw the white forefinger of Point Venus, the old lighthouse. Confused shapes untwisted into buildings. Two hours later we headed through the wide and untroubled pass into the port of Papeete, the capital of French Polynesia, and tacked back and forth, wondering where to anchor to clear customs.

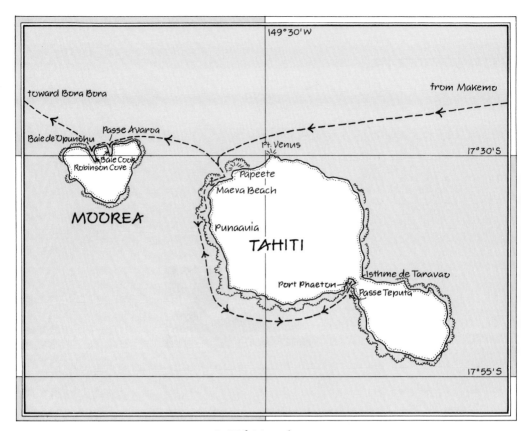

8. Tahiti and Moorea

Around us I could see a concrete breakwater, big ships unloading, shiny oil tanks, buildings of glass and masonry, and a clutch of yachts. A row of flowering trees guarded the shore, and I could hear the buzz of motorscooters and small cars in the distance.

We anchored near a yacht from New Zealand.

"Customs?" I called over.

"Take your papers and passports to the little office over there." A sunburned arm waved vaguely east toward a row of waterfront buildings.

I stood in line in a little police station while a gendarme in a blue uniform filled out forms. Then to the port captain and finally to a tiny customs office where a clerk from Paris was trying to read a dog-eared orange paperback by Graham Greene. "To improve my English," explained the customs man as he stamped my papers. "What about this Greene? Is he any good?"

"First-rate," I said. "A bit cynical, but skillful and quick. You know you have met an intelligence."

Papeete seemed quite orderly. Small cars scurried along the six-lane coastal road, which was nicely camouflaged with trees and shrubs. On the streets we saw Tahitians, Chinese, neatly dressed French military officers, civil servants, and tourists. The old post office was gone; the new one was larger, better looking, and air-conditioned. We were told that you could call London or Paris by simply picking up a telephone in the lobby. The downtown stores were chockablock with goods priced much the same as in the United States. We saw that marine supplies, once impossible to find, were now displayed in neat rows (shackles, solar panels, stainless steel screws, Stockholm tar) in at least four stores. There was a sailmaker and two places to haul out for bottom painting. If you couldn't find something you could always go to the Chinaman who carried everything from aspirins to zippers, from baby rattles to welding rods.

We counted seventy yachts along the waterfront. Most hailed from the United States, Canada, and France, but we saw flags from England and Germany and even from Japan and Brazil. I was surprised at the sight of five yachts from Switzerland, which I had thought was a country of skiers, not sailors. I had to get out the flag book to identify a strange flag that showed five blue stars on a horizontal white stripe that was flanked above and below by horizontal blue stripes.*

The yachts ranged in size from *Blackjack* (twenty-one feet, two tons) to *Camelot* (seventy-nine feet, sixty-six tons). We saw all rigs and all sorts of designs. Wooden boats. Fiberglass yachts by the dozen. A few ferrocement heavyweights. Smooth, unpainted aluminum hulls from France. Many hard-chine steel yachts with the wavy lines and uneven joints of amateur construction. The percentage of metal hulls was increasing each year, and almost every boat had aluminum spars. Some of the vessels were shiny and new; some hogged and decrepit. Some were so burdened with outboard engines, motorcycles, plastic jugs, cockpit dodgers, windsurfers, gas bottles, flapping awnings, spray dodgers, deck boxes, sail bags, hammocks, wind generators, and miscellaneous junk that I wondered how anyone could possibly sail or even see out.

The contrast between the yachts was astonishing. A sleek yellow trimaran with pencil-thin hulls sat next to a beamy Norwegian gaff cutter, an original Colin Archer from Risør, Norway. The trimaran was built of thin wooden strips glued with epoxy and reinforced with carbon fibers. The Norwegian had double-sawn frames and planking suitable for an Indian fort. Yellowbird's mast was a featherweight bendy aluminum extrusion, quiveringly supported by hairlike wires. The Norwegian's spars were stumpy, with the scantlings of cannon barrels, and anchored in place with a forest of wires as thick as your thumb. Yellowbird's sails were laminated from paper-thin

---

* Honduras.

Mylar and Dacron, programmed for scientific stretch. The Norwegian's sails were vertical panels of hand-sewn flax that made you think of blankets. The Norwegian's stores included potatoes, salt beef, and bread baked in a coal stove. The trimaran's crew ate nut paste, freeze-dried pork chops, and dehydrated fruit. It was the traditional sailors versus the scientists. Leif Ericson and Company against the astronauts. Each regarded the other as an oddity, but the crews had a drink and a few laughs together and found that they were very much alike.

We saw all kinds of sailors. Each had come a long way across the sea. There were bronzed, muscular teenagers. Young women with lovely legs. Thirty-year-olds who had somehow escaped from the nine-to-five. Retirees with nifty captains' caps, weak white beards, and wives dutifully plodding behind. The tough loners, the vegetarians, the big drinkers, the old veterans, the know-it-all beginners, the nonstop talkers, the nuclear protesters, the rich and the poor, the excited and the disappointed. The variety was fascinating.

Margaret and I had sailed to Tahiti fifteen years earlier, and we saw many changes in the fleet in front of us. The number of yachts was roughly six times greater, and in general the boats were newer and bigger—say an average of thirty-eight to forty-four feet—and represented investments of perhaps four or five times as much. The vessels were increasingly complex and typically had wheel steering, a hefty four-cylinder diesel engine, an elaborate galley with a gas stove, a hot water heater, a pressure water system, a shower, and a ten- or twelve-foot inflatable dinghy with a twenty- or twenty-five-horsepower motor. We saw auxiliary generating sets and electric windlasses and even washing machines and water makers. Many yachts had both wind vane steering systems and electric autopilots. People proudly showed us their ham radios, VHF sets, automatic radio direction finders, and satellite navigation equipment. Refrigeration was commonplace as were banks of instruments to indicate apparent wind, boat speed, velocity made good, compass averaging, and so on.

The price of all this complexity was high both in dollars and maintenance. The captains complained bitterly about the never-ending boxes of equipment going to and from manufacturers and the difficulties with air freight, postal deliveries, foreign payments, customs problems, and delays. Refrigeration was a particular curse, and complaints about failures and poor operation were almost universal. I don't mean to say that some of this equipment is not useful, but there is a point at which a person must declare "No more!" Otherwise instead of the gadgets helping the captain, the captain becomes the slave of the gadgets. After all, you can judge wind direction perfectly well with a ribbon at the mast top and learn to estimate wind speed by looking at whitecaps. You can live without radios and bathe in the tropical seas. Excellent bread can be baked on a simple galley stove. Hanked-on sails are less costly, more reliable, and have better shape than roller furling sails, which may not work at all. The simplest is the most foolproof and certainly the cheapest and most maintenance-free.

One day in the post office Margaret and I accidentally overheard an American woman's telephone call to the United States. The lady was in tears. "Everything is too complicated and too expensive," she wailed. "This is supposed to be paradise, but our trip has turned into one problem after another. The radar doesn't work anymore, the haulout was a disaster, and there are so many jobs to do on the yacht that we have no time for the Tahitians. We're heading back to Hawaii." The poor woman seemed very distressed because she had so looked forward to the trip, which because of boat projects had become tedious and unpleasant. I felt sorry for her, and I thanked my lucky stars that *Whisper* was a simple vessel and easy to sail.

Not only did the equipment complications cut into sailing time and enjoyment, but I felt that yacht crews were far less expert than earlier. Nowadays they almost always used engines near ports and seemed to have entirely given up the fun and challenge of working in and out of complicated anchorages under sail. If the engine didn't work they called for help over the radio. Additionally, the present-day Magellans traveled to the same ports, stopped for long periods, and then went to the next major stopping place where they again anchored in tight little clusters to compare notes and experiences. Were the natives friendly? Who knows? Few sailors ever met any.

We spent six days in Papeete. Like all visitors to French Polynesia, we had to show either a return air ticket to our home country or post a bond to guarantee our outward passage. I deposited $1,300 at the Banque de l'Indochine, which was to be refunded when we left. We carried a sail to Voilerie Pacifique to have a panel replaced. We had experimented with a genoa that had a foot that could be reefed. However, we found that the tied-up foot was no good at all because head seas bashed into it and not only worked the ties loose but threatened to destroy the lower part of the sail. As a practical matter we found it quicker to change to a small headsail.

We did a little food shopping, and Margaret bought lengths of brightly patterned cotton material for wrap-around pareus that she liked to wear. We had several meals on other yachts with new and old friends. We discovered that the long-term Papeete harbor sailors had developed an astonishing social program, which included Tuesday luncheons, Thursday beach barbecues, Friday night fish fries, and Sunday morning brunch plus parties aboard various yachts, endless visits, and advice sessions. This was pleasant up to a point, but we chose not to get too involved because we wanted to visit other parts of Tahiti.

We saw several yachts that belonged to the Greenpeace movement and were protesting against French nuclear testing on Mururoa Atoll. The yachts had tried to sail to the test site but had been forcibly diverted to Papeete.

High viewpoint for a new island

The authorities, savvy to the appeal of political dissent, treated the yachts cautiously and with patience, smiled bleakly, and hoped they would go away.

On September 12th we sailed a few miles to the west side of Tahiti and anchored at Maeva Beach, which looked out at the island of Moorea ten miles to the west. At sunset the distant mountains flamed with dancing browns and filmy yellows, and one could almost imagine a mythical ship with burning sails that rocked slowly on a vast and golden Pacific.

We had had a paint failure on *Whisper*'s starboard side near the midships waterline. To be able to work on the area, we ran the main boom out on the port side at right angles to the hull and hung various anchors, pieces of chain, and jugs of water at the end of the boom to heel the yacht to port. When the wind was calm we sanded the blistered area and daubed on paint. While the paint was drying we went ashore and jumped on a truck to go to a Tahitian wedding in Punaauia. The sister of a Tahitian man we had met was getting married.

"Would you come?" he asked.

"By all means," we answered.

"Les trucks" were the main transport of the islands and great fun to ride. Each truck started from the central bus station in Papeete and went to one of the outlying districts—Papeari, Hitiaa, Papenoo, or wherever, the schedule depending on demand. Each vehicle had a covered wooden back with two facing benches that ran lengthwise and could seat about forty people depending on how many watermelons, shopping baskets, chickens, guitars, and big Tahitians were on board (empty baby cribs were tied on top; fish at the back). The trucks were all nicely painted in bright greens and reds and yellows. Each had a sound system that played Tahitian music at maximum loudness. When le truck was full, it started up, the music began to play, and the Tahitian women adjusted their straw hats. Everybody smiled, and we sped along a route with flowering trees and wide-leafed plants and shrubs redolent with perfume.

It was the nicest bus line in the world.

We didn't quite know where the church was and got off at the wrong stop, so we had to walk three or four kilometers. We soon found that strolling along Tahiti's flower-covered lanes is not the worst walking in the world. We passed all sorts of lush flowers and blossoming trees, fruit-laden mangoes, and brightly colored hedges. We stopped to look at a house, and an elderly Tahitian woman waved us up to the porch for a glass of iced tea. We arrived at the church a little late, and the service was half over. The pews were filled with nicely dressed Tahitians who were busy looking at one another and smiling at small and large jokes. The priest's biggest job seemed to be to keep order by trying to look serious and glaring at noisy youngsters. The formal vows were soon over, and the service finished with a couple of quick hymns. The wedding party then assembled on the front steps of the

Tahitian dancer

church for the official photograph, a moment to be immortalized in a picture that would hang in the house for years.

The men wore white shirts, ties, dark suits, and shoes, and had flowers in the right lapels of their jackets. The suits, however, were ill-fitting, with the trousers generally too long and the jacket sleeves too short for the powerful Tahitian shoulders. It was obvious that the suits were borrowed from Uncle Tati, taken from a secondhand rack, or rescued from the bottom of a trunk. Everybody knew this, which made it even funnier as the Tahitians pointed out one another's worn elbows and wrinkled trousers. Nevertheless, the men were reasonably dressed and as proud as they could be. The women looked trim in long white dresses and white high-heeled shoes. They wore earrings, strings of white beads, and circlets of white flowers in their hair, and carried white bouquets on their left arms. From the constant shuffling of the shoes, however, it was obvious that the big Tahitian feet hated shoes. The bridesmaids were in back laughing together and waiting to bombard the bride and groom with showers of rice. A few children scampered about dressed in finery. Now the photographer had everyone set. Look at the camera. Hold it! Presto! And it was over. The party relaxed. Coats and ties were peeled off; the women kicked off their tight shoes. The wedding group moved to the newlyweds' house where tubs of iced beer and food and guitars were ready. The celebration was called a *bringue* and everyone made merry. The first order of business, however, was to get rid of the business suits and the long dresses and slip into cool pareus. . . .

Back at our anchorage we got acquainted with Val Schaeffer, an energetic American who owned an enormous green dragon named *Camelot*. She was a wishbone ketch seventy-nine feet on deck and built of steel by Abeking & Rasmussen in 1952. *Camelot* was huge and deluxe and a bit run down. She was the only yacht I've ever been on that, in addition to all the usual things, had an honest-to-God piano bar and a bridal suite (with mirrors). Val, a former X-15 aircraft test pilot, claimed that he and his girlfriend Marsha (who were to be married the following week in Boston, where Marsha had already gone) ran the vessel by themselves and did deluxe chartering ($6,000 a week for a man and his party, whatever that meant).

"I made the mistake of spending all my money for *Camelot* and never thought about what I would use to run her," moaned Val. When we met him he was expertly laying out two three-hundred-pound fisherman anchors all by himself so he could leave *Camelot* and go to Boston to get married. Val produced a bottle of 151-proof rum, and we toasted the bridegroom, *Camelot,* and distant Marsha. We wished the captain good luck in all future enterprises.

On September 20th we sailed south along the west coast and then east along the south coast to the Isthme de Taravao, about which we'd heard vague and wonderful reports. We had been assured by the harbor rats in Papeete that because of the contrary current and headwinds we would never be able to sail there, and if we did, the impenetrable reefs would defeat us. I bought a French chart and we studied the pilot book. The thirty-four-mile route didn't look difficult, but you never know, so we started early, reefed down when necessary, and pushed along as best we could. We got to our target and through Passe Teputa nine hours later. The reefs on the south side of the peninsula were a nasty lot, and I was pleased to have the detailed chart. We slipped into Port Phaeton, an irregular-shaped inlet a half mile wide that

cut deeply into the island for about two miles. Our anchorage was surrounded by a basin of land roughly one by two miles, hemmed in by heights
on three sides and by a complex of reefs on the fourth. We were landlocked
in the only hurricane anchorage on Tahiti. Five yachts swung easily at
anchor, one near us and four in the northeast corner. A country road ran
partway around the shore, and here and there we saw small houses—perhaps
a dozen in all. An occasional automobile rumbled in the distance, and a
fisherman trolling from an outrigger canoe paddled slowly past us.

Every day or two we rowed ashore and walked to the road and shops
on the narrow isthmus to the east. Our first stop was always the Tahitian ice
cream stand, then the baker, the butcher, and the grocery store. The shopkeepers were easygoing, business was slow and unhurried, and the whole place
was pleasantly remote. Sometimes Margaret and I walked in different directions. I would go looking for photographs while she went to the post office
or the shop that sold yard goods.

One morning I was out in the country and I passed a crew of tough-
looking Tahitian laborers. The men had picks and shovels and were hacking
away at a slide that partially blocked the road. The workers were barefoot
and wore shorts, and their bodies were streaked with mud. They used their
picks and shovels in a determined, faintly ominous manner, and I felt a little
nervous when I walked around the slide and passed close to the sweating

Tahitian house and shore line, Motuovini

workmen. I tried the greeting *ia-ora-na,* but I rather mumbled the words, and no one seemed to hear me. At least there were no replies.

All at once a child came running down the road, tripped over something, and crashed to the pavement. The little girl got up screaming and crying. Her sobs were heartrending. The road gang immediately threw down all the picks and shovels and rushed to the little girl. One man scooped her up and began to comfort her. The other laborers crowded around the girl, patted the child's head, and muttered reassuring words. They took turns holding her and jostled her with tenderness. I couldn't help but smile at the love and affection that poured out from the tough road gang into the sobbing little girl who gradually dried her tears, released herself from one of the big men, and skipped off down the road. The workmen went back to their picks and shovels. Tough men indeed!

We had heard about the Gauguin museum, so after breakfast one day we walked six kilometers southwest to the new buildings at Motuovini. Gauguin spent six years in Tahiti at the end of the nineteenth century before sailing to the Marquesas, where he died in 1903. His work in Tahiti was important and enduring, although he was despised by the authorities and the French settlers. Today, almost four generations later, Gauguin, along with van Gogh, Seurat, and Cézanne, is considered to be one of the founding giants of modern art. If you walk through the villages and look at the people and the flowery countryside, it's easy to see where Gauguin got his colors and ideas. How strange it is that on the island where Gauguin was scorned while he lived, a splendid memorial to him should open sixty-two years after his death. The museum is built around a series of visual displays that recreate the life and work of the artist in a surprisingly effective manner. When we visited Tahiti there were no original Gauguins in the museum. However, Margaret and I met Gilles Artur, the director, who told us of his plans to borrow three or four originals and display them in a new wing.

From *Whisper's* anchorage in Port Phaeton we looked toward the north and west where tall grasses rose stiffly along the shore. Behind the grasses, low shrubs crowded the foreshore and grew around the bases of the coconut palms, whose smooth trunks climbed fifteen to twenty meters before erupting in sunbursts of spreading fronds. In back of the palms a miscellany of trees marched up the steep slopes. In a few places the branches of casuarina trees swayed lazily. Higher up were low trees with horizontal branches, and in the distance we saw a ragged crest six hundred to one thousand meters high. Slim cascades tumbled from a few high points. My eyes were filled with the impossible-to-describe greens of Tahiti: dark, light, edged with yellow, thinned with brown, mixed with gray, trembling with silver. . . .

Suddenly it was raining. The flickering greens (those damned greens again) became more intense and heavy, almost as if they had a core of black. The ribbon cascades widened out to waterfalls now tinged with brown as bits of topsoil washed toward the sea. Water poured from *Whisper*'s awning into buckets and into the water tanks. A gust pushed the yacht in a half circle, and I looked to the south—out beyond the booming reef to the sea.

Two nights earlier we had visited a large ketch owned by an American with a Tahitian girlfriend. Or, more precisely, a live-in vahine who adored Mr. X. The pleasant Tahitian girl was about to have a child fathered by the American, and she was thrilled at the prospect of a white baby. He was sixty-five; she was twenty. The American was a widely traveled, well-off, retired businessman. The girl could neither read nor write and had formerly worked in a laundry. They communicated in halting French that neither spoke well. He was thinking about learning some Tahitian, and she was picking up a little English. She dreamed of sailing off into the blue, but one wondered how she would navigate or even read the compass. The plot was pure Somerset Maugham, and one shook one's head at the foolishness of passion. Beyond, far out beyond, the restless sea boomed on the reef.

. . . .

CHAPTER SEVEN

Notes from
Margaret's Journal

OCTOBER 6th. 19 miles. We're off for another two or three weeks of sailing and another two or three thousand miles. We rushed around all day on Tahiti getting the yacht ready and dealing with supplies, the clearance, and last-minute letters. I'm very tired. In order to get under way, we sailed across to the north coast of Moorea in the late afternoon and slipped through Passe Avaroa into Baie de Cook, where we have anchored in the shelter of the reef. Behind us the tops of the green mountains disappear into the clouds. This place gives me a feeling of magic.

OCTOBER 7th. 14 miles to noon. We sailed from our anchorage to the head of Baie de Cook with the mountains rising close above us on both sides. I steered while Hal played the mainsheet as gusts of wind danced down the slopes. Delicious scenery climbed up all around us, and the sailing on the smooth water was perfection. Some determined farmers, probably Chinese, are raising pineapples on the incredibly steep slope far up a mountain on the west side of the bay. Unbelievable. No Polynesian would even go up there. We glided past *Hippo,* the Swiss yacht that was anchored next to us at Maeva beach on Tahiti, and *Chant d'Alize,* also Swiss, which we last saw in Brazil. The number of Swiss yachts is amazing. We then sailed out into the ocean and along the reef for two miles and nipped into Baie de Opunohu, the second deep bay on the north side of Moorea. We made a few tacks up to Robinson Cove near the head of the bay where we anchored fifteen years ago. I thought of our old friends on the blue yacht *Procax* from Belgium and little *Calypso* from Australia. Where, oh where are they now? Clouds covered the sun, and the mood of the place was overcast and somber. It matched my feelings about leaving Tahiti and Moorea. I could have stayed forever.

OCTOBER 8th. 98 miles. At 0700 we picked up the green cones of Huahine and Raiatea, two more gorgeous islands in the western part of the Society group. I feel sad not to visit them. Sailing near land demands close attention, which means that someone must be on deck every minute.

OCTOBER 9th. 70 miles. I scored a big success with hotcakes made of half whole wheat flour and half white flour. Good with canned butter and maple syrup. A couple of platefuls stuffed the captain until the afternoon. At 1500 we were near Bora Bora, so we slipped into the lagoon via Teavanui Pass and anchored for the night. Even from two miles away we can see many new buildings and hotels in the main village. The place looks like a travel folder.

OCTOBER 10th. 51 miles. Awoke to the smell of kerosene, which we traced to a leak in the new lantern from Shanghai that we bought in Papeete. Nicely painted but poorly made and impossible to fix because the pressed metal joints were faulty. We heaved the lantern over the side. We passed Maupiti, the last of the French islands. A small place with a little volcanic mountain ringed by a coral reef. The pass at the south end looked narrow and dangerous with some nasty breaking seas on the right-hand side. Heavy rain showers. I can't stand to have the radio on because the Tahitian music makes me think of the island and I start to cry.

OCTOBER 11th. 96 miles. A steady southeast wind and long, even seas. We're going nicely with the vane steering. At last I can relax and do a little sewing. I'm trying to make a Vanuatu flag from scraps of cloth. Why do new countries choose such complicated designs?

OCTOBER 12th. 124 miles. Hal made a masthead fly, which is a great help in judging wind direction. It's simply a meter of blue ribbon sewn to a horizontal plastic disc—the size of a silver dollar—which pivots at the top of a twelve-millimeter-diameter aluminum tube about a meter long that we hoisted up to the masthead. I believe the Dutch call such a thing a wimple. We made it from odds and ends on board, so the cost was nothing at all. So far the wimple works to perfection.

During the afternoon we had heavy rain and no wind for a few hours. We topped up the water tanks, bathed, washed our hair, and collected three buckets of water for clothes rinsing. We catch the rainwater, which runs down the mainsail to the boom and then forward along the footrope slot in the boom to the mast. The water then pours into a large cylindrical funnel lashed to the back of the mast underneath the boom. A hose leads from the funnel to the deck filler for the tanks

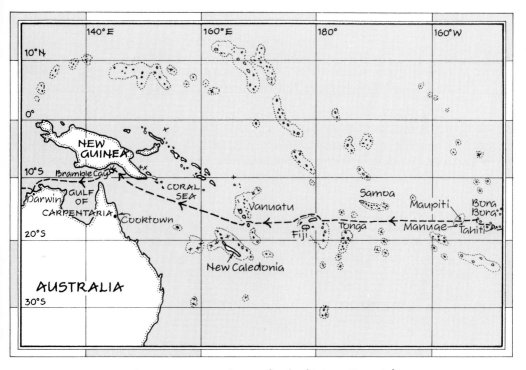

9. The western South Pacific (Tahiti to Darwin)

or into a bucket lashed to the starboard shrouds. We let the rain rinse everything before we collect the water.

Hal and I have both been on deck keeping a careful lookout for Manuae, which we think is about fifteen miles to port. We planned star sights, but clouds rolled across the sky at dusk. The motion of the sea is a little upset, which suggests that we may be close to the atoll. We changed to the fore-and-aft rig so we can reverse our course quickly. Passing low and unlighted islands at night is a worrying business.

OCTOBER 13th. 92 miles. We had the mainsail down for a few hours to replace a broken leech line.

OCTOBER 14th. 150 miles. The captain is in a bad temper, and I am staying out of his way. He has been working on the mainsheet traveler, whose aluminum parts have corroded and frozen up. A lot of violent hammering, sawing, and cursing. I don't know why men have to swear so when they fix things. Hal has replaced the aluminum limit stops with an arrangement of Dacron line to take the shock of the main boom traveler's movements when we tack or gybe. At least the line won't corrode.

OCTOBER 15th. 130 miles. Finished *Out of Africa* by Isak Dinesen. A 1937 book set on a coffee plantation in Kenya. First-rate. Lovely descriptions and good insights into the lives and feelings of the African people of her era. I enjoyed the book in spite of some recent snarky remarks by V. S. Naipaul, currently the darling of the critics, who writes scathing social criticism. It's unfair of Naipaul to attack an author who wrote of an Africa of two generations ago when the social climate was light years away from today. I wish the perceptive Isak Dinesen could have met Naipaul. She might have gentled down his snotty remarks.

OCTOBER 16th. 115 miles. My birthday. The day started out with a double rainbow at 0630. When I awoke from my morning sleep, I heard Hal rattling around in the galley trying to bake a cake. His batter didn't rise properly, and the cake finished up burned at the bottom and raw at the top. The remains looked like volcanic debris or a chemical experiment. We ate it as chocolate pudding. Before we left Tahiti Hal took me out to a nice restaurant and bought me a dress to celebrate this day.

OCTOBER 17th. 138 miles. Our wedding anniversary. Not that we ever celebrate. Hal doesn't believe in wedding anniversaries. He likes to celebrate birthdays. This afternoon I worked on my Vanuatu flag. Meanwhile Hal read aloud from *Alice in Wonderland.* He is very tired today. He took star sights last night, but the stars he shot had declinations too high for H.O. 249. He worked them out from H.O. 208, which is a longer method. One sight was a planet that he did not recognize, so he tried working out Mars and Saturn and then discovered that the planet was Jupiter. He also started off with the wrong day, which meant that he had to discard all of his first calculations. Today he is suffering from eyestrain. Reading from *Alice* was light relief.

OCTOBER 18th. 158 miles. So much of this long-distance sailing is ridiculously easy. You simply blow along in front of the wind out in an ocean somewhere. The main problem is not to run into anything. That's why you stay away from the shores, which often mean rocks and coral and problems. The insurance people who restrict vessels to twenty-five miles from shore have got it all wrong. The rates should go up near shore and down at sea.

Just now my problem is what to do with a great stalk of bananas—fifty or sixty luscious Tahitian bananas—all enormous and all ripe. I can't stand to throw away fresh fruit, particularly when it's so good. Today for breakfast we had banana French toast. For lunch we had fried bananas. For supper we ate a curry with a banana garnish. Tomorrow I plan banana crepes for breakfast, bananas with canned cream and sugar at lunchtime, and bananas in an instant pudding to finish off supper. Hal and I both like bananas, and we have been eating two or three off the stalk every day. Also I am drying half a dozen. In spite of all this, however, I still have half a stalk. Too bad we don't have a monkey on board.

OCTOBER 19th. 142 miles. After dark we saw a loom of light from American Samoa, seventy miles to the north. The easterly wind has gradually eased, and the windless sails slat and bang. In the middle of the night I was sitting in the cockpit when a black bird, a noddy, landed on the starboard life ring just behind me. I was half asleep, lost in my thoughts, when a great fluttering of wings startled me. A phantom had come to roost. The noddy was smooth and sleek, probably a young bird, and entirely black except for a grayish-white cap on his little head which he cocked in the most engaging manner. The bird stood watch with me for about two hours and then was suddenly gone.

OCTOBER 20th. 61 miles. Light wind most of the day. We put a few stitches on the old number two genoa and replaced a bronze hank that had worn to paper thickness from rubbing on the headstay. Wonderful Samoan talk coming over the radio. I don't understand a word, but the flow of the words and their tuneful sounds are lilting and delightful. At sunset Hal sighted a volcanic island ahead and a little to starboard. According to a star fix I worked out at 1920, we are forty-five miles from a Tongan island named Niuatobutabu.

10. Fiji and Tonga islands

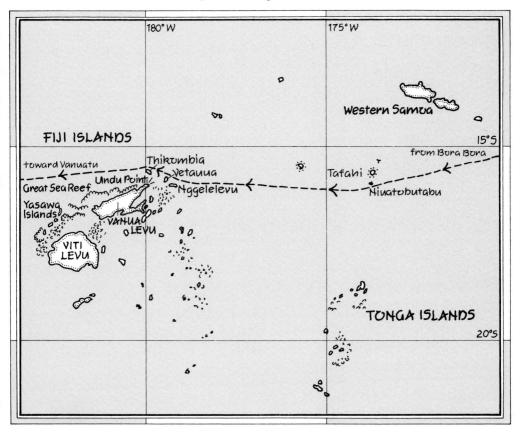

OCTOBER 21th. 118 miles. A long night. One of us kept watch every minute. The wind was unsteady, which meant the wind vane needed attention. At 0345 Hal—who had been looking into the darkness for several hours—managed to see the dim volcanic cone of Tafahi against the northern horizon and the low lump of Niuatobutabu a little later. There was no moon and it was quite black, but after a half hour in darkness it's surprising how well you can see. Once past these islands we're clear for the next three hundred miles.

OCTOBER 22nd. 146 miles. We sleep a lot during the day. Generally one of us naps in the morning while the other does a few chores or reads. Then in the afternoon we change roles. It's more important for someone to be awake at night when the visibility is less, and there is a greater chance of running into land or another vessel. Presumably a ship will see us more easily during the day. When I'm off watch I can go to sleep immediately. I try to get three or four two-hour naps every twenty-four hours, although it's not always possible. I like to keep a credit balance of sleep.

OCTOBER 23rd. 132 miles. Hal took a round of star sights at dusk last night because we were approaching the northern islands of Fiji. Hal likes working out star sights and always finds the plotting exciting. First he draws one position line. Then he pencils in a second position line that crosses the first and gives us a fix. The third position line is the critical check. If it goes precisely through the cross of the first two, then we know exactly where we are. Generally the three position lines make a small triangle called a seaman's cocked hat, the center of which is presumed to be our position. Of course the fixes don't always work out. In that case, the navigator hunts among his figures for a mistake. Sometimes when there is a problem, Hal and I change places because a new pair of eyes can often quickly spot a foolish mistake in arithmetic. I suppose that fourteen out of fifteen fixes are precise, however. It's amazing that we can find our way around the world from imaginary lines to distant stars so far away.

I had a good sleep in the afternoon and took the first watch. The night was squally, and at midnight we were overpowered, so Hal pulled down the mainsail. We still went along at five knots, but we steered a straighter course, although we rolled more without the mainsail up. The first streaks of dawn came at 0420, but it wasn't until the middle of the morning that we saw the westernmost lump of Nggelelevu Island ahead. By noon we were going along the northern edge of the atoll under full sail with a good breeze. However, we made poor time because an adverse current or a tidal stream was running against us. Apart from three scraps of land at the eastern end of the island, most of the atoll is a horrid, submerged reef. Hal watched it from the top of the mast. By the middle of the afternoon we had passed a second island, a sandy wooded islet called Vetauua from which twenty-five blue-footed boobies flew out to inspect us and our fishing lure. A little later we saw Thikombia, a small island ahead to starboard, and we began to pick out peaks and valleys on the big island of Vanua Levu to port. At 2200 we saw the group flashing light on Undu Point on Vanua Levu, about ten miles away.

Wahoo for dinner

OCTOBER 24th. We lost this day forever because we crossed the international date line. Now in east longitude, our time suddenly went from twelve hours behind Greenwich (early) to twelve hours ahead of Greenwich (late). This sounds simple, but every time we cross the date line we get into arguments about whether to add or subtract. As we traveled westward across the dateline Hal was positive that GMT was twelve hours ahead of ship's time. I said that GMT was twelve hours behind the ship's time. I had to get out Bowditch to prove my point. I won.

OCTOBER 25th. 120 miles. A scorching sun. We have been cooling off with buckets of seawater and washing a little laundry. The amount we can do depends on how much fresh water we have for the final rinse. We soak and wash clothes in salt water with liquid detergent and then rinse the clothes in more salt water to get rid of the soap. Finally, we wash out the salt with a rinse or two in rain water. The salt must be washed out; otherwise the clothes will never dry, because salt particles attract moisture.

We are out of sight of land, although we are aware of various Fijian islands near us. There is a frightening sixty-mile-long reef about twenty miles south, so we are continuing west. We were becalmed for two hours during the afternoon and went swimming.

OCTOBER 26th. 116 miles. My lips are quite sore. I have tried every kind of lip salve, antichap ointment, skin balm, magic grease, and more recently a special lipstick with an ingredient to block the sun. I have used zinc ointment, but the white paste looks ghastly. Nothing seems to help. I wonder if I lick the coatings off? Perhaps I should put something on more often—say every hour.

The sea has been a little rough and mixed up even though the wind has been a steady fifteen knots from the east. A while ago part of a wave skipped aboard and poured through an open portlight into my bunk. Now I am trying to dry my sheet. We are certain that the upset seas have something to do with The Great Sea Reef and the Yasawa Islands south of us. Probably a tidal change, because later in the morning the seas eased off.

OCTOBER 27th. 139 miles. Chicken crepes for lunch. Thin, sugarless batter (beaten eggs, milk, and water poured into flour, salt, and baking powder) cooked on a smoking hot frying pan for one minute each side. Then stuffed with chunk chicken (a small can), seasoned with a little tarragon, and heated in a cream sauce (melted butter, flour, and milk). Raves from the captain.

Overcast and gray. Weather threatening. Wind up a bit, so we double-reefed the main and put up a smaller jib. Still going along at five to six knots or so. Large seas with some of the tops tumbling in white foam. Waves filled the cockpit several times in the morning. We handed the double-reefed mainsail and have been going west-southwest under the staysail and working jib. At noon we were 225 miles east of Efate Island, our target. Every now and then *Whisper* sheers off course a little and water rushes along the deck into an open portlight. We have been trying to keep at least one portlight open to give us some fresh air because of the crushing tropical heat, but it's a losing struggle. Hal slipped on the wet companionway steps and bruised his left toes. He is limping around and will be wearing shoes for a few days.

OCTOBER 29th. 145 miles. The gale has continued, and the seas have built up. During the night I was worried about the yacht getting knocked down, so I woke Hal and we screwed down the tops of all the lockers with heavy goods underneath. Fortunately Hal drilled all the lockers long ago so it took only about ten minutes to pull

11. Efate Island, Vanuatu

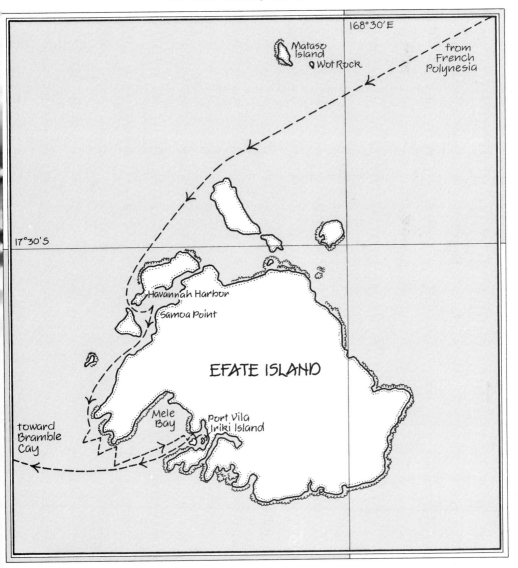

out the little can of stainless steel fastenings and screw down the tops. I feel more secure now. Also we have both companionway washboards screwed in place and all the portlights closed. At 1430 our dead reckoning position was forty-five miles east of the Shepherd Islands, close enough for a lee shore with darkness coming on. We decided to stop, so Hal winched up the trysail, I pulled down the working jib, we sheeted the staysail to port, and lashed the tiller to leeward. Now we are jogging along on the port tack at one knot or so heading southwest while we make lots of leeway.

OCTOBER 30th. 99 miles (to anchor). At daybreak we sheeted the staysail to starboard and began to sail fast again. Since we needed to keep a careful watch and the seas were quite large, Hal decided to steer by hand. A little after 0600 he saw a cone-shaped island on the west horizon, and by 0700 various other bits of land began to appear. The wind was still thirty-five or forty knots from the east, but the seas were bigger and noisier, with plenty of white streaks and tumbling tops. By mid-morning we were south of Mataso Island and Wot Rock, a distinctive large thumb, and had put up larger sails for more speed so we could reach Port Vila by nightfall.

Efate began to appear out of the clouds to the southwest. The island is high and dun colored, some twenty miles across, with low, rounded mountains and upland valleys. Here and there I saw dark patches of trees. Although the latitude is comparable with Tahiti's, Efate hasn't the sensuous greenness and the incredible steep-faced mountains of Tahiti. The rolling curves and soft browns of Efate give it a relaxed feeling I found easy to admire. Certainly in appearance the island belongs to the higher latitudes. I would think it a good place to raise cattle.

By noon we were surfing down long seas near the island. Hal yelled with excitement as we roared along and had a great time steering. Hal is more of a daredevil than I am. I would have shortened sail instead of increasing it, but his tactics worked and we soon got close to land. By early afternoon it was obvious that we would never reach Port Vila before dark so we turned into Havannah Harbor on the northwest side of the island. Havannah Harbor—remote and beautiful—is five miles long and very deep. The Admiralty pilot book suggested anchoring at a place called Samoa Point and taking a line ashore to keep from blowing off into deep water. We found the place, anchored in forty-five feet over white sand, and rowed a line ashore to a tree. We had a quiet supper and turned in.

During the night I looked out. The bay was perfectly still and the full moon so bright that I was able to see the sandy bottom and the rocks and stones forty feet beneath the yacht. We were floating in midair. I had never seen the shadow of *Whisper* on the floor of the sea by moonlight before. I could even make out the separate parts of the anchor chain as it fell away from the bow in a long necklace of links. My moonlight walk on the deck was like a dream. Was I still asleep?

. . . .

CHAPTER EIGHT

Where Is Vanuatu?

I was an orange bird high above a green lake. I circled around and around in a tight spiral to gain lift from an updraft of rising air over a hot sandy beach on one side of the green lake. Suddenly I had a muscular spasm. One of my wings was locked ("Do birds get muscular spasms?"). Around and around I circled. Higher and higher. The green lake was getting smaller. The air was thin ("Do birds need oxygen?"). By now the lake was only a dot far below. Still I was climbing swiftly. Was I to become the first bird in space? Was I . . .

"Helloooo out there."

"What's that?" I said.

"Helloooo. Can you hear me?"

The orange bird and the green lake were gone. I was waking up. Someone was shouting from shore. By now Margaret and I were awake and on deck. I rubbed my sleepy eyes. A man was waving and calling from the beach. "OK, OK. I'm coming," I answered.

We rowed ashore to find a small, dark-skinned Melanesian on the beach. The man was extremely friendly and shook our hands with great solemnity and deliberation. He and I examined each other closely. The Melanesian looked hard at my white man's large nose and at my soft brown hair. He studied my light eyebrows and my thin lips. Meanwhile I stared at a flat nose, kinky hair, furry eyebrows, and thick lips. When both of us were finally satisfied we relaxed and smiled at each other. The man, a fisherman, showed

us his nets and spears. "I have a stall in Port Villa where I sell my catch," he said proudly.

"You speak very good English," I said.

"My French is really better," he replied shyly.

A truck pulled up on the shoulder of the dirt road, and four Melanesians got out. "This yacht is from across the ocean," said the fisherman to his friends.

I explained that we had come from America and more recently from Tahiti.

"In 1942 and 1943 we had the American navy here in Havannah Harbor," said the driver, who wore a bright yellow shirt.

"Sometimes there would be two or three hundred sailors in swimming at once," added another man, the oldest, recalling the time of forty years before. "We were all hired to help the navy. We had plenty of work and lots to eat. We were fascinated by the war, but it was scary."

When we asked how many villages were on Efate, the men conferred among themselves in a strange tongue.

"Oh, about forty villages with maybe one hundred people in each, but we're not sure," said Yellow Shirt.

"What language were you speaking just now?" I asked.

"The Melanesian that we use in our village."

We already knew that the general language of Vanuatu was pidgin English or Bislama, which we had heard on the radio. "Do you all speak French, English, Melanesian, and Bislama?" I asked.

"Oh yes," said Yellow Shirt. "Most of us need to speak four languages just to get along."

"What about eating missionaries?"

"Not now," said Yellow Shirt with a smile. Everyone laughed, but my laughter was perhaps a little forced and uneasy as I realized we were outnumbered two to five. "Not now," he said. "All that was long ago. Nowadays it's better to eat French filet, entrecote, or escalope de veau from the Paris butcher shop in Port Vila if we have extra money. Generally, though, we eat fish from the sea, local beef, or maybe pork if someone in the village kills a pig."

How you learn through travel! How stupid I had been! I had looked down on Melanesians as Stone Age inferiors, when in reality many of these splendid fellows spoke four languages as a matter of course and were as friendly as could be. Instead of carrying spears and grunting, these men wore digital wristwatches and knew more than I did about satellites and videotape

Melanesian carving, Vanuatu

devices. The natives listened to the world news every night, read newspapers avidly, and worried about taxes and the competence of their prime minister. If anyone was inferior and prejudiced it was I. Instead of being hostile, these men were kindness itself. Would Margaret and I visit their village? Did we have plenty to eat? Did we want cooking oil or water or fruit? Or a ride somewhere?

"If you're short of anything we can bring it out to you," said Yellow Shirt as he drove off in his truck.

A few days later Margaret and I sailed around to Port Vila, which was only twenty-four miles away. We thought it would be an easy five- or six-hour trip. As we rounded Devil Point and entered Mele Bay, however, the southeast wind increased to thirty-five knots. We had only seven miles to go and would gradually get into more sheltered water toward Port Vila, so we kept on course. Since the chart showed a mass of overfalls south of Devil Point, we sailed close to the land to try to avoid the worst seas.

Once again we were down to a deeply reefed mainsail and the number three jib. The wind picked up to forty knots and blasted down from low clouds. We were over on our ear and pitching heavily.

"What is this?" I shouted to Margaret. "I thought we were in the heavenly tropics where the gentle trade winds always blow at fifteen knots!"

"Maybe these are the augmented trades that people are forever talking about in the West Indies," she shouted as the wind whisked her words away. "Look at the wreck on the lee shore behind us to port."

I turned and swallowed hard when I saw a wooden inter-island ship sitting on the rocky shore a quarter of a mile behind *Whisper*'s port quarter. The big waves were sweeping directly toward the wreck. Although we were heeled to thirty-five degrees and rolling almost every sea on board, *Whisper* slowly worked eastward. Little by little we angled away from Devil Point and the wreck, crept across Mele Bay, and tacked past the entrance buoys to Port Vila. By now we were in smooth water and sailing faster but still heeling a lot in gusts. My face was stiff with salt, and my left hand ached from holding the tiller so hard.

Jesus, what an afternoon! And this was supposed to be a pleasure trip! One thing about sailing is that it's always full of surprises. Whenever you think you're as safe as a clam in a mud bank, the world collapses around you. Sailors ought to be contrarians; certainly things happen opposite to what you plan.

We saw no signs of ships or fishing boats or yachts inside the mile-wide harbor. "Where is everyone?" said Margaret as we dropped an anchor off the waterfront and clawed down the sopping sails. A minute later a Zodiac inflatable dinghy with a big outboard rushed up alongside us and stopped. The four yellow-jacketed figures on board all began to talk at once.

"Haven't you heard the news?" shouted one of the men above the others. "Tropical storm Jodie is bearing down on the island. You had better move behind Iriki Island," he said, gesturing toward the south. "Put out your hurricane anchors and tie ashore like everybody else."

Iriki Island is a hilly, wooded islet a half mile long near the center of Vila Harbor. A north-south small-boat channel about 250 meters wide lies between the islet and the mainland. No storm seas can reach this channel, which was dotted with twenty yachts and half a dozen work ships, mostly on the islet side. The vessels faced eastward away from the islet and were held in position with bow anchors toward the opposite mainland and stern lines that ran to casuarina trees on the shore of the islet. We selected a place at the south end of the line between a big Cheoy Lee ketch and an Australian sloop, dropped twenty fathoms of chain, and rowed two stout stern lines ashore. We then laid out two additional bow anchors on long warps, stripped off the sails, dropped the spinnaker pole, unrove the halyards, put all loose gear below, and sank the dinghy. Once again—as in Bermuda—*Whisper* was sleek as a seal.

The weather was overcast and rainy, and the barometer remained high at 1007 millibars. According to the few words we could understand from the radio announcer who spoke in Bislama, a storm with sixty-five-knot winds was centered in the Banks Islands 225 miles to the north. Since the wind was light and we had done all we could, we turned in at 2030, tired from the long day and the anchor drill. The night was utterly peaceful. In the morning when I looked out, a man in an outrigger canoe paddled past, and we began to see people on the other vessels. The crisis was over. By noon a customs officer had come out in response to our yellow flag and had cleared us. We were sent ashore to the immigration office to have our passports stamped.

Port Vila, a main settlement and the capital of Vanuatu, is a town of 9,000 people spread out along pleasant green slopes that rise above the eastern shore of a large natural bay. Dozens of stores, small shops, and government buildings face the main waterfront road and climb the lower hills. A cruise ship was in port, and a hundred Australians puttered about the streets in the warm sunshine taking photographs and buying souvenirs. We changed a traveler's check into vatu—the local currency—and bought lamb chops at the Paris butcher shop. Margaret filled a canvas bag with fruit and vegetables at the big outdoor market while I picked up two bottles of French wine.

We learned that Vanuatu—which means "our land"—is made up of forty small mountainous islands spread out over some 94,000 square miles of the western Pacific south of the equator. The islands—with a population of 120,000—run from Aneityum in the south (20°18′) to Torres and Vat Ganai in the north (13°03′). An imaginary rectangle 215 miles wide and 435 miles from top to bottom would just fit over the whole group. The early history of the islands is a tale of five horrors, one stacked on another:

1. Blackbirding (kidnapping for forced labor abroad).
2. Greed (the cutting of sandalwood, a rare timber whose heartwood yields a fragrant oil. The Chinese burned sandalwood in religious ceremonies and were willing to pay high prices for it).
3. Disease (influenza and measles, which decimated the population).
4. Drunkenness (liquor from traders).
5. Religious intolerance (native customs versus missionaries).

One of the most shameful aspects of the white man's influence all throughout the Pacific has been the feuding—which still goes on—between Christian missionaries of different faiths, each of whom claims to have the real word. When you read the mournful history of the New Hebrides you marvel that the Melanesians were able to survive the arrival of the white man. The human organism is tough!

Modern Vanuatu was born in 1980 from the wreckage of the awkward New Hebrides condominium, a hopeless political arrangement of dual sovereignty that was set up in 1907 by France and England to protect the interests of their nationals, who were running plantations that raised copra, coffee, cocoa, and cotton. With two systems of courts, two police schemes, two high commissioners, and two languages, the government was bewildering, not only to the natives, but to the French and English themselves.

Hebridean land rights have always been a big problem. In Europe and America land is used for agriculture, grazing, minerals, recreation, and sites for homes and buildings. In Vanuatu, however, a man's prestige and questions of local politics are intimately tied up with land control. Ninety percent of Hebrideans—or ni-Vanuatu, as people born in Vanuatu are called—are small farmers whose land gives them an inordinate sense of security and a feeling of pride and identity. These concepts are quite unknown in the West, where an acre of land is sold like a cake of soap or a barrel of nails. The ni-Vanuatu have a complex system of renting land to people outside their home villages and think in terms of primary, secondary, and other rights. A man raising root crops, for example, may pay a small yearly charge to the owner of the land. Surface crops such as coconut or breadfruit trees or banana plants, however, signify more control, and these rights may or may not be granted. And so on. The arrangements are complex, hard to reduce to written words, and their adjudication would test the wisdom of King Solomon himself. Basic land rights generally stay with families or small villages that may have used the land for centuries. White men who thought they were buying land might only have gotten minor rights. As you can imagine, severe disputes

Four young women with ribboned dresses, Port Vila

arose over these problems, augmented by imprecise land boundaries and language difficulties. Even with independence, thorny problems remain.

In the small Port Vila museum we saw some fine Melanesian carvings, decorative clothing, plaited headdresses, and ceremonial masks (wood with feathers and grasses). We saw even better native work in a shop run by longtime English resident Nora Cahill, who would not tolerate tourist junk in her store. Nora dealt mostly with artists from the outer islands and often got carvings and masks at the close of native ceremonies. We bought an eighteen-inch black hardwood carving of a Rom, a stylized human face with exaggerated Melanesian features that represented a secret society in North Ambryn Island. The carving was done by a twenty-six-year-old deaf man named Obed Talepu.

Although we heard a lot of French and English spoken in Port Vila, many of the Melanesian clerks in the stores used Bislama. Success meant knowing the key word in pidgin English. We needed a new cockpit fire extinguisher for *Whisper,* so I went shopping. No one in the stores understood the word "extinguisher." I tried "put-em-out-fire," "fire-stop-um," "smash-em-flame." No luck. In one store a group of eager clerks surrounded me, all trying to help. One man produced matches, but that wasn't it.

Someone gave me a box of barbecue fire starter. No! Another clerk disappeared and came back full of smiles waving a cigarette lighter. No! Then the manager thought he understood and triumphantly appeared with a can of lighter fluid. No! I kept striking matches and blowing them out while trying to gesture that I wanted to put down the flame. Did I want a fan? No! A half-dozen black heads shook sideways in puzzlement.

Finally I went to the library, where I was told that the word for fire extinguisher is "killim-fire." Once I had the word the rest was simple. The clerks at the store exploded in laughter when I asked for a "killim-fire," which was quickly supplied. Henceforth, whenever I appeared in the store I was known as the "killim-fire man."

Bislama is a musical language with rich and pleasing sounds. A person who speaks English often thinks that he can understand Bislama at once because of many familiar English words, but pidgin is deceptive. You pronounce every vowel and soon get used to word compressions and grammatical shortcuts (some very short). Many of the words and expressions made us smile.

hat blong me	my heart
tok swit	to flatter
tok kros	to scold
krae long	to mourn
toktok blong mared	discussion about a marriage
gudtaem	good weather
olfala blong mi	my father
hed gavman	head government officer
fiva	fever, malaria
tabu blong smok insaed ia	no smoking inside here
blakman blong ostrelya	aborigine from Australia
kolwata	drinking water
joklet	chocolate
lektrik aesbokis	electric icebox or refrigerator
aeskrim	ice cream
brekemdaon	break down, destroy
mekem fani long	to play a joke on
mixmaster blong Jesus	helicopter
nasonal sing sing blong Vanuatu	national anthem
small box blong musik	tape recorder

A few saltwater crocodiles lived on some of the outer islands. Occasionally one of these big creatures would grab an unsuspecting child playing near the water. Parliament had a long discussion (broadcast on the radio) about whether the crocodiles should be protected and saved, or whether they should be shot to protect the children. During the debate we kept hearing the phrase "krokdile tekem picinini."

It was in the New Hebrides that the mysterious cargo cult of John Frum arose. When the Americans came during World War II, the natives were incredulous at the endless number of big ships that arrived and spewed forth cases of canned food, trucks and automobiles, great stacks of building materials, boxes of guns, bulldozers, whiskey, refrigerators, unlimited gadgetry, and so forth. John Frum, so the strange belief goes, is the American who will return—perhaps like Jesus Christ—with the ships one day and dispense endless largesse to all. Every Friday a few of the men, suitably juiced up with kava, pray for John Frum's return. Often small boys are sent to prominent hilltops to watch for the ships and to report back to the elders. Jesus Christ? After two thousand years they ask, "Why he no come?"

We tied *Whisper* alongside a venerable wooden ketch named *Phobus,* veteran of two trips around the world. Her new California owner, Reese Clark, was happily hammering away on a new hardwood deck, a mammoth undertaking on a remote island in the tropics. Reese had several local black men working for him. One man complained that he didn't like to use an electric sander "because it makes my hand sick." We borrowed an electric grinder to knock off *Whisper*'s old deck paint and brushed on new paint and sand.

I had a new book in production in New York and had been solemnly promised that the galley proofs would be waiting for me at the post office when we arrived in Tahiti. The proofs were not there. When I telephoned New York I was told that the proofs would be sent to Port Vila. "Without fail. You can count on it," said my editor. The timing was critical because each day of delay meant that we might miss the seasonal southeast trade wind that we hoped would carry us through Torres Strait north of Australia. Also, we wanted to get west as soon as possible to miss the hurricane season. When we arrived in Port Vila, however, the proofs were not there. I telephoned New York on November 10th, and was horrified to learn that the galleys had not even been sent and that the book was about to be printed. It took six days for page proofs to arrive from New York and four days of day and night work to deal with them. On November 22nd I sent off a 2,500-word telex from the impressive new Port Vila communications center to finish the annoying business and collapsed in my bunk with a ghastly migraine headache.

I was guilty of dealing with things that one goes sailing to forget: contracts, deadlines, rush work, arrangements with other people, editing problems, complicated telephone calls. . . . It was awful. But one needed to earn money somehow. I was so shattered by this experience that I was unable to write a line for an entire year.

We liked Vanuatu and hope that it will prosper. The country earns modest foreign exchange from exports of beef, fish, and cocoa, and some from tourism and offshore banking. Both England and France contribute to the budget. The ni-Vanuatu are proud of their new country and full of exuberance. I liked the sight of every chair in the small library in Port Vila filled with men reading books and newspapers. The people we met were embarrassingly honest. There was no tipping in restaurants or taxis, and all prices were fixed (no bargaining). If you forgot to pick up your change in a store, one of the clerks came running after you.

The prime minister of Vanuatu was an Anglican priest named Father Walter Lini, a Melanesian from Pentecost Island. He was a good speaker with a confident and relaxed manner. There was some minor squabbling by a few opposition politicians ("Lini is becoming a dictator"), but in general Vanuatu seemed under reasonable management. A new country needs a firm leader to give it direction and push. Long ignored by the West, the small countries of the Pacific have begun to seek their own ways. Lini has led his young country into the nonaligned movement, and does business with Cuba and Vietnam. Vanuatu refused to sign the recent South Pacific nuclear-free treaty because, according to Father Lini, "it's far too weak." He accused Australia of duplicity because though it signed the treaty, the country exports uranium.

One day I heard an address in which Father Lini entreated his widely separated island people to work together, to think together, and to achieve together. "It's the first time many of us have been together in a group," he said. "We can't solve every problem overnight, but we must cooperate and keep working until confusion becomes order and until our big problems become small."

These were grand words that might apply to anything, but as I heard the mellifluous phrases of Bislama roll out and watched the little groups of men and women listening to their leader with respect and awe, I felt a little tinge of excitement. The bright eyes of the Melanesian audience were full of hope for the future, and full of pride that one of their own people was their leader.

CHAPTER NINE

The Search for Bramble Cay

I think it's impossible to grasp the true size of the Pacific until you sail across it in a small vessel.

- The distance from Ecuador—on the west coast of South America—to the east coast of Australia is 7,800 nautical miles. From Ecuador to China (Guayaquil to Shanghai) is 8,872 miles.
- The distance between Cape Horn—at the southern tip of South America—and the Aleutian Islands, at the edge of the Bering Sea far to the north, is 6,480 miles.
- The 64,000,000 square miles of the Pacific hold 46 percent of the earth's water.
- The Pacific's average depth is 3,841 meters. The bottom of the Marianas Trench is 11,036 meters below the surface of the ocean, much deeper than Everest is high.

But such numbers are meaningless. People think the Atlantic Ocean is large. However, if you take a world atlas and a pair of scissors and snip out the North Atlantic and superimpose it on the map of the Pacific, you will find that four North Atlantics will fit on the Pacific quite easily, and you will still have a lot of sea room left over. It's when you creep across the Pacific at 100 or 125 or 150 miles a day in a toy boat that you finally begin to realize how small you are and how big the ocean is. And if the wind goes light and your daily runs decrease, the ocean gets big—bigger—very big.

So far in the Pacific our travels were:

Panama to the Galápagos	11 days+ (1,230 miles)
Galápagos to Tahiti	30 days+ (3,702 miles)
Tahiti to Port Vila	24 days (2,648 miles)
Total	66 days (7,570 miles)

Now we were headed for Torres Strait, the shallow, island-studded channel between northern Australia and New Guinea that leads to the Indian Ocean. We had 80 percent of the Pacific behind us and 1,876 miles to go.

We sailed west from Port Vila on December 1st. The date was late, and we were on the edge of the cyclone season in the western Pacific because of the delay caused by my book problems. The carefully prepared sailing calendar that we had worked out to maximize fair winds and to miss the storm seasons was already in shreds. However, a light southeast trade wind still blew steadily, and we hoped for a speedy trip to Torres Strait. Once at sea we logged 410 miles on the first three days. Then, as we feared, the steady trade wind faltered. Each day of slow sailing took us deeper and deeper into the hurricane season. We still had a few weeks in hand, however, and were already more than 1,000 miles west of Fiji, which seems to get the worst storms.

It was the third evening out at dinnertime when we had the explosion. We had caught a small dorado on the trolling line, and I quickly filleted the shimmering fish. Margaret was below in the galley rolling the fillets in beaten egg and bread crumbs while the cooking oil was getting hot in the big cast iron frying pan. I sat in the cockpit removing the cork from a bottle of white Mateus wine from Portugal. A friend had given us a nifty new cork puller which consisted of a jumbo hyperdermic needle and a tiny air pump. In practice you stuck the hollow needle through the cork and worked the handle a dozen times to pump a little air under the cork, which gently lifted it out. The device was clever and we liked it. But on this night the cork was stubborn. I stupidly pumped away while I idly looked at the thick glass of the bottle as I had done dozens of times before. All at once the bottle blew up with a tremendous bang. A thousand slivers of green glass and a shower of white wine burst into the air and sprayed all over me, the cockpit, the companionway steps, and even up into the mainsail. Fortunately I was wearing sunglasses.

I was so startled that I was speechless. I couldn't believe what had happened. Margaret's head popped up in the hatchway. "Has the mast come down? Have we hit a whale? Have we been rammed by a submarine?"

"No, the cursed wine bottle blew up because I pumped in too much air," I replied weakly. "Look out for your bare feet. Glass is everywhere." I spent the next hour with the floor brush and dustpan cleaning up shards of brittle glass. I have no recollection of eating the fish or of the entire evening because I was so startled by the explosion. I was miles away in a private dream world when my universe was suddenly dynamited in a green flash. It took hours for me to calm down. . . .

In the light wind we changed to our largest sails. Soon we were banging and slatting on a calm ocean. On December 5th we did seventy-seven miles; the next two days we logged fifty-nine and sixty-two miles. Sailing between two and three knots with light following winds meant that the apparent wind was often too weak to operate the wind-powered self-steering device properly. Then we steered by hand.

The sun burned down from a cloudless sky. We wore big straw hats, drank lots of water, and gybed the rig from one side to the other as zephyrs of baffling winds appeared and vanished. Sometimes when there was no wind we sheeted the mainsail in tightly to keep the main boom from slatting and banging. Even so, when the yacht rolled on a swell, the metal reefing grommets at the luff of the mainsail slammed against the trysail track with great clanging noises. We bandaged the grommets with rags to keep them quiet.

Malaria is the world's most prevalent disease and a nagging problem in the western Pacific. To fight this curse we took 300 milligrams of chloroquine once a week. The chills, fever, anemia, jaundice, and worse are caused by parasites that infect the red blood cells. These microscopic parasites are usually passed from one person to another by an infected anopheles mosquito, which flies at dawn and dusk. Unfortunately, a particularly virulent chloroquine-resistant strain of the parasite, named *Plasmodium falciparum,* is fairly widespread in the Solomon Islands, New Guinea, Indonesia, and elsewhere. To stave off falciparum (cerebral) malaria you need to take a second drug (we took Maloprim) in addition to the weekly chloroquine. We carried (but did not take) Fansidar and quinine sulphate for treatment in the event of falciparum. If a high temperature occurs, it is vital to take the drugs at once because when nausea and vomiting start, it may be impossible to keep the necessary medicines down. Then it's death in two or three days.

The disease is no joke, and these sentences are not exaggerated. Margaret's brother Leonard died from malaria, so it is a kind of family horror. In addition, we heard of a death on a yacht on passage from Papua to Cairns, Australia (the people thought the man had had a stroke, but the autopsy showed cerebral malaria). The yacht *Polette,* sailing in the western Pacific, reported that in a single month she had met twenty-seven yachts. Sixteen had malaria on board; two of the cases were falciparum. *Polette*'s captain, Basil Campion, lost thirty pounds and had a temperature of 103° for thirty-five days.

It's well known that you can be in trouble after leaving a malarial zone because you may be (or probably are) carrying the parasites in your body. You must continue the weekly drug dose for five weeks to get rid of the cursed disease.

On December 8th we sailed 112 miles. We were halfway across the Coral Sea, slowly making westing in light winds. To keep cool we poured buckets of seawater over ourselves. I found this too slow, so I jumped into the sea.

[From the log] 1640. Clocks set back one hour. Earlier this afternoon I went over the side for a cooling dip, and with a face mask looked at the underside of the hull. We were going about four knots, and I needed to hang on to the rope ladder with a good grip. I was surprised to see two dozen small fish about six inches long, some silver and some reddish, that seemed to be drawn along by the suction of the hull, perhaps like bicyclists are helped by the suction of a truck. The fish seemed to be tearing along and swimming a great deal faster than normal (I wonder what the hull speed of a six-inch fish is?).

I also noticed a lot of small bubbles rolling along the surface of the underbody from forward aft. The bubbles were tiny, two or three millimeters in diameter. There were thousands of them, and they seemed to be produced endlessly. I thought of my friend Rod Stephens, the naval architect, and wondered what he would have said about the bubbles.

The next day we logged eighty-one miles. We looked at rain, lightning, big cumulus clouds, and shearwaters and terns. We had seen no whitecaps for ninety-six hours. In such paltry winds it was astonishing that we were moving at all. I thanked my lucky stars for *Whisper*'s streamlined hull, folding propeller, and smooth bottom. Maybe all that work in the boatyard was worth it. That evening as the sun fell into the sea we were fascinated by a dark, spindly waterspout that did a snake dance at the west end of a rain squall far in the distance. A little later we got position lines from Achernar and Alpheratz, two stars that sounded like the name of a vaudeville act.

On December 10th we were 365 miles east of Cooktown, Australia, and 175 miles south of the Louisiade Archipelago at the east end of New Guinea. Our ocean was deserted; we had seen only two small coasting vessels since Port Vila. We sat in the shade of the mainsail, played chess, and ate popcorn.

For the next two days we had light northwest winds. Our course was roughly west-southwest, which put us 70 miles from the unlighted shoals of Diane Bank at noon on December 11th. Since we were south of our course and didn't want to approach land at night, we tacked to the north-northeast. The distance made good toward our goal was miserable; in fact, we were actually sailing away from Bramble Cay. Although we were 180 miles southeast of the giant island of New Guinea at noon on December 12th, we could plainly smell forest fires burning and the scent of hot ashes carried by the hazy northwest wind. Finally on the next day the wind backed to the north; we tacked at once to the west-northwest. We had 550 miles to go.

At 0200 on December 13th I stood in the main companionway, my favorite place, from where I could see in all directions. The moon was hidden behind low clouds, and the horizon was inky black. "What am I doing in the middle of the Coral Sea at midnight halfway around the world from my home in America?" I wondered to myself. Sometimes it seemed so stupid to be traveling to obscure islets at the ends of the earth.

That night I was full of doubts and uncertainties about sailing around the world. It was idiocy, madness. Or was it? Could it be the greatest adventure of all? A way of meeting the whole earth, of shaking hands with the people of two dozen strange countries? Or was it escapism, a kind of running away from a family, a home, junk in the attic, a secure job, and a personal empire? But wait a minute! I was an adventurer, and I was not running from anything. I was simply a writer collecting new experiences, a man on a lark. I had become intrigued, I had fallen in love with the endless challenge of making a sailing yacht perform well. It was enjoyable to take *Whisper* from place to place as I directed. Sailing was fun, a rapture. I liked it immensely. People were forever telling me how dangerous it was to go to sea and cluck-clucking about the hazards. I didn't think it was risky at all, certainly much less than driving an automobile on a freeway.

I wrote in a journal every day, but maybe there was a second, *unwritten* logbook, a kind of mysterious notebook—a typewriter of dreams—that belonged to the silent stars and the brooding sea. Both were giant and untouchable; both were intimate and all-embracing.

The wonderful sea had enchanted me from my first day of sailing. In spite of its power and obstinacy, the sea was beautiful beyond hope. I thought of a shower of backlighted spray at the bow. The cry of a circling seabird. The caress of water on my fingertips when I dangled my hand over the side. The pinkish streaks of clouds at dawn. The hard rim of the blue horizon. The rumbling of power when a big wave swished past. The familiar pinpricks of stars in the night. It was all beyond words and photographs. Only my unwritten log could keep pace with the silent mysteries and glimpses beyond the edges of my private world.

How had I become a sailor? As far as I know, no one in my family was a sea captain, a sailor before the mast, a passenger on a ship, or even a dockside laborer. None of my forebears, I believe, had ever even *looked* at the sea. My home was in middle America, where the important things were steel production, the making of automobiles, going to church on Sunday, a regular job, spring floods on the Ohio River, summer picnics, and baseball. My great-grandfather (on my mother's side) was German and Dutch. He lived on Price Hill in Cincinnati and was drafted into the Civil War. My father, whose antecedents may have been Swiss, was born in West Virginia, where his family farmed. My roots in America go back three or four generations, possibly more.

I was born in Cleveland, Ohio, a grimy industrial city in the north-central part of the U.S. My father was a talented musician and a successful orchestra leader; my mother dutifully kept house while my father alternated between two dance orchestras. My earliest memories are of terrific arguments between my parents, of being taken to nightclubs where my father was playing, and of my domineering grandmother (on my mother's side), who evidently contributed to the collapse of my parents' marriage. My father took a new wife to another city, where he soon had an orchestra. My mother and I moved in with grandpa and grandma. It was during the Great Depression, and my mother had trouble finding work. She finally got a job as a telephone switchboard operator and earned eighteen dollars a week (hamburger was eighteen cents a pound, gasoline cost thirteen cents a gallon).

I was bright for my age, and when I was ten I was placed in a special class at Willard School. After a year we moved away from the school and my "major work class," as it was called, to Lakewood, a suburb of Cleveland, where I was put in an ordinary fifth grade. About this time I discovered model airplanes, which were to become the mainstay of my life for the next twenty years. The economy was a little better in 1938, and my mother became a switchboard operator at an aircraft engine parts company (her pay was twenty-two dollars a week), where she met and married the head of the shipping department. My stepfather and I were mutually terrified of one another, but he was good to me, although we were never very close until he got quite elderly. During World War II he was occupied with his job, now expanded with war contracts, and with my mother, who had begun to drink too much. I learned to play the saxophone.

During junior high school I made dozens of model planes. I began to enter contests for engine- and rubber-powered free-flight models, and some-times I won a prize. My three years of junior high school were happy years. By the time I was in high school I always carried a notebook and worked on new model plane designs. I read all the model magazines, and sometimes I wrote to the editors. Often I worked on my drawings and calculations in class. My schoolwork suffered accordingly. Once I was so engrossed in a new design that I failed to notice my Spanish teacher suddenly standing above my desk. She made me wear a dunce cap and then threw me out of class. "You'll never amount to anything," she shouted, furious at my engineering drawings.

For pocket money I worked at the neighborhood drugstore after school. I continued to play the saxophone and take lessons, but my consuming interest was model airplanes, and I spent every spare minute with my models, which had become the center of my life. My stepfather worked long hours; my mother was away in bars. My balsa and tissue creations were the focus of my existence, a substitute, perhaps, for an intimate family life. By now I was involved with racing models that flew in a circle and were guided by wires from the center. I teamed up with an engine manufacturer, and we won trophy after trophy and set a national record for high speed. My name appeared in newspapers and magazines.

In 1944 I volunteered for the U.S. Army Air Force and became an air cadet. World War II was winding down, however, and instead of being trained as a pilot I became a mechanic and flight engineer. I flew mostly on B-25s, on which I logged 1500 hours. Before my discharge I was responsible for the maintenance of five aircraft. I enjoyed the work, which was easy for me.

In 1947, out of the service, I began college in Cleveland. I was still playing the saxophone and now earning an occasional check by playing in a jazz group. However, I had seen too many new horizons on my military flying trips. I was restless, and soon transferred to the University of California in Los Angeles, where I completed another year. By now I had a wife. My college studies were not easy, the schools were incredibly crowded with veterans, and from time to time I had to drop a class in order to earn money. I transferred to Berkeley in northern California, where I alternated between college, working in a bank, and building model airplanes. My long apprenticeship in models began to pay off, and I won or placed high in many contests. One day I got an offer of $125 from a magazine that wanted to publish the plans and instructions for my latest design. To think that I could get paid for what gave me so much pleasure was a real thrill.

A war erupted in Korea. The air force wanted my mechanical skills. Once again I was flying and repairing big airplanes. In 1952 I returned to college. It was a time of decision. Should I become a professional tenor saxophone player and spend the rest of my life in bars blowing smoke? Should I become an engineer? Should I become a writer? I thought I had talent in all three directions; I had to choose which way to go.

I sold my saxophone. I checked out of the school of engineering. I enrolled in the school of journalism. "I want to write," I told my professors.

My moves were all a dreadful mistake. With an engineering degree I could have gotten a good job and then written on the side from a position of solvency. But I was too proud to be logical. Or too stupid to be realistic. Maybe it's a law that writers have to start from poverty.

When I graduated from Berkeley in 1953 there was absolutely no work for journalists. My degree was worthless. Newspapers were combining and consolidating and running terrified before the strange new power of television. (Three out of five San Francisco daily newspapers went out of business.)

Public relations specialists on the scale of today were unknown. Besides, I had no experience. I was accepted for the graduate school of journalism at Columbia University in New York, but I couldn't afford to attend. I simply had no money.

I tried to work as a free-lance writer. I sold my model airplane designs to magazines, but the market was too thin to make a living. I wrote travel and general interest articles. However, it takes years of rejections to learn your way in this perilous field. I soon discovered that photographs were a vital part of nonfiction sales, so I learned to take editorial photographs. I read books, built a darkroom, and in time studied with Ansel Adams and Edward Weston. In 1954 I was a big winner at the national model airplane meet in Philadelphia. The magazines bid for my designs, and Pan American Airways, a sponsor of one event, featured me in advertisements. I was jubilant. My wife was stone-faced and glum and told me to go out and get a job.

I kept at free-lance writing and gamely sent out ideas, stories, and photographs. The writing and photographs began to replace my model airplanes. In 1956 I sold a major story to *Collier's* magazine and got $1,500 plus generous expenses. Wow! A little later the *Saturday Evening Post* featured my photographs. I was on my way! Little did I know that 1956 was the beginning of the end for mass-circulation general interest magazines. Television knocked out the weekly and monthly magazines one by one. My articles and photographs were better than ever, but the New York editorial scene was a smoking ruin. Even famous editors were out of work. Instead of joining television, however, I grew to despise it. Only gradually did I realize that specialty magazines were my only hope. During all these trials I desperately needed encouragement. Instead of reassurance, however, my wife scorned my work. I craved support, not nightly arguments. My wife sounded like my Spanish teacher in high school. We got divorced.

In 1957 I lived alone in a small apartment on Nob Hill in San Francisco. At one time I was down to fifteen dollars, all I had in the world. I sat down and wrote a short wildlife article for *Westways,* a motoring magazine, and received a check for sixty-five dollars. Disaster had been close. From that low point my situation improved. A year later I was taking editorial photographs for various medical publications and writing travel articles for the *New York Times.* During the summer I did a little mountain climbing. One day Margaret, an English girl fresh from Europe, appeared in my life. We got on well, and she pitched right in and helped me with my work. When I traveled for a magazine she went with me, and we laughed at how pleasurable life had become together. On one of these trips, to Reno in 1960, we got married. I continued to write and photograph for magazines and occasionally got a good assignment, but the competition was fierce. The periodical field was being hacked apart by television and increased postal rates. I began to write a book on mountaineering in the Sierra Nevada.

The year after our marriage, Margaret and I were invited to go for a sail on a friend's yacht on San Francisco Bay. We found something fresh and exciting. I read books about sailing and discovered a whole new world. Here was travel and adventure on a grand scale. Yachting seemed to be growing; maybe I could write about this burgeoning sport. First I would have to learn about it.

In 1962 we flew to the West Indies, where we chartered a yacht from Commander V. E. B. Nicholson in Antigua. One day at sunset this genial retired naval officer met us in English Harbor. ("Will you join my wife, Emmie, and me in the speciality here? A tall rum and ginger ale with ice goes nicely about this time.") Our vessel was the *Linney,* an aging forty-five-foot wooden cutter from England with a knowledgeable English captain named Stanley Young and a black Antiguan with the unlikely name of Tyronne Scott. We sailed south to Martinique, where there were only two yachts in the main harbor, and to St. Lucia and Grenada, which were still run by the British in a sleepy nineteenth-century manner. (It seems incredible to recall that in those days a man had to wear a tie and jacket and a woman had to wear a proper dress in order to have meals in a hotel.) On St. Vincent we took a taxi to the botanical gardens, where we saw a breadfruit tree that was brought to the West Indies by Captain Bligh on his second (and unpublicized) voyage. It turned out that the blacks in the West Indies didn't like breadfruit, so the whole project was unsuccessful.

"Too bad nobody checked before ordering out the *Bounty,*" said Margaret. "A little market research would have prevented the mutiny and saved all that trouble."

Captain Young was patient with us and answered a thousand sailing questions. Talk and reading, we soon found out, were no substitute for hands-on practice when learning to sail.

The following summer we took a dinghy sailing course to learn about tacking and gybing and many things. Later in the year we chartered a yacht in Greece and sailed from Piraeus to Kos. Again we had a captain, but this time our leader (a certificated Greek mariner) had gotten his experience as a steward aboard a forty-thousand-ton Greek tanker. He knew nothing about small-boat handling. Worse yet, the yacht was woefully underequipped. I remember that we had to unreeve the mainsheet in order to have a dock line (one!) when we tied up to a wharf. On that trip we learned a lot of things not to do. *Skipper* magazine and later *Oceans* published *A Touch of the Golden Fleece,* which got a lot of laughs.

I continued to work on the mountain book, to write travel articles, and to take photographs for magazines while Margaret and I learned more about sailing. We bought an old thirty-six-foot steel sloop that we sailed on San Francisco Bay on weekends. The San Francisco Museum of Art featured an exhibition of my photographs. Finally in 1965 the book about the Sierra

Nevada, *Pathway in the Sky,* was published and got good reviews. The writing had been spread out over a number of years, and I had wasted a great deal of effort on false starts and wrong directions, but the project taught me a lot about nonfiction books. I began to think about other books.

One night in 1965 our steel sloop was destroyed in a fire. We looked forward to a replacement and finally decided on a thirty-five-foot yacht built of an experimental hull material called fiberglass. *Whisper* was launched in February 1966 at Spencer Boats Ltd. in Vancouver. Alone for the first time on an offshore trip, we sailed the new vessel south along the Oregon and Washington coasts to San Francisco. The following year we set out on an eighteen-month, twenty-thousand-mile circumnavigation of the Pacific. In those days there weren't many world-voyaging yachts, and before we sailed, our friends urged us privately to make "our final arrangements."

Margaret and I had good times in French Polynesia, Samoa, Japan, the Aleutian Islands, and Alaska. A new book *(Two on a Big Ocean)* and a sixteen-millimeter motion picture documentary film perhaps reflected our enthusiasm. People liked the film, and we lectured with it all over the United States. We handled our own publicity and had hilarious times on radio and television promoting ourselves. In 1970 we sailed to Vancouver Island and showed the film in Canada. The next year I began a series of technical sailing articles that were printed in *Yachting* magazine and in four foreign countries, and eventually became a book.

We had heard a lot about Cape Horn and, like everyone else, trembled at the name. We wondered if the reality was as severe as the tall tales. To find out we threw common sense overboard and sailed from San Diego to Nantucket via the dreaded cape. We went to the Galápagos Islands, Peru, and the Chilean channels and had many adventures, including a wreck, an emergency camp twenty-four miles from Cape Horn, salvage of the yacht, and finally a successful rounding. When I wrote *Two Against Cape Horn* and tried it out on a few friends, I discovered that without maps no one could follow the action in the book. It was incredible how many people thought that Peru was in Africa, Chile was in the Mediterranean somewhere, and Ecuador was part of Argentina. I hired a marine artist named Sam Manning who made an outstanding series of maps to sort out the places.

We worked on the Cape Horn material in various anchorages on the East Coast of the United States. The book did reasonably well, and was serialized in three countries and was eventually translated into four foreign languages. We had also made a sixteen-millimeter documentary film during the Cape Horn trip. There were problems with the film, however, because of several gaps in the coverage. Two expert editors did wonders, and the early audiences seemed to approve, but the projected costs for completion were daunting. All the proceeds of the new book and from a series of boat test articles had gone into the film. I was a writer, not a banker, and I was in over my head. We quietly shelved the film for completion at a later time and set off on a sailing trip around the world.

I had long wanted to make such a voyage, but I had planned it for the future. One day I was doing a little reading about international finance, and I was astonished at the increasing disparity between the rich and poor countries of the world. Because of the growing differences in education, the gulf was widening every year. The rich countries were getting richer; the poor got the dregs and, sullen and resentful, stood in line for handouts. What this meant in sailing terms was that more and more countries had begun to see the yachtsman only as a rich tourist, a source of plunder. Already much of Africa was a political disaster, the Philippines were dangerous, Colombia was out of bounds, Indonesia was a problem, some of Central America, the Arab world. . . . I had read of yachts being troubled by pirates and murderers and thieves in the night. Half of these accounts were exaggerated fantasy. Nevertheless, the reports were unsettling, and I knew for certain that some were clinically accurate. The wonderful sport of yachting was growing rapidly; yet on a worldwide basis the places where a yacht could travel in safety were getting fewer and fewer. Twenty years ago no one thought about security; now one's well-being in distant places was a constant topic.

If we were to make the trip the time was now. The future had arrived. We had new sails made at once. We stocked the yacht with charts, spare parts, and stores, and sailed from Maine.

All these thoughts flickered through my head from my lookout post in *Whisper*'s companionway as we glided through the black hours of December 13th in the westernmost reaches of the Pacific and entered the Gulf of Papua. A little over one hundred miles to the northwest lay New Guinea's Port Moresby. The great continent of Australia was south. I woke up Margaret as the pink fingers of dawn gently pushed away the darkness of the long night. . . .

[From Margaret's journal] December 14th. When Hal got up he decided to try the spinnaker. It took about an hour to get it hoisted. It had to have stops tied round it, and we had to get the sheet, guy, foreguy, and halyard worked out. Also we had to take down the running headsails so we could use the spinnaker pole. What a business! We kept the spinnaker up while we had wind, but it was most unsatisfactory. The wind was light so we had to steer by hand to keep the sail full. Even so, our progress was not very good. We got terribly hot from the sun, and after two hours we took down the spinnaker. We then hoisted the big genoa and staysail and were right back where we started! We hooked up the vane, and the yacht went along exactly on course. The speed was just as good if not better than with the spinnaker. To hell with spinnakers.

In spite of the spinnaker fiasco, we registered 155 miles at noon on December 15th, our best run for many days. The winds weren't particularly

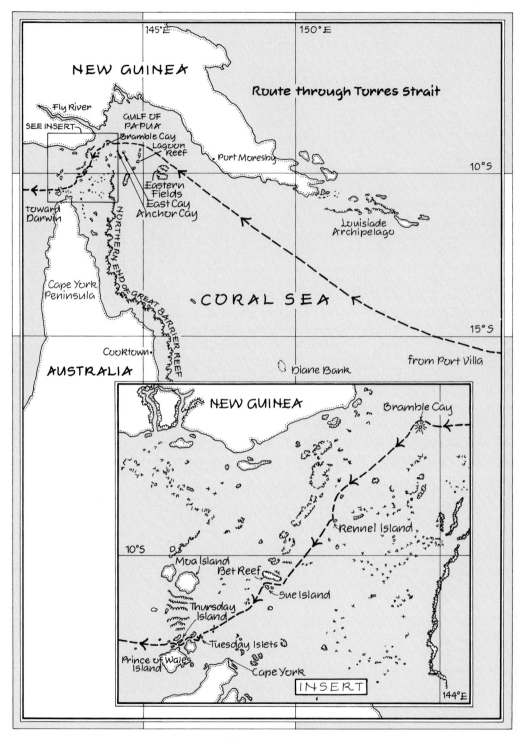

12. Torres Strait

strong—twelve to fifteen knots from the east-southeast—but the sea was fairly calm. We were now concerned with Eastern Fields, a reef complex on our port hand. I climbed to the masthead several times but was unable to see anything. At 1900 we got a star fix from Rigel, Aldebaran, Achernar, and Fomalhaut, which put us 20 miles north of Eastern Fields. At 2230 we saw a coasting ship headed north-northeast.

A round of star sights the following morning showed that we were fifty-six miles from Bramble Cay. We had passed Eastern Fields and Lagoon Reef, so we set a straight course of 271°M. for the light tower on Bramble Cay, which we hoped to see in the late afternoon. A noon fix confirmed our course with eighteen miles to go. Anchor and East Cays were twelve miles to port, but I saw nothing from the masthead. Obviously there were reefs around because the water was perfectly smooth. There was no trace of ocean swell at all. The wind was eight to ten knots from the southeast; we were running on the port tack with maximum sail set. After lunch Margaret pulled in the trailing fishing lure and found the hooks straightened out. Who had done that? Think of the power in a fish's jaw strong enough to unbend a fish hook! A few boobies and a lone tern circled around us.

Late in the afternoon, almost into the sun, we saw the spindly light tower of Bramble Cay a few miles ahead. Wonderful! We had found the place, the islet that has given so much trouble to navigators. With the sun in our eyes, however, it was hard to judge how far off we were. I wasn't a bit worried about getting too close because we were approaching from the east. Our new chart, based on a 1974 Australian survey, showed the light tower on the islet, which was at the east end of a mile-long reef. We took repeated bearings of the tower and confirmed that we were right on course approaching from the east. Our plan was to sail close to the sandy island and then to round up to the north to the recommended anchoring place on the north side. Soon we were two miles from the light tower. Margaret eased the spinnaker pole forward. I unclipped the genoa sheet from the outer end of the pole, stowed the pole, and lowered the genoa. The sun was setting, and the water ahead was a thousand slivers of reflected red. We were now one mile off. Margaret was steering and had just begun to head a little north. I was pulling in the mainsheet prior to gybing.

We struck the reef with terrific force. Our momentum carried us up on the coral for about two boat lengths before we crunched to a stop. The light tower of Bramble Cay loomed ahead of us in the setting sun, an ominous sentry climbing above a tiny islet of white sand. We were exactly on course, but we were over at a crazy angle and wrecked. Something was terribly wrong.

On the reef at Bramble Cay

. . . .

CHAPTER TEN

Hello Australia

*D*amn! We were wrecked. Or were we? A reef wasn't supposed to be in this place, but it was. Never mind. I would figure out the mistakes later. We had to get off! We would get off!

Since *Whisper* had been aground—sometimes lightly, sometimes not so lightly—many times during our sailing voyages, Margaret and I knew exactly what to do. We would put out an anchor from the stern and try to pull the yacht off the reef backwards—to reverse what had happened.

We immediately dropped the mainsail and staysail and tied shock cord to the tiller to ease the rudder, which was banging from side to side. We threw off the lashings that held the dinghy to the coachroof and tossed the small boat over the side. I jumped into the dinghy and pulled myself and the small boat along the side of *Whisper* while Margaret passed down the oars. We had an anchor on the stern pulpit, and it took only a moment to untie the lashings and drop the anchor into the dinghy. The nylon line for the anchor was on a convenient reel on *Whisper*'s afterdeck, so I reached up and quickly spooled off all one hundred meters and dropped the loose line into the dinghy. One end of this line was secured to the yacht. Then as I rowed astern of the grounded vessel the slack anchor line in the dinghy was gradually pulled into the sea. When I got to the end of the line and was in the place we wanted, I would toss over the anchor, which was attached to the other end of the line. I began to row away from *Whisper*. . . .

Only a few minutes had elapsed since we had hit the reef. Already the swift tropical night had fallen, like a heavy dark hand or the embrace of a wind that had suddenly begun to blow. In the distant western sky I could see a few bars of daylight shredding into gray. Overhead the dark vault of the sky seemed enormous; down on the black reef we were only a few dots floating on the infinite surface of space. How small and trifling I felt. How my life had changed in a few minutes! A moment ago I was a sailor on the ocean. Now I was a land person again. Were there bits of land up on those far distant stars that twinkled above us? Were there stranded sailors on reefs up on the stars too? It was all too much. No one could figure it out. The only thing for certain was that no one was near us on this sliver of forgotten land between New Guinea and northern Australia. Whatever happened now was up to us.

"Move to your right!" Margaret shouted. She waved a flashlight to indicate where the anchor was to be dropped. The tide was falling rapidly, and I scraped the oars and dinghy bottom as I went along over the rough surface. Once free of the reef, I pushed into the small breaking waves at the edge of the stone barrier, reached the end of the anchor line, and tossed the anchor into the sea. Margaret pulled in the slack and winched the line tight. But *Whisper* was hard aground, and as I rowed back I could see the mast over at a steep angle, and about a meter and a half of exposed copper bottom paint on *Whisper*'s starboard side. We would have to wait for a rising tide to get us off the horrid reef. As the tide fell, *Whisper* lay over on her port side, a dreary sight as I waved a flashlight around in the darkness. I tied the dinghy alongside the yacht, pulled on a pair of old shoes, and began to look at our situation.

We were three or four boat lengths up on a rough, fairly flat coral reef that was made up of millions of calcareous skeletons of tiny polyps. The reef was hard as flint, uneven, full of jagged humps, and totally unyielding—except perhaps to dynamite. If we were to get off we would have to float off or get off with a combination of partial floating and dragging, which meant hauling the vessel off by setting out anchors and putting tension on the lines to the anchors. *If* we got a reasonably high tide, and *if* the sea remained calm, we might be able to do it. In case the sea got rough, and heavy swells began to break on the reef, however, we would be lifted clear on one wave and then slammed down on the next. Anchors out in the direction of the oncoming swells would help, of course, but the yacht might be bashed to pieces and destroyed before she got into deep water.

The ebb continued, and the yacht now lay high and dry on the reef, which made gurgling and sucking noises as small pools of water appeared and disappeared as wavelets made their way across the black stone barrier. Here and there the reef lay quiet and exposed. The smells were pungent, unusual, strange, and not unpleasant. Perhaps like whiffs of unknown spices, or plants from mysterious greenhouses. Various small crabs and little creatures hurried along on nightly hunting expeditions. I sloshed around from side to side. Already I regretted that I had forgotten to put a couple of fenders and tires under *Whisper*'s port bilge before the yacht settled on the reef.

The wind blew at ten knots from the east-southeast. The sea was smooth with only a tiny swell. If the swell stayed down we would try to drag the yacht into the water on the next rising tide. In the meantime we laid out a second stern anchor on a hundred-meter warp. We ate something and slept a little, but life at an angle of forty degrees was not comfortable at all. Besides, we were too nervous and upset to rest. Every fifteen seconds the light on Bramble Cay flashed twice and sent two dim pulses of white through *Whisper*'s portlights. I gnashed my teeth when I thought of finally getting to elusive Bramble Cay and then crashing into it. Unthinkable!

After three hours the tide began to rise. The quiet reef started to gurgle with small waves that delicately tiptoed across the corrugated black rock. The splashing grew noisier. *Whisper* began to bump when the depth of the water got up to a meter or so. On the fourth hour she knocked hard as she lifted and sent terrible shudders through the interior. I looked at the anchor lines, which were bar tight. On the fifth hour we began to straighten up. "Only an hour to go," I said hopefully. But the high water crested and fell, and we didn't move at all. I dozed, and when I awoke I saw that the water had gone down again. Everything was peaceful and still.

I was sick at heart. Yet the wind and swell stayed light; perhaps we would have another chance. I knew that often a higher high tide is followed by a lesser high tide. With luck the second high tide would be enough to get us off. Also we would have daylight and could see what we were doing. Margaret slept peacefully on the port settee. I crept up next to her and gave her a silent kiss on the cheek. Perhaps to reassure us both.

When I awoke it was daylight. Margaret was propped up in the slanting cockpit with the chart. "This stupid chart is all wrong," she announced. "Whoever drew it has the reef on the wrong side of the cay. It's just horrible that so-called responsible people could do such things and pass them off as accurate."

Since we had several hours before the next high tide—the tide we would have to employ for our maximum effort—we looked over our situation carefully. I decided to attempt to turn the yacht toward deep water. This would give us several advantages. First of all, if we could turn to starboard about ninety degrees or a little more we would have only about two or three boat lengths to go to deep water. This scheme shortened the distance to the water by one boat length. Second, if we pulled from the bow we could use our anchor windlass to maximum effect. Third, if a swell came up, we would be facing more into it.

We got busy with the anchors. I recovered the first and second anchors that I had laid out during the night and put them out at right angles to the reef (on our starboard side) on hundred-meter lines from *Whisper*'s bow.

Next I sawed off a link holding our main bower anchor to our principal anchor chain and rowed out the anchor on another hundred-meter warp. We put out this anchor in deep water near the other two. Now we had three anchors on long warps in deep water—all on *Whisper*'s right side. It was fortunate that we had a good rowing dinghy and that I had had plenty of practice rowing and dealing with anchors. Even so I almost got swamped in the breakers several times. The rigid rowing dinghy was absolutely indispensable. An inflatable rubber dinghy would have been shredded to bits by the sharp coral, and it would have been impossible to have used an outboard motor on and off the reef.

Now the heavy work commenced. We had three anchor lines at *Whisper*'s bow. We took the first anchor line and led it through a large snatch block at the stemhead to change the line's direction so we could put it on the rope gypsy of the anchor windlass. Margaret held the turns on the windlass and tailed on the line while I cranked the old cast iron Simpson-Lawrence #500 hand windlass. The sweat poured off me, and the windlass groaned and creaked. We managed to get about four hundred or five hundred kilograms of tension. There was a chance that the tight nylon line would chafe and part on the sharp coral, but it was a risk we had to take.

When we had as much tension on the line as we could get—I was afraid that we would tear the windlass off the deck—I used a rolling hitch to tie a second short piece of line to the anchor line ahead of the windlass. I then belayed the second piece of line to a mooring cleat and unwound the anchor line from the windlass. In other words, we used a piece of line belayed to a cleat to hold the tension in the anchor line, while we freed the windlass for use with another line. Then we repeated the whole procedure with the second anchor line.

The tropical sun poured down. Everything seemed yellow: the sunlight, the coral, the early morning sea. We had to stop often for drinks of water because the work was hard. Sometimes we got a riding turn around the rope gypsy on the windlass and had to take a line back to a cockpit winch to help us unscramble the tangle. The tide was flooding rapidly, and *Whisper* began to straighten up. A larger than usual swell poured across the reef, and when we floated for an instant, the tight anchor lines swung us around a little. We had moved!

Once we had moved, however, the three anchor lines became slack and useless. We immediately bent over the windlass and worked frantically to take in the slack and put the five hundred kilograms of tension back into each of the three lines. More water flooded across the reef, and *Whisper* straightened up a little more. Now we could stand partially erect without half falling off the deck. But as the yacht straightened up, her draft increased! We lifted and bounced and moved to the right. Quick! Back to the lines and the windlass.

We seemed to be moving finger length by finger length. Sometimes I had the illusion that the anchors were dragging back to the yacht. The reef got noisier with small breaking waves. We had begun the anchor warp tension game a little after first light. By the time the sun was in our eyes we had moved one boat length and had turned the bow toward deep water. Our prospects were hopeful, but I wondered—to use Miles Smeeton's words—whether I would be found dead at the anchor windlass! Since we had now turned *Whisper,* we had straight leads from the anchors to the windlass; nevertheless, we were plagued with continual trouble with over-rides and jamming turns because of the confusion with three lines plus the smaller holding lines. A cat would have loved the tangles and snarls.

Whisper gradually floated more upright, but now when she rose and fell on a wave her rudder struck the coral with a terrific shuddering force that jarred every bit of the yacht and almost knocked over Margaret and me. Could the yacht survive such blows? Crash! Again she rose on a swell and hammered down on the coral. I thought of a pneumatic jackhammer drill destroying a concrete sidewalk. Could the keel withstand such battering?

As I worked on *Whisper*'s foredeck I happened to glance across my shoulder toward Bramble Cay, about a mile away. The cay was a smear on the horizon about four hundred meters wide, a flat hump of whitish brown sand in the sea. The cay had no trees, no water, and only a few patches of scrub green growth. The main features were a tiny abandoned hut and a spindly light tower. At the far side of the cay there was a metal pole of some kind, but I paid no attention to it until I noticed that the pole was moving! It was no pole at all but the mast of a yacht. Other people! I saw a white sail go up the mast and a hull slip out from behind the cay and head west away from us. The vessel had a low aspect rig, and I think it belonged to a small trimaran. We were a little disappointed that the people on the yacht didn't come across to help us, because just then we could have used some assistance. It seems hard to believe that a captain leaving an anchorage wouldn't have looked around and seen *Whisper,* because the visibility was unlimited, and our mast must have made an unmistakable visual point on the eastern horizon. Perhaps it was hard to see us into the sun, or maybe the other captain was busy with his departure. Our problem was that if we didn't pull the yacht off the reef and got stuck ashore without supplies, we would die without water.

"Look! We're moving," shouted Margaret. My attention was jolted back to *Whisper* as we rose on a swell and thumped into the coral. I bent to the lever on the windlass. I could see that we were on the edge of the reef, which had a slight rise before it fell off into deeper water. If we could drag ourselves over another half boat length we would be free. The swells were bigger on the edge of the reef, and we were slamming into the coral harder and harder. I noticed that the dinghy—tied alongside—had somehow

Kedging off, Bramble Cay

worked its way to *Whisper*'s transom and had gotten underneath the blade of the self-steering vane, which had punched a hole through the bottom of the dinghy. Incredible! Murphy's Law again. There was no time to deal with it now. I rushed aft and pulled the half-submerged dinghy forward and tied it out of the way.

The yacht was upright now—with her mast vertical at last—but the vessel struck the coral with the full force of her seven-ton weight on every swell. Was *Whisper* breaking in two on the final hump of the coral, or were we demolishing the coral? I cranked madly on the windlass, and we kept the tension on the lines to the three anchors. Quick! Hurry! Faster! Crank the lever! The jolts and groans and knocks almost threw us off the deck. I saw bits of plywood and fiberglass from the rudder float up. My beautiful rudder was being destroyed. I wondered if we would tear off the lead keel. A particularly big swell broke on top of us, and water cascaded over us and down the deck, scrambling the lines together. Quick! Hurry! Faster! There was a terrible final crash, a shuddering knock, a roll to port, and a scraping noise. Suddenly we were free and in deep water, away from the reef and the breaking swells. We rode gently to three anchors, almost as if we were out on a Sunday picnic in a quiet cove in San Francisco Bay.

We had escaped from the reef! We immediately pulled ourselves off another fifteen or twenty meters. I was so exhausted that I could scarcely stand up. All Margaret and I could do was to sit on the coachroof and marvel at our escape. As we sat talking an Australian NTAW patrol plane appeared and circled overhead two or three times before flying off to the west. "I bet the pilots are talking to one another about the easy life in deluxe yachts," said Margaret as we watched the plane.

Our first order of business was to check the condition of the keel and rudder. I put on a face mask and dived over the side. The keel was severely bashed, with deep scratches everywhere. Small pieces of lead poked out from the fiberglass encapsulation in a few places, and several sections of fiber-glass—the size of the palm of your hand—were gone entirely. Yet there was plenty of fiberglass holding the keel area together, and the general condition was much better than I had hoped. The lower quarter of the rudder was gone, the bottom of the rudder shaft was bent, and the lowest gudgeon on the port side was partially torn off. Yet the main part of the rudder was quite serviceable. I climbed back on board and sat down woozily. I was dizzy from exhaustion.

Margaret had been working in the galley and produced a hot meal which we ate slowly and with thankfulness. We drank lots of water. With our three anchors out, we were well tied to the earth and had ample water at high tide. Even though we were on the exposed side of the reef, the motion of *Whisper* seemed wonderfully calm.

I felt that I was in paradise itself. The saloon table was level, and as I sat eating, the cushions beneath me felt marvelously soft and voluptuous. Never had food tasted so good. A cup of hot chocolate seemed a king's potion. A few spoonfuls of pudding were a gift from the gods. To swing quietly at anchor gave me a magical thrill. I thought of a phrase from the twenty-third psalm: "Yea, though I walk through the valley of the shadow of death . . ."

Sometimes life was too exciting to be believed.

I must have fallen asleep while eating, because the next thing I knew was that Margaret was gently shaking my shoulder. "Wake up," she said. "We've got to move around to the protected side of the island to the anchorage and get away from this horrid reef. We don't want to be around here when the tide falls."

Whisper's forward deck was a mass of twisted lines. Ideally we should have recovered all three anchors and their long warps, but two of the lines were fouled around one another and all three were wrapped around coral heads. We picked up one warp and our main twenty-kilo CQR anchor. It would have taken several hours of diving to have extricated the rest of our ground tackle, so I decided to buoy the lines with floats and to return in the dinghy when we were rested and had collected our wits.

I climbed to the masthead to direct Margaret while we sailed around to the north side of Bramble Cay. The sun was high and clear. I could see the reef structure perfectly. I could also see that the chart was entirely wrong. My navigation and general approach had been good; my mistake had been to rely on a chart instead of using eyeball navigation in strange waters.

We anchored in thirty meters depth with ninety meters of line. We ate a little more and then collapsed into our bunks and slept the sleep of the dead. When we got up the following morning we noticed water on the cabin sole and traced the moisture to seepage on the port side of the hull near the chart table. I went into the water with a face mask to examine the hull and found that the leak was in the area that had lain on the reef when the yacht was on her side. The fiberglass had several deep wounds that needed attention. Years before, a friend in Vancouver, Doug Sutherland, had given us two cans of underwater epoxy. We had these two cans tucked away in the bosun's supplies. The directions said to mix part of can A with an equal part of can B and to hold the resulting mixture against the leak with an old glove. I jumped into the water and put on an old glove while Margaret mixed the epoxy. I found that it was somewhat like toothpaste and that about half of the mixture floated away. The rest stuck to the damaged area and soon got hard as stone. The leak stopped.

Since the poor dinghy had been holed, we hoisted it to the foredeck. I got busy with epoxy resin and fiberglass. We found that after the exertion on the reef we weren't moving very fast, that we were always hungry, and

that we seemed to be drinking inordinate amounts of water. On the following day we rowed around the cay to the reef to recover our two anchors
and lines. When we got to the reef, however, we found that the white marker
floats were impossible to pick out among the whitecaps and small breaking
waves. We rowed back and forth along the edge of the reef for several hours
and looked for the white floats from all angles. We simply couldn't find
them. The only thing I could do was to abandon the Danforth and Wishbone
anchors and lines and resolve to use colored floats in the future. In any case,
the loss of two anchors and a few hundred meters of line was a small price
to pay for the recovery of *Whisper.* I was quite prepared—pleased, in
fact—to make the trade, but I hoped never to repeat such a night.

The next day—after a long sleep—we rowed ashore to Bramble Cay.
Much of the cay's sand surface looked as if it had been crisscrossed by a truck
with big tires. We soon saw that the dry sand cay was a place where giant
turtles laid their eggs. When the meter-long females came ashore they made
great patterned tracks in the sand with their bodies and flippers as they
dragged themselves along. We watched one of the females head back to the
sea after she had laid her eggs. She breathed hard and had to make frequent
stops to rest on the warm sand, but she chugged along on her inflexible course
toward the sea after her stupendous effort at laying eggs. Margaret and I made
a circuit of the tiny islet and agreed that it was *not* the place to be ship-
wrecked.

Female turtle after egg-laying, Bramble Cay

On December 19th we set off to sail through Torres Strait, which runs from Bramble Cay in the western part of the Gulf of Papua (south of New Guinea) to Thursday Island, 140 miles to the southwest (at the extreme northeast tip of Australia). The 140 miles of sailing was past a series of small islands and large reefs in clear, greenish water from seven to twelve fathoms deep. The islands lay from 10 to 40 miles apart and were generally a scrap of land a mile or less long with a ragged topknot of scraggly palms and either no people or a few aborigines. We sailed during daylight on straight compass courses, anchored at night, and kept an evil eye posted for reefs. We were as wary as cats with the hounds out and plotted battleship courses until we gained back a bit of self-confidence. We had to assume that if one chart was wrong, they were all wrong.

On that same day we sailed to Rennel Island and anchored off the northwestern shore. The wind was light and the sea calm. Ashore we saw no people, only a small, tumbled-down house or two covered with rusty sheets of corrugated iron that must have made the places unbearable under the tropical sun. We examined the remains of gardens and flowers that someone had once tended with care. We looked at four tombstones, including a crude marker that showed the burial place of S. Savage. Next to him was the grave of his wife Rachel, who, according to the inscription, had died at twenty-eight and was buried in 1943. (Had the Japanese come this far during World War II? What was Rachel's story on this remote, forgotten island? I was fascinated with Rachel and wished I had had the time to look into her life.)

Rennel Island had a pleasant sandy beach but no water, and the catchment systems of the old houses had fallen to pieces. I cut four coconuts, but they were small and poor and I soon realized that the area was marginal for coconut palms because it was so dry. Even the fronds were stunted, and cracked and dry at the ends. The Australian pilot book said that the island had been abandoned because of no fresh water. I had the feeling that the rainfall was much less than in former years.

As we sailed through these waters we followed the wakes of many earlier small-boat voyagers. I had the books of Harry Pigeon (who had passed through here in 1923), Alain Gerbault (1927), Louis Bernicot (1937), Jacques-Yves le Toumelin (1951), Annie Van de Wiele (1952), Peter Tangvald (1962), and Eric Hiscock (1961 and 1974). All reported brisk winds, strong currents, and marginal anchorages in Torres Strait.

One of my favorite accounts was by Harry Pigeon, a quiet American who sailed around the world twice by himself in a gaff-rigged wooden yawl named *Islander* that he put together with his own hands. Harry lived simply and loved to go ashore in foreign places. When he stopped at Rennel Island in 1923, he met Tom Savage and his family.

Giant clam *(Tridacna gigas)*, Rennel Island

"They owned the island," wrote Harry, "and turned out the best it afforded for me. After I had eaten I went for a walk, and found the island a wonderful place. Like many others in Torres Strait, it was just a reef with a sandbank on it crowned with coconut trees. There were nautilus shells and cuttle-bone strewn all along the shore, and beautiful shells everywhere on the beach. Out beyond, where the falling tide had left the reef bare, a troop of great white pelicans with black wings stalked gravely about. Sea-gulls, that I had not seen in the South Sea islands, were flying here and there.

"I had cut my hand while husking a coconut on the way over from Yule Island," he continued, "and it was now inflamed with some kind of New Guinea infection and very painful. If I was to save my thumb, something had to be done, so I went on board, and spent the rest of the day and most of the night soaking my hand in hot water and permanganate. . . .

"My hand was still sore the next day, and I was tired all over, so I stayed at Rennel Island and enjoyed the hospitality of the Savage family. Tom's mother gathered leaves to bind on my sore hand. They brought out the pretty shells they had gathered, and gave me all I would take. Tom gave me a splendid pair of gold-lipped pearl shells, and his sister a pretty pandanus basket to carry the shells in. They came out and admired the *Islander,* and Tom said she was stronger than any boat in Torres Strait. The next morning, when I sailed, they ransacked their garden for green corn, sweet potatoes, and pumpkins for me to use on my journey. They came to the shore and bade me an affectionate farewell, and as I sailed away into the west a rain-squall swept down and blotted Rennel Island and its people from my sight."[4]

The next morning the winds were light and it took us all day to sail *Whisper* forty miles to Sue Island. The sun scorched down and we seemed to be moving on a nautical desert. We drank water, chewed salt tablets, and tried to hide under big straw hats and long-sleeved shirts. Near the navigation light on Bet Reef we passed a big three-masted fishing trawler that lay wrecked and rusting. Various small high-speed launches began to zip past us, either fishing or on errands between the villages on the islets. The blacks in the outboard-powered aluminum runabouts were very dark-skinned and quite spirited, and waved and shouted as they rushed past us at full throttle. Sue Island is three-quarters of a mile long, and sits on the end of a three-mile reef. We saw a dirt airstrip, a church, a community health center, a scattering of houses, and half a dozen aluminum boats drawn up on the beach. We didn't go ashore because we were still suffering from the effects of the reef incident.

We had hoped to make Thursday Island the next day, but we had moderate head winds from the west. Because of tacking and sail changes, the best we could do was to get to the Tuesday Islets, forty-four miles farther. This put us ten miles from Thursday Island—our entry port for Australia— where we hoped to repair the yacht. There was a lot of coral around the

Tuesday Islets. Fortunately the late afternoon visibility was excellent, and from the masthead I was able to direct Margaret to an anchorage sheltered from the west wind.

During the night I woke up with a twinge of pain in my lower back. I felt uneasy and went out and sat in the cockpit for a little while before going back to my bunk. An hour later I awoke with a terrible pain in my right kidney, something I had never known before. The pain became excruciating, and in a short while I lay writhing on the cabin sole. I almost fainted and was half in shock. I took an Empirin-codeine tablet, but I lost any good from it by retching up the medicine. I woke up Margaret and together we looked up the symptoms in the *International Medical Guide for Ships*. The descriptions matched my problem perfectly. I was passing a kidney stone ("agonizing pain"). The treatment was rest, lots of water, a hot water bottle, and an injection of morphine.

We had carried six vials of morphine for years but had never dreamed of using the drug. Now its availability was urgent and vital because the pain was overpowering. Margaret quickly filled a syringe from an ampoule and stuck the needle into my bottom. It was no time for delicacy. I lay on my bunk soaking wet and gasping for breath. I drank lots of water and vomited half of it back. Margaret put a hot water bottle on my lower back. Either the morphine began to take effect, or I had passed the kidney stone (the pain comes when the stone enters the ureter), or maybe it was a combination of both. An hour later the crisis seemed to have passed. I had a good sleep, and in the morning I felt no pain at all. I seemed perfectly normal and ready to sail. Margaret called me Captain Junkie.

Since Thursday Island was only ten miles away, our move was quick and simple. We anchored off the southwest corner of the small island and hoisted the Australian and yellow Q flags to the starboard spreader of the mast. Half an hour later a launch filled with officials appeared alongside.

"Welcome to Australia," said the first man. He handed me forty large printed forms to fill out.

. . . .

CHAPTER ELEVEN

Land of the Aborigines

*T*hursday Island is a government outpost at the northeast tip of Australia, and is the dividing line between the Pacific and Indian oceans. This tiny island—less than two miles long—was once a busy fishing center for pearl and trochus shells, which were used for buttons, knife handles, and jewelry. The increased use of plastic, however, wiped out the industry, and the one hundred ketch-rigged fishing luggers that Alain Gerbault counted in 1927 during his sailing trip around the world dwindled to just fifty boats when Eric Hiscock sailed through in 1954. Now we saw only a single lugger, and there was little employment for the local blacks who had once crewed the vessels and dealt with the shelling.

When the launch came out in response to our yellow signal flag, customs, agriculture, and medical men climbed aboard. In Australia, yachts are treated the same as big ships, and we were instructed to fill out more than three dozen forms. The paperwork was overwhelming, and if the customs and agriculture officers had insisted on the fine points of every regulation we would have had to surrender all medical drugs, weapons, and most of our food. We were allowed to put the revolver and a number of forbidden cans (good enough for us to eat but capable of infecting Australian cattle, it was claimed) into a locker that was taped shut with an official customs seal. Though the officials were pleasant—and profusely apologized for the red tape—the bureaucrats had obviously gone wild. Each form was a different size—to take one small point—which made it impossible to assemble the forty separate sheets. Some accepted carbon paper, some not. We wrote out exhaustive lists, in triplicate, of every scrap of food on board. We promised not to sell the ship's gear, nor to seek employment. We swore that we were not drug addicts or alcoholics, and, yes, we had sufficient funds so that we would not become wards of the state. Someone even took a color photograph of the yacht in case we tried to sell the vessel without paying duty. I began to think that I was an invader from another planet.

In spite of my complaints about the paperwork, however, I was thankful when the doctor asked us about our malaria precautions. Margaret and I had been taking chloroquine for ordinary malaria, but we learned that falciparum—cerebral malaria—was well known in the Torres Strait area and in Indonesia. For routine prevention of this new super-malaria we were instructed to take a drug called Maloprim once a week (instead of chloroquine). Dr. Holt gave us a little talk and left a sheet of typed instructions. In addition, we were told to carry quinine sulphate and Fansidar and to take them *immediately* if we got sick and had a high temperature.

"Pay attention to this," said Dr. Holt, waving an earnest forefinger. "Falciparum can kill you *stone bloody dead* in forty-eight to seventy-two hours after you first feel ill."

We were sent ashore to the immigration office, where we were handed more papers to fill out, and asked for our passports and visas. I had assumed that Westerners would be welcome in Australia, so I had never thought of applying for visas outside the country. I was exempt, as captain of the vessel, but Margaret—even with a British passport—had to pay thirty dollars.

Thursday Island had wide, dusty streets and lots of empty, deserted houses, and reminded me of an abandoned motion picture set for a Western movie. The little settlement seemed full of idle black men and their families, most of whom lived on weekly government checks, and when we walked past the ramshackle, unpainted houses we were often saluted by a black man with a beer can in his hand. These "black fellahs," as they were called, were usually very slim, and when you saw them at a distance—silhouetted against a light background—their legs and bodies made unreal, sticklike figures. The men we met were always polite except when overwhelmed with beer. We heard that the population on Thursday Island was 3,000, but the census man must have totaled that number when pearling was at its height.

At the Torres Strait's pilots' office, John Walker listened to my tale of trouble at Bramble Cay. He got out the latest Australian chart (#840, dated 1978), which showed the one-mile reef *east* of the islet. John and I compared his chart with my American chart (#73552, dated 1976), which showed the same reef one mile *west* of the cay. I had bought the American chart in 1982, but it failed to have the correction shown on the Australian chart.

(Later, when I wrote to the Royal Australian Navy, Commander J. J. Doyle, the deputy hydrographer, answered from North Sydney that a correc-

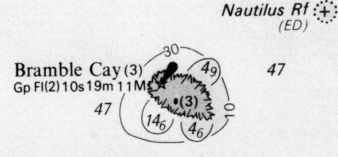

33

38   46

Nautilus Rf ⊕
(ED)

30

4₉

(3)•

Bramble Cay (3)
47

47

Gp Fl (2) 15sec 19m15M

14₆   4₆

31   35

45

39

⚓ Black Rks
(1)

Innocents aboard: We approached Bramble Cay using the chart at the top (U.S. chart #73552). Although the light was poor, we figured to home in on the light tower, which was clearly visible. Little did we know that the chart showed the mile-long reef on the wrong side of the light. The Australian response: Corrections are always supplied with a chart. The U.S. response: Drop dead. The corrected Australian chart at the bottom of the page clearly shows the reef between the light tower and an approach from the east.

33

Nautilus Rf ⊕
(ED)

5

30

Bramble Cay (3)   4₉   47

Gp Fl(2)10s19m11M

47   •(3)

14₆   4₆

31   35

45

39

⚓ Black Rks
(1)

tion had been issued in 1977, and that corrections affecting a chart were *always* supplied with a chart. The U.S. policy, replied Mitchell Kalloch of the Defense Mapping Agency in Washington, D.C., is to sell out-of-date charts—six years in this case—and let the buyer worry about the corrections, even if a mariner is a long way from the corrections office. This idiot policy had almost cost us our lives. *Caveat emptor.*)

I walked to the hospital for a checkup and got acquainted with some friendly Australian medical people who invited Margaret and me to a Christmas party. At the marine radio station I was invited to a second party, and at the meteorological station we were asked to a third. I began to realize that Thursday Island was a lonely posting for the civil service workers from Melbourne and Sydney, and that new faces were a discovery.

I met a boatbuilder named Jimmy Peddell who offered to help with repairs to *Whisper.* Unfortunately it was only a few days before Christmas, and everything was about to shut down until January 4th. In addition, the most suitable marine ways on the island had three broken arms in the main cradle, and its hauling winch was not working because of a broken part in the cable mechanism. The local machine shop was making a new part, but there were problems, and the shop had already closed for Christmas. Besides all this, the tides were low and unfavorable for the next ten days. Jimmy Peddell was keen to repair *Whisper* and obviously knew a lot about fiberglass, but he shook his head at the outlook.

"If you can I'd try to limp along to Darwin," he said. "Time's not on your side in this place, mate. Everything's against you, and you're liable to have to stay here till spring. If you can you'd better go while the wind is with you."

The heat on Thursday Island—at ten degrees south—was severe, and I felt like a panting horse as I walked along the dusty streets. The southeast trade was still blowing, although reduced in strength, and liable to quit any time. We decided to take Jimmy's advice and push on to Darwin. We hurried around and bought a few fresh stores, and I got the broken steering vane gear mended on the afternoon that the welder closed for the rest of the year.

We sailed on December 24th, the day before Christmas. Darwin lay 760 miles to the west. On the first two days we logged 201 miles, which included 19 miles of favorable current. The southeast trade wind was still significant, although it was weakening, which meant only a light breeze to ease the tropical heat.

During the next few mornings we became aware of an airflow from the south that gradually veered to the northeast by noontime. This was from the direction of the Gulf of Carpentaria, several hundred miles to the south, and bounded by the hot deserts of Australia. The wind vane steering gear began to make an ominous grinding noise, a sure cry for help, which I managed to silence with some sawing and filing and a smear of grease. We began to see a few large modern fishing trawlers, presumably Australian, and at 0500 on December 27th we passed a big high-sheered Oriental fishing boat, with a rust-streaked hull, fluorescent lights, and a clothesline full of shirts. A little later a sea snake, almost two meters long, with athwartships stripes of dark yellow on a green body, wriggled alongside the yacht for a few minutes. (What did such a creature find to eat so far out at sea?) The wind was getting less and less, and with all the drag from our damaged hull we managed only sixty-five miles. The big news of the afternoon was the arrival of dinner—a scrappy blue and silver wahoo—on our fishing line.

During the next three days we averaged only seventy-nine miles a day in poor winds and increasing heat. Margaret complained of "sweat running into my eyes," and she sewed a sweat band that she wore around her head. We poured buckets of seawater over us to cool off, but the sea was so warm that the water wasn't refreshing at all. The trade wind had disappeared, the barometer was low and steady, and we looked at towering clouds, fiery sunsets, squalls, and rain showers—the conditions of the doldrums. One morning we collected four buckets of fresh water for clothes washing, filled the teakettles, and put the drain hose from the mainsail into the water tank. The electric log began to have mental problems and started to give double readings, so we pulled in the rotator, padded the deluded instrument in white rags, and packed it away in the asylum of a box to recuperate.

We kept track of our position by star sights and continued westward about seventy miles north of the Australian coast. One afternoon we watched hundreds of screaming birds circle wildly around a school of silver and blue tuna, which were churning and splashing and jumping clear of the water. We changed course to pass through the melee and hoped for a tuna on our line, but suddenly the birds and fish were gone.

[From the log] December 30th. One thing that sailing teaches you is patience, and to laugh at yourself. The trip from Vanuatu has taken us almost a month at sea, mostly in light airs and calms. You must keep a sense of humor and lightness in these conditions. Otherwise you'd be a candidate for the nuthouse. This morning at 0800 we were sailing nicely with a west wind. Suddenly at 0805 the wind switched to the north. Good! Now we were able to lay the westerly course. At 0810 the wind stopped. At 0815 it was back in the west, and by 0820 had confused itself (and the despairing helmsman) and had hopscotched back to the north. Now at 0825 it is calm. Heavy rain showers are circling to the southeast, east, and north. Thunder is rumbling in the north. At least the sun is hidden by the clouds, and the air is cool. Will we get to New Year Island today? We must!

The wind stabilized, and by midnight we were far past the winking light on tiny New Year Island. We marveled at twenty-five porpoises that were running along with us—dodging from side to side and in front of the yacht—blowing, surfacing, splashing, making sucking noises, jumping entirely out of the water, and having a great time under the full moon on a perfectly smooth sea. Such joyous creatures!

A little later—at 0130 on December 31st—I looked through my 7 × 50 Nikon binoculars and could plainly see the smudge of Cape Croker in the moonlight. In mid-morning, when I got up from a nap, Margaret pointed out the remarkable four-fathom patch of Jones Shoal that stood out like a beacon in the sea ten miles offshore, and gave us our precise position. At the western end of the Cobourg Peninsula the wind fell away to a trace from the northwest. *Whisper* sailed very slowly and seemed to be towing an underwater log. Certainly a strong tidal stream was running against us. Since we weren't getting anywhere and it was late in the day, we headed for an anchorage at the east end of Trepang Bay to wait for wind and tide and to have a good sleep. I climbed to the masthead to watch for coral. We crept in slowly and passed a green turtle more than a meter long, the biggest I'd ever seen. After we anchored I dived into the tepid sea and discovered that the water was a slimy green soup and as cloudy as ink. When we had come in I thought I was judging water depths and the absence of coral. All I had been doing was looking at opaque, jade-colored water at thirty-one degrees Celsius.

13. The Northern Territory

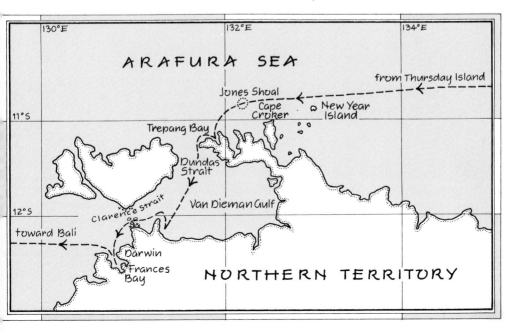

From the anchorage we looked at a harsh desert of sloping beaches, wrinkled cliffs, corrugated tablelands, and dome-shaped hills. A few stunted trees bordered an ancient river bed. The landscape was all light and dark browns—browns mixed with yellow, with red, with gray, with blue, with everything, but still the browns of a scorching desert whose bleakness stretched away towards the ends of the earth, a compound of heat and dryness that only the Australian aborigines could tolerate. A white man might last a day or two. The aborigines had survived for ten thousand years and wanted mostly to be left alone. Their survival was based on stealth, cunning, and incredible expertise at taking kangaroos, wallabies, possums, squirrels, goannas, emus, crocodiles, porcupines, and birds, mostly with spears hurled with a sling. The aborigines ate adders, dogs, pythons, and turtles, and fished for barramundi, mullet, trevally, and snapper. They knew water holes and native medicines and how to make their own weapons and shelter. They had meetings, celebrations, fights, taboos, and both respected and laughed at the rights of others. Their society had wise men and rogues, artists, ne'er-do-wells, and ordinary providers. A rich culture lay hidden in those bleak desert hills.[5]

It took two days of tedious sailing to work through tide-swept Dundas and Clarence straits and Van Diemen Gulf to Darwin. Generally we sailed in sight of a shoreline, but the deserts were so bleak and look-alike and the navigational aids so infrequent that it was hard to keep track of our position. Once we had to take celestial observations to find out where we were. We finally anchored in Frances Bay on the morning of January 2nd. The trip from Thursday Island had taken nine days. We had anchored three times and averaged eighty-four miles a day.

Now, in a twinkling, we had landed in a modern city. We were astonished at the lack of transition—the abruptness—between the trackless desert and Darwin. We rowed ashore in the dinghy and walked up a little hill. All at once we crossed the city limits. Before us sat hundreds of parked cars, shiny and new, bumper to bumper. Incredibly, a man on a little scooter was going around writing out parking tickets! After spending days sailing along the edge of the trackless desert and seeing no one, to suddenly come face to face with people and cars and traffic and policemen and stores and even a modern shopping mall was a shock.

Darwin was a city of 60,000 on the north-central coast of Australia, the capital of the hot and arid Northern Territory, an enormous area of half a million square miles. The city was bright and new, with excellent government buildings and apartments and houses, because the place had been totally rebuilt after a cyclone had leveled the entire city on Christmas day in 1974. We found a first-class library, a stunning new museum, and a casino where we watched the gamblers play a coin-flipping game called Two-Up.

Except for a little fishing, Darwin was entirely a government community of civil service workers and a few service industries. Civil service jobs were considered hardship postings, and the people got extra pay, a one-month vacation, and even yearly air fare to Sydney or Melbourne or Perth, the "real" parts of Australia. The people in the service industries—often Oriental or Greek immigrants—stayed in Darwin for only one reason: to make money. All the food, clothing, supplies, furniture, building supplies, hardware—*everything*—was trucked in from the big cities in south Australia, and was marked up to ensure a big profit. It may be unkind to use the word "rip-off," but the prices even shocked the Australians. The heat was truly formidable, with extreme temperatures and humidity, and every office and store and house was air-conditioned.

We didn't want to settle in Darwin. We wanted to repair *Whisper* and get on with our trip. Darwin had no marinas, no docks for small vessels, no suitable boatyards, no marine ways for yachts, and no Travelifts. There were four meters of tide at springs, so it was easy to dry out alongside a big dock or wharf and work on the hull for one tide; however, we needed to get on land and to have access to water and electricity.

I walked to the harbor office to pay my respects and to ask for information, but I was dismayed at the harbormaster's response: "A yachtie, eh. Piss off," he said.

The yacht next to us in Frances Bay was a fifteen-meter ferrocement ketch named *Myambla.* We got acquainted with the owners, Bill and Sheila Shorter, and had a few meals together. Bill taught school. Sheila, a lady with a strong personality, was a secretary to the chief minister who was in charge of the Northern Territory. Bill kindly took Margaret and me on a tour of the boatyard facilities.

We got a cordial reception at the Darwin yacht club, but its anchorage was open and exposed. To get out of the water at the club we would have needed a crane to lift the yacht on a truck, the truck to carry the yacht to a work area, and finally a crane to lift the yacht down. This would have cost $350 each way, in addition to problems of land space, shelter from the weather, water, and electricity.

After considering several places we finally hauled out at a do-it-yourself yard (G & M) run by a pleasant French-Canadian named George Lasette. We hired a crane ($160), which plucked *Whisper* out at the top of a spring tide. We blocked up the yacht and set to work. It was against the law to live on board, so we took the cheapest lodging we could find—a single room in the local YWCA, which cost $120 a week. We rented a small car ($110 a week) to chase supplies.

Whisper needed repairs to her rudder, keel, and the port side of the hull. The rudder was the most complicated, so I started on it first. The shaft was almost 3 meters long, and to drop the rudder required a hole 1 meter deep. Unfortunately George's yard was built on fill material of old bricks, stones, throwaway pipes, decrepit lumber, and soil, all compacted together. As I dug I kept running into plaster, bottles, and sharp pieces of metal. I was finally stopped by cement blocks that were impervious to my crowbar and ordinary hammer. My only hope to finish the digging was to get a jackhammer—those noisy horrors used to break up street pavements—and 125 meters of hose plus an air compressor. As I struggled with the heavy and unwieldy jackhammer in the terrible heat, I thought of the glories of sailing and of the people who dreamed of yachting and trips to paradise. . . .

With the rudder finally out and at a machine shop, I turned to the keel. I took a big grinder and cut away the broken material until I got to sound

Jackhammer drill, Darwin

fiberglass. With scissors I cut out fiberglass mat and roving, saturated the pieces with polyester resin, and began to build up new sections of keel. I hired a man to help me, and was surprised at how fast he was. After two days, however, I discovered that my assistant was using cheap body putty that he covered with a quick layer of fiberglass. I told him that I didn't want slipshod repairs, but he continued, so I had to fire him and grind out all his bad work.

The heat and humidity were overpowering, and the sun blazed down while Margaret and I worked in clouds of fiberglass dust. By now our skins were the color of old leather saddles. Every morning we bought a gallon of cold mango-orange juice which disappeared by twelve o'clock and had to be replaced for the afternoon. We never seemed to go to the toilet; everything inside us poured out in torrents of sweat.

I had heard vague talk about big crocodiles ever since I had been in Darwin. I pooh-poohed all this as inflated exaggeration. One Sunday we went to the new territorial museum, and I happened to look at the crocodile exhibit. My hair stood on end when I saw Sweetheart, a *five-meter-long* muscular horror of teeth and waiting eyes and warts, reputed to have eaten a few people. The size, the jaws, and the bulk of such a monster were stupifying. The damned thing seemed to be three-quarters of a meter wide across the shoulders, but maybe I exaggerate. Fortunately Sweetheart was stuffed, not alive. The exhibit also had a large steel bait box that had been attacked by a crocodile and reduced to a mass of metal fragments. After seeing all this I was *very careful* about walking in the grass near the water at the boatyard.

Little by little I covered *Whisper*'s exposed lead ballast with a heavy sheathing of fiberglass and began to grind the area into a fair shape. The problem was the bottom, which was difficult to get level and smooth. I found a new helper, a cruising sailor named Jeff Lemon, who knew nothing about fiberglass but who was an excellent worker and good at following directions. I soon had him using a grinder together with a spirit level and a straightedge.

By now we had become good friends with George Lasette, the owner of the boatyard, and his girlfriend Penny Giles. Penny liked dogs and was a ready friend of strays. There were always half a dozen in the yard, and every morning George and Penny and the hounds (much sniffing, tails wagging) came to check on our progress and to cheer us up as we drudged away in the heat and dust. We used the town laundry, whose owners, Bob and Thelma Claydon, took an interest in us. The Claydons, veterans of the Australian outback, were dismayed at the auto rental charges and insisted that we use one of their cars, which was a generous gesture. Bob and Thelma were always ready with a cheerful greeting and were full of stories about living in the bush. We were touched by the friendliness and generosity of the Shorters, the Claydons, and George and Penny, who fed us, and took us on picnics, and on Sunday trips to the interior.

Repairs, Darwin

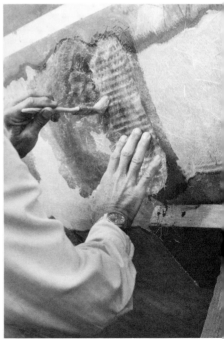

Meanwhile I removed the interior woodwork on the port side of the saloon and reinforced the damaged area on the inside. With Margaret's help I re-glassed the after saloon bulkhead in place with six layers of 150-millimeter wide tape set in epoxy resin, and through-bolted the taping to the bulkhead with bolts on 150-millimeter centers. I repaired the hull on the outside and began to smooth it for painting. We carefully ground the keel into shape, and I added more fiberglass and Marine-Tex as needed. The machine shop straightened the rudder stock and milled a new bottom gudgeon from a spare casting that I luckily had on board. I rebuilt the lower part of the rudder, and on a bright Tuesday morning we slipped the whole rudder assembly back into the hull. While the glassing and grinding had been going on, Margaret had prepared the topsides for painting. One morning at dawn—before it got too hot—we rolled and brushed on the first of three coats of topside paint. A few days later we hired a sign painter who did a splendid job on *Whisper*'s name. The yacht began to look like her old self.

We were taken out of the water on January 12th. Five weeks later a crane lowered us into Frances Bay. We hurried out to the anchorage and rejoiced at being afloat. We were as good as new.

One day a streamlined-looking ketch named *Marathon* motored in and anchored next to us. She flew the blue and yellow flag of Sweden, and her masts were festooned with a dozen antennas and electronic devices. Three lively Scandinavians, one incredibly named Leif Eriksson, were trying to sail around the world in twelve months. According to Captain Eriksson, the yacht was paid for by Swedish advertising companies. As *Marathon* sailed from big city to big city she was met by advertising representatives and their clients, who were taken for sails and given hospitality on board. Everything was high tech, precise schedules, speed, and rush.

Captain Eriksson—who said that he had suffered a heart attack in the past—told us that he was one of the most experienced racing sailors in the world. *Marathon*'s rig was tall and looked strong, but the Swedes claimed to have sailed the yacht so hard they continually broke things. We were shown fractured blocks and a useless vane steering gear. We were told of four severe knockdowns, damaged rigging, and broken wires while sailing to Sydney. We heard about night spinnaker runs between atolls in the Tuamotus. One of the men made little jumping motions as he spoke, and all three seemed to be on the ulcer circuit. Their general story was that anyone can have a free fifteen-meter yacht if he is clever enough to get commercial help. Eriksson said that *Marathon* had at least two of everything: two engines, two satellite navigation devices (sat-navs), a mass of radios, autopilots, off-course alarms, all sorts of wind instruments, five guns, three motorscooters, three inflatable dinghies, radar, a water maker, electric cooking, etc. The captain said the yacht could motor at ten knots, his special sails enabled him to sail closer to the wind than others, how he spoke with Sweden on various radios every few hours, and so forth.

"Do you need such a big engine?" I asked. "With all your skills perhaps you could do without . . ."

"Yes, yes, of course," answered Eriksson crossly. "Anyone who sails without an engine is mad, crazy."

Our foreign acquaintances sat in *Whisper*'s saloon drinking white wine and talking nonstop about how they had to rush to Cape Town for appointments with advertising agencies and industrial clients, and about real estate deals in Spain. By chance I happened to mention that I had special sailing directions for the hard run between Durban and Cape Town. I was surprised how fast Captain Eriksson asked for a copy.

"Those Swedes are certainly keen sailors," said Margaret when they were gone. "I'm exhausted after listening to them for two hours. I wonder what they do for pleasure?"

The next morning *Marathon* headed for Durban. As the yacht left, the blond sailors swooped past us with their engine going full throttle. We all waved goodbye.

A few days later an old yacht named *White Foam* sailed in and anchored where *Marathon* had been. *White Foam* was ten meters long and had been built in Ipswich, England, in 1937. She was carvel-planked with a tall Bermudian cutter rig, a small doghouse, almost a plumb bow, and a short counter that angled up sharply at her stern. She was engineless, with old sails, old gear, rust streaks everywhere, and persistent leaks both above and below the waterline. During the trip her rudder had developed twenty-five degrees of side play. The owner suspected that the bottom gudgeon was gone, and by diving he managed to brace the fittings with old rigging wire that he led vertically upward from the base of the rudder to each side of the cockpit.

John and Jill Semple—who must have been in their thirties—had sailed this small vessel all over the Indian Ocean with practically no money and only a few charts. Their voyages were slow, and the windless seasons were a trial, but the Semples didn't care because they enjoyed the trips *for the pleasure of the sailing itself.* It didn't matter when they started or when they arrived. They took things as they came.

"On the trip here from Singapore we were close to a nasty reef one night," said Jill. "We could hear the waves breaking, and there was very little wind. It was a nervous time, but after a few hours a breeze came.

"It may sound foolish," continued Jill shyly, "but we try to follow our dreams. We haven't got very big goals, and we're only small people, but we're doing the things we like, and maybe touching the edge of things. John and I are quite happy together, and we're content to look at the waves and the birds and the clouds and to visit the different islands."

Margaret and I marveled at the Semples' gentleness and peace of mind. They had very little materially, but a great deal spiritually, and it seemed to me that they got much more out of life than the frantic Swedes on *Marathon.* John was an electrician and had come to his home in Australia to earn money and to repair *White Foam* before starting out again.

Since Margaret and I were bound for the Seychelle Islands, we asked the Semples about the main harbor and any special problems. The next day John brought over a sketch chart he had made for me that detailed the entire Port Victoria area together with a list of his friends. He had lots, and I knew why.

. . . .

CHAPTER TWELVE

Where Is Bali?

*W*e sailed on April Fool's Day, sad to leave our new friends behind, but happy to see the last of the Australian bureaucrats and their humiliating paperwork and petty regulations that assume foreign sailors are indigent criminals. We had spent $4,907 for repairs and living expenses while we were in Darwin, yet before customs would give us our ship's clearance we had to pay a $10 departure tax, a sort of final red flag designed to make a visitor swear off Australia forever.

Our course to Indonesia and Bali ran roughly west and a little north through the same soupy green sea that we'd seen since Torres Strait. The wind was light, but *Whisper* glided along nicely with her smooth bottom and new paint. She steered much better with a proper rudder and a straight rudder shaft, and we soon left the desert coast of Australia behind. The barometer was high and steady, the sun broiled down, and the visibility was extremely good with clear skies and a few wisps of upper clouds. We passed fishing boats from Australia and Taiwan seeking prawns and the tasty barramundi, one of the best fish anywhere. Although it was hot, it felt good to get to sea again, to have peace and quiet and fresh air, and to be away from the crush and noise of a city.

Fishing canoe, Padangbai, Bali

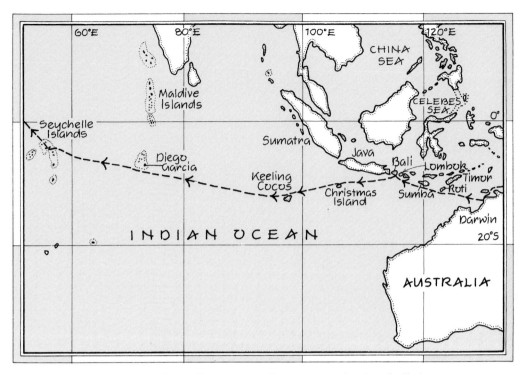

14. The Indian Ocean (Darwin to the Seychelles)

We were rested, well stored, and ready for Indonesia. But was Indonesia ready for us?

In order to sail to Indonesia—a country with a population of 166 million people on 13,500 separate islands—you were supposed to have a special sailing permit. A few years earlier one's embassy helped get the permit, which consisted of permission from the Indonesian navy for a foreign vessel to visit the country. To get this you applied forty-five days in advance and supplied a list of ports you planned to visit plus the exact times of arrival and departure at each port. Since we had no knowledge of Indonesia and no idea where to go, I found such a list impossible to make. Ostensibly the permit was a way for a suspicious military government to check on strangers who, God forbid, might be spying on the rice crop or be enemy agents from Bolivia or Upper Volta. Of course the visitors might be tourists who would bring desperately needed foreign exchange to poor Indonesia. The permit was conditional on "a check of the intended foreign vessel and her crew." How, I wondered, could a man in Jakarta possibly find out anything about a tiny foreign yacht somewhere at sea?

Formerly this elusive permit was gotten by one's embassy, as I said, but now the task had been taken over by a ship's agent in Jakarta who charged

$185 for the permit, which took six or seven weeks to get. The record of the agent was poor, however, and many people who applied and sent the $185 never got the permit, besides wasting a lot of time. I telephoned the agent in Jakarta to ask about the permit, but I was transferred from person to person. The last man on the line suddenly hung up. I had gotten no answers at all.

After listening to various stories in the sailing community in Darwin, I decided to sail without the permit. Some of the strongest opinions seemed to have little factual basis. One person claimed that the permits had been abolished. We heard that "one can always get five days." Someone else told us that Bali had a quasi-independent status, and some authority regarding visitors. In any case, if we were denied visiting rights I was prepared to continue sailing westward in the Indian Ocean.

In spite of the attraction of coastal villages, new people, remote anchorages, and exciting scenery, we had little desire to see the rest of Indonesia. We were a bit uneasy about our safety, which was probably foolish and based on scanty information. Yet a nagging concern for our well-being lurked in the back of my mind, particularly after pirates in the Sulu Sea killed Lydia Tangvald on the American yacht *L'Artemis de Pytheas* with a blast from a shotgun. On the radio program for merchant seamen on the BBC we had heard repeated tales of Indonesian piracy in Phillip Channel near Singapore. I was not keen to sail where murderers and pirates had more power than the police. Bali, however, was said to be safe.

I had considered stopping in Timor because I remembered reading about this Portuguese island in my history books when I was a schoolboy. It was in the main port of Kupang on the southwest corner of Timor that Captain Bligh had landed in 1789 after his 3,700-mile voyage in a twenty-three-foot open boat with eighteen men following the *Bounty* mutiny. Now Portugal had cleared out, and the central Indonesian government had been involved in a military action of some kind against the people of this former European colony, who were unhappy with their new status. There were ugly rumors, but facts were hard to get because journalists were forbidden. The Indonesians sternly warned outsiders to stay away. We skipped Timor.

According to *Ocean Passages for the World,* the recommended sailing route from Darwin to Singapore (for November to April) is a complicated and lengthy track northward via the Banda Sea, the Molukka Sea, and round the northern tip of Sulawesi into the Celebes Sea. Then through Basilan Strait to the Sulu Sea, to the China Sea via Balabac Strait, and finally to Singapore. This intricate sailing route went past all sorts of places with exotic-sounding names and made me think of the stories of Joseph Conrad and Somerset Maugham. However, since Bali was a thousand miles to the west-northwest

Mountains of Bali and fishing canoes

from Darwin (and halfway to Singapore, on a clear and uncluttered track), we struck out boldly for the island and trusted that the predicted northwest winds would not be strong.

On the first two days we had runs of 128 and 112 miles. Then 44 miles, with twelve hours of calms and drifting while we crossed Baldwin Bank and looked at clumps of yellow gulfweed. By now the sea was its usual deep blue with lots of birds and fish. Once while becalmed we went swimming, but the sea was as hot as water in a bathtub and measured 34°C.—94°F.—when we dropped in a thermometer on a string. On April 5th we logged 46 miles on a sea that was as smooth as a sheet of glass. Our little private world was calm and peaceful. I couldn't stand to think of interruptions of any kind.

[From the log] April 6th. 0015. We're near the Sahul Banks, which according to the chart have a least depth of seven meters. I will feel easier once past this problem. After our experience in Torres Strait, who can trust a chart?

0045. I turned on the depth sounder and got a reading of 2 fathoms. We stopped the yacht immediately and heaved the lead, but found no bottom at 6 fathoms. Back on course. Maybe the sounder really read 102 fathoms.

0520. The depth sounder now reads 12 fathoms. We can clearly see a bottom of white sand in a deep blue sea in the early dawn.

We averaged fifty-nine miles a day for the next four days with trifling winds from the southeast. Sea snakes—black on top and yellow underneath—occasionally wriggled alongside and stuck up their heads for a look at us. I don't know who looked the harder—Mr. Sea Snake or us. One afternoon we had a visit from fifty dolphins, leaping and splashing and squeaking as they crossed and turned and dived. Each morning before dawn a bright satellite passed overhead. "I wonder what the three wise men from the east who saw the Christmas star above Judea would have thought of satellites?" asked Margaret.

During the calms it was fun to watch the life in the sea. Once a chambered nautilus shell floated past with a small crab on top and two little fish underneath in the shade of the shell. Sometimes dorados streaked after flying fish and chased them into the air. The wings of the flying fish made the most wonderful patterns on the still water when the little fish ran for their lives and left the water for short flights. The dimpled wing tracks lasted for only a second or two; then the magical crisscrosses were gone. Had the flying fish been grabbed by the swift green streak that was the mark of a dorado?

We watched two enormous Japanese bulk carrier ships. One was black and carried iron ore from Australia to Japan. The second was a gray, high-sided bulk carrier that took automobiles and trucks from Japan to Australia. It seemed incredible that the Japanese could take away iron ore, bring back finished automobiles, and finally leave with a load of money from Australia, which appeared to lose twice and gain once, if my logic was correct.

The islands of Indonesia appeared dimly to starboard. First Timor, then Roti, and later Sumba. High, brownish-green, with tops of smooth mountains showing between faraway layers of clouds. We saw the sails of small fishing boats rising and falling on distant swells. Each boat had a single A-shaped lateen sail with the apex pointing forward and down. From a distance the white sails made me think of dancing butterflies.

On April 11th we logged 117 miles before a light easterly breeze. According to a vertical sextant angle of Mt. Talariu on Sumba, we were 21 miles offshore. The weather was unsettled, and we began to see rain, squalls, and sheet and fork lightning. Soon we had fresh water from the mainsail funnel running into the tanks. We washed out a couple of buckets of laundry in salt water and hung the clothing on the lifelines so the rain could rinse out the salt.

Now Bali was getting close. On April 12th we did ninety-nine miles, still running before a light easterly wind that was turned on and off by a dozen squalls that had us running the sails up and down. "Absolutely wretched weather," I wrote in the log. "Rain, calms, more rain, swell, and no wind. Slat, slat, slat. I hate it!" We finally put the mainsail down entirely and ran along under a single large headsail. Then as the squalls came and passed we merely speeded up or down. "This works well," I noted. "I must remember to put the mainsail down more often when squalls are astern."

To our north the thinnest and weakest of grays gradually strengthened into darker blurs of substance that grew into mountains on the island of Sumbawa. At dusk we lay becalmed. A little before midnight a breeze floated south from the land and lifted us along to the west.

Dawn was lovely. The backlighted clouds to the east were shards of pink and white glass in front of the most fragile of blues. Above and closer, a black frigate bird circled around and around.

By noon we had run eighty-three miles. To the north on Lombok Island we could see smooth green mountains whose long steep slopes gradually fell away to abrupt cliffs that plunged into the sea. At mid-afternoon we were bouncing around in rough water in the strait between Lombok and Bali. We were close to our target, but the hour was late, the tidal stream was against us, and the wind fell away to nothing. We saw lots of junk in the water— plastic trash, a crab who was getting a free ride on an old sandal, and what appeared to be grass clippings. During the night we were pushed back and forth in the big tidal flows of Lombok Strait, which was wide and deep but a little scary in the darkness. We had heard of small vessels that had stopped on the Indian Ocean side for the night, and in the morning had found themselves in the Java Sea north of the islands. With the help of light land breezes, however, we managed to work *Whisper* toward the Bali side, and by mid-morning we were at the port of Benoa on the southeast coast. The chart and sailing directions and buoys were confusing, so I climbed to the masthead to sort things out.

A Balinese village lay on the south side of the entrance. Ahead of us to the west I looked down on the main channel where two dozen tiny outrigger canoes floated quietly while their owners tended fishing lines or threw out little nets. Each boat had a single sail, and the separate triangles of white and yellow and red and green made accented patches of color on the muddy waters of the estuary. Although *Whisper* was bigger and had the right of way, no one moved. We had obviously been seen, but not a single person paid the slightest attention to us or our horn, so we had to dodge around the impassive fishermen.

Fish traps made of bamboo poles and palm fronds dotted the south shore, and a rabble of launches, ferryboats, masts, awnings, flags, and new and old fishing boats rested in and out of the water. I looked across to a white sand beach on which a hundred outrigger canoes lay panting in the moist heat, like spindly insects. A garish Hindu temple with a top like a silver umbrella rose above the village. The houses were crowded together and mostly low, squarish, and white, with red tile roofs. Behind the settlement ran a thick ribbon of coconut palms and shorter trees of dark green.

Weaver, Bali

Children raced around on bicycles and shouted, and I could hear the sounds of hammering across the water. I watched slim women with dark hair carrying heavy baskets along the quay. Old men sat smoking and talking. A smell compounded of fish and incense and drains drifted up to me.

I realized that the Javanese settlement that lay before me was not make-believe, but the heart of the Far East, a scheme of life that had gone on for hundreds, perhaps thousands of years. The scene was something new to me; yet I had the feeling that it was what I had expected, that somewhere in my subconscious I *knew* this world. Was it from reading, from old motion pictures, or from my imagination?

We sailed past the village, turned a little to starboard, and anchored near two other yachts in a place we were directed to by three men in an Indonesian coast guard launch that suddenly appeared. After we got the sails down, our first move was to put up the cockpit awning to block out the sun to ease the great wave of tropical heat that swept over us inside the harbor. The men in the launch sent us ashore to see the harbormaster.

"Do you have the security clearance?" were the first words of the clerk inside the harbormaster's office. When I said no, the man was shocked and said that we would have to come in on an emergency basis. The clerk's job seemed to be to prepare a reasonable story and to fill out various papers for his chief. One form wanted to know if we had any *important news*. We were also asked whether we carried parrots, monkeys, gunpowder, or opium, and what quantity of each.

Wayan Dira, the harbormaster of Benoa, was an impressive fellow in a well-tailored, loose-fitting gray uniform. He welcomed us in his second-floor office, which had a view and cross-ventilation, and sent someone out for cool drinks. Dira was different in appearance from the usual boyish-looking Indonesians—taller, with different racial strains, and he seemed a cut above his assistants, both in intelligence and manner. He spoke some English and quickly put us at ease. Margaret and I had made an effort to be reasonably dressed and groomed, and we told Dira about our trip around the world. We asked if we might visit Bali for a few weeks and buy a few supplies since our trip westward had been so slow. The harbormaster was upbeat and positive. He immediately picked up the phone and called the immigration chief and put in what we hoped were some good words.

I was given a form to be signed by various departments, so I visited the customs, port administration, police, navy; and quarantine offices, which were close by. The immigration department was in the city of Denpasar, about five miles north. To get there we took a small bus called a bemo. Benoa was the end of the line where all the drivers and bemos waited for ferry passengers and seamen. As soon as a couple of foreigners like us hove into sight the drivers made a beeline for two easy marks. We had been told to bargain sharply.

"Where going?"

"Suci station in Denpasar."

"For you a fare of 5,000 rupiahs."

"No."

"How much you want to pay?"

"500 for two people."

"500! 500! OK, 2,000 and go direct. No stopping for passengers."

"No."

"Final offer. 1,000 special for you."

"No, 400."

"OK. Get in."

(The fare was 20¢ each.)

Bali is a big island, and on a map is shaped something like the head of a dog facing west, with a left-to-right dimension of 78 miles. From top to bottom the island measures 48 miles. On a land area of 2,095 square miles, there are 2,300,000 people, which makes the island one of the most densely populated anywhere. Yet in traveling around, the first impression is one of spaciousness and room, with high, smooth-flanked mountains and lots of rice fields, often neatly terraced and bordered with graceful coconut palms. The rice fields are green, an incredibly light, penetrating green that is at once peaceful and pleasant and buoyant, if such words can be used to describe a color.

The people of Bali are small and slim, with delicate features, brown hair, and hazel eyes. We saw a great deal of walking, and it was usual to see women along the roads carrying large loads balanced on their heads. We never heard an angry word.

Denpasar was crowded with people who rushed in all directions. The jammed intersections overflowed with buses, small automobiles (some with three wheels), motorscooters, bicycles, pushcarts, taxis drawn by small horses, and women who carried baskets, bundles of reeds, sacks, packages, and boxes on their heads. It seemed that the commerce of Bali moved on the heads of the women.

We met with the immigration authorities who stamped our passports for a two-month visit. We were told that we could stop at Surabaya and Jakarta on Java, and Medan in North Sumatra if we wished. A few days later, however, we were summoned back and informed that we should only have been given seven days or a little more. Nevertheless, since our passports had been stamped, we were welcome to stay for two months. I think we were lucky.

Indonesia as a whole is Moslem, but the Balinese are Hindus whose devoutness is a fundamental part of everyday life. The island has hundreds of temples and shrines, and the people use sacred statues, holy books, puppet plays, masked dramas, cremations, operas, and ballets as vehicles of religious

Religious procession, Sampidi, Bali

expression. Almost every day we watched religious processions, some with hundreds of nicely dressed Balinese adults and children. The women often carried elaborate decorative offerings on their heads, and a procession of forty or fifty immaculately groomed women with meter-high displays of flowers, fruit, and bright cloth and ribbons held above their heads was an amazing sight. At first I found it hard to believe that women could support such unwieldy loads on their heads. We soon learned, however, that the young and old carried these offerings—sometimes for miles—with enthusiasm and love. It was common for the driver of a crowded bus or taxi to stop his vehicle and get out and put a few flowers on a religious statue as he drove on his rounds. No one showed any impatience at such stops; indeed, a passenger or two sometimes joined the driver to add a token offering of food or woven leaves.

Everyone we met seemed to enjoy the active daily throb of religion with pleasure and gusto and a sense of joy. I couldn't help but compare what I saw in Bali with the dogma, ritual, and heavy-handed gloominess that accompanied most Christian worship in the United States.

Balinese plays and dancing were a delight. For example, we watched the Barong play (and others), which dealt with a fight between good and evil, with buffoons and villains and heroes dressed in flamboyant costumes that represented mythical animals and spirits. Sometimes the clowns and jesters hopped around the stage in overblown, feathery costumes and comical masks, or dressed as horses or elephants. Even in a strange language it was all outrageously funny, and everyone died laughing.

At some point, however, a slim and elegant dancer glided onto the stage. She wore a towering crown of ornate gold leaf and fresh frangipani flowers. Her disciplined body was sheathed in brocaded fabrics overlaid with wrappings of silver cloth and hangings of ornamental gold. The dancer always had an incredibly smooth face, and she held her hands and arms and arched fingers in unusual, contorted positions. She seemed not a woman at all, but a creature who was a phantom, a marvel, a princess from beyond.

Twisting like a jerky, stylized puppet, she glided and swooped and turned in a circle that seemed illuminated by a special sunbeam.

The girl danced to the music of a fifty-piece gamelan orchestra whose tinkling bells, metallophones, gongs, hand cymbals, accented drum beats, squeaky flutes, and two-string violins produced a curious cocktail of jingling, percussive sounds. By itself the ornate dancing of the young woman was only a pleasant curiosity. The syncopated clanging of the gamelan orchestra grew repetitious to my Western ears after a few minutes. Yet the dancing girl *plus* the shimmering ornamentation of sounds stirred up my feelings and became something new and different. Suddenly I smelled the jungle. I heard antiquity. I felt primitiveness. I became aware of smoldering power. Was there something to these religious statues after all? Or was I simply attracted to

Barong dancer, Bali

the girl? I had succumbed to fantasy. Yikes! What had this performance done to me?

One night we sat in a darkened hall lighted with flickering torches to see the Kecak, or monkey dance. Again a traditional story was filled with pretty dancers, a bizarre king, and various comics and clowns who rushed in and out of the story. The words were impossible, but the theatrical effects were numbing. At the climax a hundred men sat in a circle swaying back and forth in unison in a kind of rhythmic trance while they intoned a chak-a-chak, chak-a-chak sound. As the dramatic action heightened, the performers seemed to become possessed by their roles until they entered a world of make-believe. The music went faster. The swaying grew quicker. The hands clapped harder. We saw a blur of naked arms raised toward the center. Soon everyone was screaming in a sort of frenzy, a kind of ecstasy and trance. What was going to happen? How long could this go on? Now the men were really screaming. Then bang! The dance was suddenly over. The audience and performers stood up, laughed nervously, and got ready to go home. I was in a cold sweat and emotionally exhausted.

Another night we saw a traditional shadow play. The puppet master, who was also an ordained priest, manipulated the flat, two-dimensional puppets with sticks from underneath. The puppets themselves were made of leather, somewhat filigreed, and vaguely resembled Egyptian pharaohs. The dialogue was in poor English and accompanied by two musicians who played gong xylophones. The puppet master stood behind a large flickering yellow flame (shielded to keep it from burning him up) that lighted a white translucent screen. The various puppets were brought into focus against the screen while a story about the spiritual world unfolded.

The plot concerned a powerful man we will call Mr. X. who wanted to marry a beautiful nymph. The gods refused to allow the marriage, so Mr. X threatened to attack the heavens. The gods sent the nymph to find the secret of Mr. X's power. The nymph discovered that Mr. X's weak spot was his tongue, so, like vulnerable Achilles, Mr. X was killed by an arrow shot into his weak spot. In the end the nymph got to marry the hero who had been asked by the gods to prevent the attack in the first place. Got it?

The dialogue and action included various counterplots and intrigues and made good theater. What surprised me was that even with the language problem and the jawbreaking names of the characters, the show grabbed my attention from the start. The rage, jealousy, scheming, lust, power, and duplicity came through on the primitive flickering screen just as on Broadway or on television. We were told that this shadow play was a thousand years old and had been performed for fifty generations!

Everywhere we traveled on Bali we met painters, woodcarvers, batik stencilers, weavers, potters, and metalsmiths. Their skill and dedication were astonishing, but where the artists sold their wares was a mystery. Some of the output went to the Balinese. Most was for tourists. Yet there seemed to be too many galleries and shops and showrooms. The woodcarvers often did large (say twenty-five- or thirty-centimeter) three-dimensional pieces with incredibly complex carvings *all the way through*. The carvers used long, thin chisels and industriously hacked away—first from one side and then another—on interior details that it would have taken an X ray to see. A large amount of woodcarving was used to decorate temples and religious structures that were renewed from time to time.

The paintings tended toward Balinese figures and green landscapes with dozens of trees and shrubs, each painstakingly drawn with fine brushes, somewhat in the style of Rousseau. Masses of detail and thousands of pastel brush strokes covered every bit of every canvas. The galleries seemed to have hundreds of such selections; meanwhile the artists were busy painting more. We watched goldsmiths tapping away. The weavers deftly sorted colored threads. The magic fingers of potters transformed globs of clay into smooth pitchers and vases and cups. The batik makers traced delicate patterns on fine cloth with tiny pitchers of hot wax. . . . Bali seemed the center of the artistic world.

One day we were on a bus that raced along a narrow road in the northern part of the island. The driver was going much too fast, but young

Painter, Bali

drivers are all the same. We rounded a curve in the dirt road and suddenly—just ahead—all the passengers and the driver were horrified to see a flock of ducks being shepherded across the road by a woman herder. The driver braked heavily, but there seemed little chance of stopping the rickety bus in time to save the ducks. As quick as the wink of an eye, the herder flicked her crook in front of the leading duck, who turned back and led the flock from the road just as we creaked to a stop.

The driver leaped from the bus. The woman herder hurried toward the driver. I expected a terrible confrontation. Instead, the driver congratulated the herder on turning the ducks. The herder congratulated the driver on stopping quickly. Each smiled at the other. We continued on our way with the driver and passengers excitedly congratulating one another on life's good fortunes. Only in Bali!

The food shopping in Denpasar was first-rate. We bought all the usual fruits and vegetables, and we tried such exotics as the rambutan, blimbing, and mangosteen—fruits whose delicious tastes are beyond all words. For twenty-seven cents we got a 250-milliliter container of tasty jamlin juice (in a sterilized plastic box with a drinking straw). Many foreign foods were produced under license and, because of low labor costs, were cheap. For example, we bought Carr's Water Biscuits, a sailing staple, in large metal cans and found the quality even better than the originals from England.

Instead of buying a new burner for a kerosene stove, we got an entire single-burner Primus stove and burner for eleven dollars. To buy kerosene and diesel oil, however, required patience. We rowed our jugs ashore and took them on the bus to a gasoline station. The oil was then measured out by the dealer, who used a small pitcher that was endlessly refilled. We carried the jugs back to *Whisper*.

There were lots of tourists on Bali, but unless the local people were employed at the big hotels or worked in art galleries they paid little attention to foreigners. On the buses we kept meeting young Balinese people who spoke a little English. They were often shy, but curious about strangers and asked us endless questions. Why had we come to Bali? Did we like it? Had we seen the best temple up on Gunung Agung, the high mountain?

I thought it was fun to bargain with the bemo drivers over the bus fare. When I got to know the drivers better, however, I discovered that their little game was desperate. My friend Pipi told me that his bemo cost 3,500,000 rupiahs ($3,627). Pipi paid the Chinese owner 7,000 rupiahs a day for the use of the vehicle plus gasoline, which meant that he needed fifty fares a day just to break even. On many days he lost money. No wonder the drivers hustled!

During our stay we had made friends with Nyoman Adnyana of the tourist bureau. One day Nyoman invited us to Sempidi, his village, to see a special religious ceremony. Again we saw a cock fight and a procession of women carrying offerings on their heads. We smelled incense in the temple and watched a white-robed priest kneel on a raised stone platform. We listened to a gamelan orchestra and drank endless cups of tea.

The next day Nyoman came aboard *Whisper* with his son. "Stay with us and write a book about gentle Bali," he said. "We'll find you a nice hotel and . . ."

"Don't tempt me. I love it here," I said, adding the traveler's cliché: "One day I'll be back."

Our departure was hard work. First I chased around to seven offices for the clearance. Then when we hoisted the tender on board, Margaret found a nasty gash in the dinghy's hull. I was well into the repair when two visitors arrived and had to be entertained. Finally when I started to winch up the anchor I discovered that the chain was encased in fiendishly hard barnacles that were covered with horrible slimy creatures with long white tentacles and fluid sacs. It took an hour of hard scrubbing with a wire brush to clean the chain. What a relief it was to put up the sails and head out.

Two hours later, Bali began to slip away from us in swirling mists astern. We would miss its busy, intriguing life. Our visit had been wonderful.

"No thank you. I already have one."

CHAPTER THIRTEEN

Two Islands

S outh of Bali we picked up the fresh southeast trade wind and soon hurried along toward the west with a reefed mainsail and a small jib held out with a spinnaker pole. Our course was clear, the air was fresh, and the breeze whisked away the cobwebs of harbor living. Hurrah for the open sea!

From Bali—just east of Java—the Indian Ocean runs almost unbroken to the east coast of Africa, 4,500 miles away, some 18 percent of the entire distance around the world. Our course was roughly along the latitude of ten degrees south, and we expected the warm trade wind to be at our back for the whole way. After the poky passages from Vanuatu to Darwin, and from Darwin to Bali, we hoped for good sailing.

On the first day we logged 129 miles in front of a squally twenty-two-knot wind. Initially we couldn't get the wind vane to steer properly. I fiddled with it for almost two hours before I looked over the stern and saw that the wooden water blade had struck something and was in splinters.* While Margaret steered I pulled the vane assembly from its mount at the stern and installed a spare blade. We then stopped *Whisper* completely so that we could

---

* This is supposed to be impossible because of a breakaway scheme. However, if an obstruction strikes the blade from the side (or you pick up a heavy fishing cable that pulls obliquely) when the water blade has swung to an extreme position to port or starboard, the force tends to pull at right angles to the breakaway fitting. This is a rare occurrence, but when it happens something has to give, and in this case the wooden blade simply split and broke away.

bolt the whole vane assembly back in its mount while there was no water pressure on the blade. Soon we were going full speed again. The vane steered perfectly.

By noon on the second day we had logged another 130 miles. The sea was rough and the wind squally. We had the mainsail down and the trysail up to stop the downwind rolling. In the late afternoon a linkage rod in the steering vane snapped with a bang. I fitted a spare, amazed that two parts had broken on successive days when we had used the vane for years without any trouble at all.

Unfortunately I was ill with a fever of some kind. I felt ghastly and presumed that it was the beginning of the end. My head ached, I was as weak as a kitten, my stomach was upset, and every half hour I ran to the toilet. I was an absolute mess. Even worse, my ears kept ringing. I was sure that I had malaria. I felt very sorry for myself.

At 0700 on May 10th I staggered up on deck and poled out the number three jib (nicknamed "bullet," a nine-ounce sail whose Dacron material was as stiff as corrugated iron). Then I collapsed in my bunk. Margaret wrote in the log that the poled-out jib worked well with the trysail, and that the steering vane was much less pressed. By 1700 the wind and seas were down. I felt better and had begun to eat a little. We dropped the trysail and hoisted the double-reefed mainsail.

By the next morning the squalls and lumpy seas had eased off. My fever seemed to be gone, but I was astonished at how weak I was. When Margaret and I unreefed the mainsail and put up a larger jib, I let her do most of the work; yet I panted with fatigue. While we were on the foredeck, four red-tailed tropicbirds came streaking toward us, shrieking with excitement. They circled around and around the yacht at high speed half a dozen times and then rushed off, as if they were late for an appointment. At noon Margaret announced that we had logged 145 miles in the last twenty-four hours. That evening I tucked a reef in the main, which didn't seem to slow the yacht at all. Later I put in a second reef when squalls appeared astern and blotted out the stars. The sailing was certainly brisk.

At twelve o'clock the following day we began to keep a careful watch for Christmas Island. Soon I was able to see the high dark mass of this T-shaped 10-mile-long island that belonged to Australia but seemed to be within the geographical limits of Indonesia. The swells grew steeper, and presumably felt the island ahead, which was getting closer. Margaret and I were uncertain whether to stop or not. We were making excellent time and at noon had logged 155 miles (which included 15 miles of favorable current). Soon we were at the northeast tip of the island and sailed into the wind shadow of 335-meter Headridge Hill. The sea became calm, and we loafed along into Flying Fish Cove, the main anchorage. Suddenly Margaret was at the bow pointing toward a boatload of workmen who were waving at us and gesturing where to anchor. I shoved the tiller down and rounded up. "Dump the jib and staysail halyards," I shouted. I let the mainsheet go, and walked forward and dropped the anchor. It was the 124th time that we'd anchored on our circumnavigation.

Though our visit to Christmas Island was short, we were still nailed by Australian officialdom. The process was less painful than usual, however, because the key person was an attractive woman police sergeant named Kathy Burdett who not only had a nice smile and a zippy figure but drove me around in an air-conditioned car. Sailors need to be thankful for small mercies.

The next day Margaret and I had a look around the island—which had some surprisingly dense forests—and bought a few special postage stamps, often a major business on remote islands. Many of the cars on Christmas were old Mercedes-Benz automobiles from Singapore, which had a rule that required owners to get rid of their cars when they became five years old. Australians on Christmas were able to buy the cars cheaply and didn't have to pay Australian taxes. Every other vehicle was a jaded Mercedes.

Christmas Island's only business was the mining and shipping of phosphate, which was used for agricultural fertilizer. Three hundred Europeans lived on the island together with 2,000 Chinese and 500 Malay workmen, each in separate enclaves. According to Camilla Yates, the wife of the administrator, the island's phosphate reserves would last only ten more years. Although the phosphate company had begun to sell a lower grade of fertilizer to Malaysia, the profitable days seemed over because of a world surplus of the chemical. "Another big problem," said Camilla, "is that we're only allowed to ship phosphate to the Australian mainland in expensive Australian vessels."

Flying Fish Cove was a poor anchorage, but since it was the best on the island it had to be used, even though enormous swells from the north sometimes rolled in. Ships couldn't anchor but were obliged to go out to sea each night and stand off. The swells sometimes lasted for weeks, and then abruptly stopped. On a day when the sea was calm, the ships came in alongside the phosphate works and were tied to enormous mooring buoys with heavy cables. It required six motorized barges and sixty men to handle a ship, the buoys, and the cables for a single mooring operation. Long cantilevered arms from shore with big delivery pipes were then swung over the vessel, and the loading commenced. The scheme was reasonably fast, but the arrangement was awkward, antiquated, and certainly labor intensive.

What was hair-raising for a visiting mariner was to watch how the motorized barges were handled. As soon as the barges finished with a ship, the tenders motored to the boat jetty, where a crane lifted each barge up on the wharf to a little railroad car, which ran on tracks leading to the land. Each barge was then shoved up the tracks and across the shore road into a specially reinforced marine building whose big doors were slammed shut like a bank vault as soon as the barges were inside. All this was necessary to keep the barges from being destroyed by the sea.

The harbormaster, a red-bearded Scotsman named Jim McMaster, showed me the high-water marks of huge breaking waves up on the shore and a frequency graph of the swells, which occurred randomly and without warning. This nasty business was reported as far back as 1688 when William Dampier complained that his men on the island couldn't get back to the ship because "the Sea fell on the Shore so high." Was someone trying to tell a stranger something? Yes. Get away from this place![6]

On the morning of May 15th—with a great sigh of relief—we headed west again. Just as we were getting under way in Flying Fish Cove, a skinny fish almost half a meter long, blue with two yellow stripes, jumped into the cockpit and startled Margaret, who was busy steering at a crucial moment. I was forward at the mast coiling halyards.

"Lunch has just appeared," she shouted. "Come back here and deal with this fish before he jumps back into the sea." While I was knocking the fish over the head with a winch handle, a group of frigate birds attacked our masthead wind direction ribbon—the wimpel—and tried to tear it off. I blew the foghorn to chase away the birds. Everyone seemed to be attacking *Whisper!*

We had a good breeze from the east-southeast and soon were running nicely before the warm trade wind. A few hours later Christmas Island was only a dot astern. Ahead of us lay the vastness of the Indian Ocean. Where we were headed there were no ships, no planes, and no fishing boats. The first land was tiny Keeling-Cocos, more than five hundred miles to the west. We had been in Bali only a week earlier, but its complex culture and busy life seemed light years away.

I adjusted the sails and went below. I got out the Red Sea charts and settled down with a book called *Confessions of a Red Sea Smuggler* by Henri De Monfreid. The author was a high-flier among adventurers and had written a hair-raising, can-it-be-true? book about hashish smuggling under sail in 1915. I had read the book before, and it was an old favorite. Now I had the opportunity to go through it slowly and trace each movement on my charts. I wanted to see if the story made sense when compared with real places. The book was good, and as I turned the pages I felt like a bee sipping nectar from a flower.

It's astonishing how a sailor's ears pick up the sounds of trouble at sea. On our first and second days our runs were 158 and 110 miles. On both days I heard a mysterious squeak from time to time, a noise that I finally traced to a shackle that held the mainsail tack to the gooseneck fitting at the forward end of the main boom. The stainless steel shackle had not only chafed the metal tack fitting and the sail grommet, but was all bent and twisted from the strains of thousands of miles of sailing. I replaced the shackle with a dozen turns of light nylon line. The lashing—which could stretch a little during shock loads—was strong, quiet, and kinder to the metal parts.

For the next three days (runs of fifty-two, fifty, and fifty-one miles) the wind veered to the northeast and blew fitfully or not at all. We were becalmed about thirteen hours. On the morning of May 20th I looked up at the most extraordinary sky.

[From the log] 0925. The sky is an encyclopedia of clouds unlike anything I have ever seen. Stratus and nimbus—the rain clouds—lie on the near horizon. Then fragments of stratus higher up. In the distance I can see cumulus and cumulonimbus whose tops appear to spread into high-altitude streaks. The feathery ice crystals of cirrus five miles up are higher still. The streamers at the tops of the cumulonimbus are shredding and spreading out toward the southeast like old rope ends. Much lower down, the stratus seem to be slowly moving eastward in relation to the higher clouds, which themselves are moving in other directions. When I watch all this and see each layer moving in a different direction, I get disoriented and lose my balance. It's like being on a busy city street at rush hour and watching pedestrians and two lines of automobiles moving in different directions while you are on a bus going another way. . . . The relative motions make me dizzy.

The southeast trade wind finally returned in strength a little before noon on May 20th, and we soon sped along with a steady wind. I put up an old number two genoa that had been made nine years earlier for our Cape Horn trip by sailmaker Franz Schattauer in Seattle. I had tried to sell this sail through the Bacon sail brokerage in Annapolis before we started our trip, but Bacon had rejected the sail. "Too rotten," said the expert after inspecting the fabric. Since the sail was apparently worthless, I tossed it on board as an extra. In spite of its supposed terminal state, however, the sail had pulled us thousands of miles in the Atlantic and across much of the Pacific. Now the old friend was flying in the Indian Ocean and was still intact. The sail seemed charmed. Its material was as thin as an old handkerchief, but in light winds the venerable fabric set perfectly, with nary a wrinkle. I wondered how long it would last and began to take an interest in preserving it as a relic. Whenever the wind got strong or squally I handed the sail, carefully folded it, and stored it below, nicely dried and out of the sun. In the trade wind region the old sail was often perfect and pulled *Whisper* like a workhorse.

Although we were sailing well, the weather was unsettled, with a lumpy cross-swell from the south. Rain showers drummed on deck, so we hooked up the water-catching system from the mainsail and topped up the water tanks. At 1600 our dead-reckoning position put us sixty-eight miles from Keeling-Cocos. Five hours later I turned the tuning dial on the radio direction finder to 305 kilohertz, identified the morse characters CC, and got a bearing of 265°–275°. Somebody was out there, and we were right on

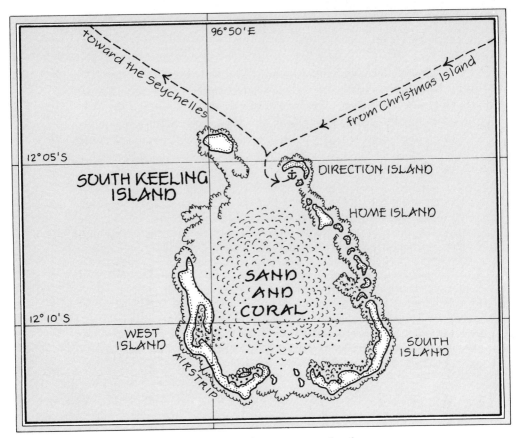

15. Keeling–Cocos Island

course. After the Bramble Cay fiasco I took care to have plenty of sleep before any landfalls. Now I was wide awake and determined not to run down on anything in the dark.

By 0300 we estimated twenty-eight miles to go, and at 0430 I saw lights and the rotating airport beacon. I stopped the yacht, changed to a small jib, fell off on the tack away from the island ahead, and went to sleep. At 0740 we were both up and refreshed and sailing nicely toward a low atoll with coconut palms. By 0900 we were abeam of Home Island and could see small houses. An hour later we rounded Direction Island at the northeast corner of Keeling–Cocos.

When we reached the entrance to the lagoon on the north side of the atoll, we headed south-southwest and were soon in the coral with depths of six fathoms. Just then a rain squall swept around us and we could see nothing. I doused all sail and anchored. As the squall moved on, an Australian in a small open boat passed us and suggested a route to the best anchorage. Forty-five minutes later we anchored in three fathoms of turquoise water over white sand in front of Direction Island, whose crescent-shaped beach and nodding palm trees seemed too perfect to be true. The protection for *Whisper* was complete, and we were all by ourselves. Margaret and I sat on the foredeck with cups of coffee and marveled at our good fortune at finding such a lovely rest stop in the eastern part of the Indian Ocean.

Keeling-Cocos, discovered by Captain William Keeling in 1608, is an oval-shaped coral atoll about 720 miles south of the equator.* The island is at ninety-seven degrees east longitude, on a line with Rangoon, Burma, far to the north. This remote drop of land in the sea measures 7 miles from north to south and 6 miles east to west. Most of the atoll is a shallow, coral-choked lagoon; only at the northern end is it possible to anchor ships and small vessels. The land itself consists of small islets ¼ to ½ mile wide around the perimeter of the island.

Until a few years ago tiny Keeling-Cocos was one of the most remote places on earth. The island was first settled in 1827 by a Scottish sea captain named John Clunies-Ross, who got the idea of collecting copra from coconut palms. For labor, Clunies-Ross imported Malays from Indonesia. He built a village on Home Island, an islet on the eastern side of the atoll, and set the Malays to work. In times past each man collected and husked five hundred coconuts a day. The women then split the nuts and removed and dried the white meat, which was bagged and shipped to market where it was used for soap and cosmetic oils. When we were there, the fifth-generation John Clunies-Ross had a Malay force that numbered 310.

From 1901 onward, Keeling-Cocos was also a link in international cable routes. For many years an outpost of the Eastern Extension Telegraph Company—manned by English technicians—was stationed on Direction Island. For a time it was also the site of a radio navigation transmitter, a boathouse, and air-sea rescue launches. The men who ran these isolated facilities were always hospitable to visiting yachtsmen, who brought with them a touch of the outside world. With improvements in worldwide communications, however, the various stations were no longer needed. By 1970, Direction Island was uninhabited; the buildings were torn down.

In 1944, during World War II, the Royal Air Force hacked out a small airstrip on West Island on the opposite side of the atoll from Clunies-Ross. Later the runway and buildings were improved, and in the days of piston-engine Constellations, Quantas Airways used the 2,600-meter strip as a refueling point for flights between Australia and Mauritius, which in the early 1950s was the longest overwater flight in the world. Today there are no commercial stops. However, the facility is useful as an emergency airstrip and a strategic military presence. "An unsinkable aircraft carrier in the Indian Ocean" was the phrase we heard. In recent years the Australians—no doubt

---

* To add to confusion, the island is sometimes labeled Cocos-Keeling, Cocos, or South Keeling. Tiny North Keeling Islet is fifteen miles north and uninhabited.

with American support—have upgraded the airport and have stockpiled fuel for an occasional Orion observation plane. When we were there the island controlled all radio traffic for commercial flights between Sri Lanka and western Australia. Instead of a handful of maintenance men and radio operators, however, we were amazed to find 250 Australians.

"It's a good example of Parkinson's Law," commented Eric Hiscock in 1974. "The Australians look after the airstrip, but the airstrip is little used except by the plane which comes from Perth every two weeks to bring food and other supplies for the people who run the airstrip. There is a hospital, a school, a golf course, and other amenities."[7]

We had been advised to put up our yellow Q flag and to wait for officials. Sure enough, in a little while a launch appeared and two friendly Australians began the usual apologies for the forms we were asked to fill out. Not only did we have the regular official baloney to deal with, but we were told that Keeling-Cocos was a "high quarantine station," which meant that entering foodstuffs were controlled and that all garbage had to be taken ashore and burned in a special place. We learned that breeding livestock—say a prize bull from Canada—was occasionally flown to Keeling-Cocos and kept under quarantine in case the animal was diseased. However, since visiting yachts anchored four miles from the animal quarters—protected by double fences—and there were no quarantined animals in residence, we thought the regulations were a little overdrawn. Nevertheless we were visitors, so each day we took our garbage ashore to the designated place, poured oil on it, burned it, and dropped it in a special pit where it was checked by a quarantine man who came all the way from West Island.

The local administration launch was the *Sir Zelman Cowen,* a fifty-foot twin-screw diesel vessel that was constructed of aluminum and had been built in 1982 at a cost of $240,000. The ship was originally designed to be sixty-two feet long, but twelve feet were chopped out of the middle by an administrative decision in Canberra to save $8,000. Unfortunately the shortening ruined both the appearance and the performance. When it came time for the vessel to proceed to Keeling-Cocos, it was found that the shortening had another effect. According to Australian rules, the ship was two feet too short to be allowed to go to sea under her own power, so she had to be shipped at a cost of $40,000. The local crewman hated the vessel because of her shortness, which made it difficult to handle stretcher cases from passing steamers. The *Sir Zelmen Cowen*'s propellers extended below the keel, which meant that if she touched any coral (sooner or later at an atoll) the propellers would be destroyed immediately. Already this had happened.

We got acquainted with Nelson and Abedin, two Malay boatmen who were in charge of a smaller launch. One afternoon they came aboard *Whisper* for a cup of tea. Both were quiet and reserved and looked at *Whisper*'s cabin with the greatest of interest. They were born on Keeling-Cocos and had never been away, so our little vessel was full of strange things from a world beyond. Their English was fair, and we heard about their job, local fishing, their wages, and the Home Island Cooperative, to which all the Malays belonged. The administration paid each man two hundred dollars a month, which went to the cooperative, which in turn paid each man forty dollars. However, the cooperative furnished housing, electricity, and other things, so the only expense was for food. "The lagoon is full of fish," said Abedin. "and we can get as much as we want." Before they left they signed *Whisper*'s guest book in good handwriting and drew a coconut palm and an island sailing sloop.

The Australians who worked at the airport and quarantine station had much leisure time and often took small boats across the lagoon to the beach on Direction Island to camp and swim and have picnics. Lots of them visited us on *Whisper* and in turn invited us to their homes near the airport on West Island. We spent many hours with Bill and Jill Blake, the relief doctor and his wife. One night we showed a sixteen-millimeter film of *Whisper*'s trip around Cape Horn to a group of our new friends.

We heard much talk about John Clunies-Ross, a subject that violently divided the Australian community. The Australian government had recently bought out Clunies-Ross for Aus. $6.25 million and ended his copra business. The United Nations was about to conduct a vote among his Malay workers to see whether they wanted (1) to be independent, (2) to have a free association with Australia, or (3) to integrate with Australia and become citizens. The labor government was supposed to be neutral; in reality it was lobbying energetically for the third option, so Australia could gain full control.*

The conservatives among the Australians liked Clunies-Ross and defended his copra operation. "He and his family have run the plantation for generations with practically no restrictions and no outside assistance from any government," they said. The liberals hated Clunies-Ross and said that he was a feudal baron who should be stripped of his land and power. "His Malays work as slaves," they said.

One night at dinner we would hear praise for Clunies-Ross. The next night at another dinner Clunies-Ross would be damned. I couldn't believe that such nasty, divisive pettiness could exist on a tiny island. One evening after a particularly bitter diatribe against Clunies-Ross, I spoke up to our hostess:

"How can you say all those things about a man who has lived on this island all his life?" I asked. "You've been here only a few months. Have you a special intelligence service? Have you ever met him?"

"I shouldn't want to," she sniffed. "He's a monster."

---

* The third option passed.

Direction Island, Keeling-Cocos

The next day Margaret and I went to Home Island to meet the monster, who in the flesh seemed a perfectly normal and pleasant fellow to me. John Clunies-Ross was fifty-eight years old, a little above average height, and lean and fit. He was clean-shaven, and dressed in the same sort of light shirt and cotton trousers that I wore in the tropics. His large house and garden were delightful. It was in this same house—when newly built—that his grandfather had welcomed pioneer small-boat sailor Joshua Slocum in 1897. We met Clunies-Ross' daughter, son-in-law, and grandchildren, and sat under a quiet arbor in the garden and drank fresh limeade.

John Clunies-Ross was well educated and was used to looking after his family on a remote island, not the easiest of tasks. He had run a large coconut plantation, supervised the Malay community—for whose welfare he had deep feelings—and had business interests on Christmas Island and elsewhere. When a hurricane devastated Keeling-Cocos or copra prices were low, Clunies-Ross drew on his funds from the Christmas Island phosphate company to help out the settlement.

As we talked he was a bit reticent at first, but he gradually opened up when we spoke of sailing and distant places and things other than local island politics, which must have been a relief to him. He invited us to have lunch with his family.

"What's really going on here?" I finally asked before we left. "I've heard nothing but talk about you since we arrived."

"It's nothing very complicated," said Clunies-Ross. "Instead of letting me and my family and my workers stay here and lead the lives we have for generations, the government wants the island for a military base. To get me out they've started a whispering campaign against me. They want me and the Malays to leave so they can run the place as they please.

"In the old days I used to have a good press. Now I'm compared to an 1850 slave-owning plantation owner in the southern United States. Once the government is down on you and the popular liberal press thinks you're an ogre, it's hard to change the drift."

I enjoyed meeting Clunies-Ross, but time was not on his side. He was right, and I respected his judgment and position, but he was born fifty years too late. Now he was pursued by a pack of mean and petty government hacks who treated him shabbily because they saw him as a symbol of independence, which they neither possessed nor could understand. Instead of confronting him with the military reality, they sneaked around and tried to gain their ends by guile and deceit. I thought their conduct was disgraceful. I was glad that I had met some of them so I could know what manner of men they were.

Margaret and I sat on the beach at Direction Island. _Whisper_ lay fifty meters in front of us, secure to two anchors in smooth water that was colored a dozen tints of turquoise. We dug our toes into the white and powdery sand and watched tiny crabs the exact color of the sand scuttle across the beach. A little earlier we had been swimming and looking at rainbows of small fish. Above us the palms sighed heavily in the strong trade wind that had been blowing for days. For a moment we felt glad that we were not out at sea. Now a second yacht had come into the anchorage, a Polish ketch named _Matylda_ with two men and a woman on board. The woman hated sailing but loved dogs and owned a large Irish setter that she tried to keep secret from the quarantine inspectors, who finally learned of the dog and were speechless with rage.

It was almost the end of May. The year before, sixty-two yachts had visited Keeling-Cocos on their way across the Indian Ocean. The peak month was August, with eighteen. Now with only two in the lagoon I wondered if traffic was falling off. What was to be the future of this beautiful atoll that was so lovely and quiet? Would it become another naval base? A few million dollars could clean out the coral and deepen the lagoon. The dredged material could be used for new land on which to build warehouses and barracks and ammunition dumps. The palms could be cut down to make room for roads. Nuclear submarines and missile-carrying frigates could anchor where *Whisper* was now. Like Diego Garcia farther west, I suppose yachts would not even be allowed to stop. But who would want to come to look at a dead island and dreary military machines? I began to feel like Clunies-Ross and to think that I too had been born too late. Was there still a place for a wanderer to go?

CHAPTER FOURTEEN

Across the Indian Ocean

*T*he distance from Keeling-Cocos to Port Victoria in the Seychelle Islands off the east coast of Africa is 2,563 miles. By the third day—June 3rd—we had already logged 462 miles, with runs of 146, 152, and 164 miles. The southeast trade wind was strong and squally and blew between twenty-two and twenty-nine knots. We had started out with a double-reefed mainsail, the staysail, and a poled-out number three jib, but we were overpowered, and it wasn't long before we pulled the mainsail down and hoisted the trysail. Later we handed the staysail. The sea was rough, and plenty of water flew across the deck and into the cockpit as *Whisper* hurried toward the west.

Before we left I was slightly cowed by the wind. We had sat on *Whisper*'s foredeck and watched the palm trees on Direction Island leaning and swaying and the fronds swishing together as the squalls marched across the lagoon. My heart turned to chicken soup, and my resolve collapsed. The passage ahead was long, but once out at sea I found that the strength of the wind and squalls was less than I had thought. The thing was to simply go! The reality was often easier.

One afternoon we tuned the radio to the BBC and listened to a description of the Derby—the great horse race—at Epsom Downs in England, on the opposite side of the earth. There was lots of action on a wet field in front of Queen Elizabeth and an enormous crowd. The announcer got so excited and his voice grew so high and squeaky that I was sure he would fall over dead from nervous agitation. Horse racing and a posh society seemed so elitist and trivial and so far from us in the middle of the Indian Ocean. I wouldn't have traded places with the queen for anything.

The wind continued a steady Force six from the southeast, and on the fourth day we ran 157 miles. When the wind freshened we found that the trysail often made the yacht head up into the wind a bit. The windward steering vane line then tugged at the tiller to make us bear off. We obviously lost ground when the course was not steady. As an experiment I handed the trysail, and hoisted the forestaysail and sheeted it flat to keep us from rolling so much. To my surprise this scheme worked well, and we flew along hour after hour toward the west. However, all this sounds as if the wind was steady, which it was not. It surged in strength, and we were kept busy running our small sails up and down.

Since we were driving the yacht hard, the steering vane worked hard too. The tiller lines from the vane moved back and forth through the small blocks thousands of times. Chafe eventually became a problem. I moved a stern anchor to the coachroof to get it away from the vane lines and greased the lines with anhydrous lanolin where they passed through the sheaves. I put light oil on the bearings of the sheaves. Every hour we checked the leads to make sure the lines didn't rub on anything. The anhydrous lanolin—a sheep derivative that we nicknamed "sheep dip"—was super stuff. A big pot of it from the pharmacy had cost only a few dollars, lasted for years, and was good for lines, blocks, bearings, stiff leather, chapped lips, and dry hands.

We seemed to be roaring along; yet it was surprisingly comfortable below in my bunk. I had soft pillows, a canvas lee cloth to keep me in place, and always a good book. Our sleeping scheme was to take naps a couple of hours long throughout the day and night. One of us was generally asleep except at mealtimes or during sail changes.

On June 5th our noon position was 157 miles farther west. The ocean was still rough, and every couple of hours a wave rumbled on board and filled the cockpit. In the afternoon the wind dropped a little, so we hoisted the trysail. The tension on the single part sheet made the line as hard as a piece of iron. Once I happened to stand up in the cockpit just as the yacht rolled. The sail gybed, and the sheet cracked me smartly on the head.

We had four kinds of seabirds flitting about: storm petrels, noddies, tropicbirds, and a melancholy gannet. The sky began to clear a little, and we saw bits of blue. We managed to open the front hatch a little for fresh air. By midnight the sea was not so rough. At dawn on June 6th we got up the double-reefed mainsail, and at noon (143 miles)—with the wind and sea lighter—we shook out one reef and flew two small headsails. There was still a big ground swell, but the wind had moderated. A little later we heard four strange thumps on deck. Margaret looked out and discovered that four squid—each about the size of her hand and silverish with red appendages—had attacked the yacht. There was black ink all over the port deck.

Sometimes the sea seemed a little calmer, and we opened a portlight for ventilation. Sooner or later, however, a wave skipped on board and water splashed below into a bunk, which caused shouts of outrage, a quick closing, and mopping up with a sponge and a bowl.

Since we sailed without refrigeration, one of our sailing staples was canned corn beef, perhaps an out-of-favor product, but delicious nonetheless. Margaret often used it in spaghetti sauce or cold in sandwiches. Sometimes she sliced it, and dipped it in a beaten whole egg and bread crumbs before frying it. She also made a kind of stew with onions, cabbages, potatoes, and chunks of corned beef. Many years before, a Chinese author friend named Charles Leong had given us a book named *Seven Immortal Flavors*. It was on this passage that Margaret happened to leaf through the book and got the idea for pineapple corned beef sweet and sour. The results were splendid—a meal that was delicious and tangy with just the right combination of spicy smells, and a taste that wrapped itself around my tongue. The recipe:

> 1 12-ounce can corned beef (the usual size)
> 1 egg
> 1 cup flour
> ½ teaspoon monosodium glutamate (MSG)
> 2 cups vegetable oil
> 1 8-ounce can pineapple chunks
> 1 medium green pepper (nice if available)
> 1 teaspoon soy sauce
> ½ cup sugar
> ¼ cup catsup
> ½ vinegar
> 2 tablespoons cornstarch

Cut the corned beef into squares as wide as your thumb. Dip each square into the beaten egg. Then coat the pieces with a mixture of flour and MSG. Bring the vegetable oil to a boil, and slowly spoon in the pieces of coated beef. Fry until golden brown on all sides—about five minutes. Remove the chunks of cooked meat and drain on a paper towel.

Put the soy sauce, sugar, juice from the can of pineapple, catsup, and vinegar in a deep skillet, stir well, and bring to a boil.

Separately, mix the two tablespoons of cornstarch with two tablespoons of water to make a paste. Gradually add this paste to the sauce. Continue to boil the sauce and stir until it thickens. Add the cooked corned beef, pineapple chunks, and sliced green pepper. Keep mixing everything for about five minutes or until all the ingredients are very hot.

Serve with hot steamed rice. The recipe is enough for three or four portions. Leftovers are excellent the next day.

[From the log] June 7th. 0145. A ship! The first since Timor. She could be on the run from the Horn of Africa to Australia's Cape Leeuwin. About five miles north of us. We are tearing along and overpowered, but the steering vane is managing. Let her rip! Hang on!

At noon we were sailing hard on a splendid blue sea with lots of white horses around us, and we chalked up a run of 169 miles, *Whisper*'s best ever. I estimated a favorable current of 27 miles, the difference between the noon fixes for June 6th and 7th, and what the log read. We turned the clock back one hour and were just five hours ahead of Greenwich time. Later that day I saw a large brownish-gray fish, perhaps three or four meters long, lazing beneath the surface. I wondered if it was a black marlin. Zane Grey would have liked the sight.

On June 8th we did 167 miles. The wind eased off to about fifteen knots from the southeast, so we hoisted the full mainsail and put up the ancient genoa. Would the venerable sail stand up to the trade wind once again? We would find out. At noon the island of Diego Garcia was about 450 miles ahead, a little to the north of west; Victoria, Mahé, in the Seychelles was 1,420 miles on a course of 288° true. In the afternoon Margaret polished the oil stove while I cleaned squid ink from the decks. Then I took a bath with seawater and Vel soap, which made a good lather. After I dried myself I put on clean clothes and felt quite superior. However, my ego inflation was short-lived, because as Margaret noted in the log: "Hal took a wave while watching the sea. Soaked. Ha-ha!"

During the next four days we sailed 571 miles before the steady trade wind. Life was pretty easy. Our hardest work was speculating whether the old genoa would last until the Seychelles. One day while Margaret was mixing bread dough in the galley, I had the staysail down for a few repairs. I sat at the chart table opposite the galley with the sail spread out around me while I sewed. Suddenly a flying fish flew down the hatch, slithered along the sail, and almost ended up in my face. I let out a great shout of surprise, which startled Margaret, who turned and accidentally dropped her bread pan on the sail. In a twinkling the sail was covered with flour into which the flying fish was hopping around.

"He's ready for the pan," I shouted.

"Get that fish out of here," snapped Margaret. "He'll ruin my bread. I don't want it all smelly!"

By this time I was laughing so hard that I almost embarrassed myself. It was a funny morning.

On June 11th at 1555 we were about one hundred miles south-southeast of Diego Garcia when a large cargo ship, the *Gulf Shipper* of the Lykes Line of New Orleans, appeared astern and began to approach us. The vessel bristled with radio and radar antennas. I guessed that she was an intelligence or patrol ship on charter to the U.S. Navy. I put up a large U.S. flag, and the ship responded in kind. The *Gulf Shipper* began to sail a parallel course close to *Whisper,* but unfortunately approached on our windward side, which cut off our wind and maneuverability. The captain, dressed in navy khakis, spoke to us through a megaphone and asked if we needed water or a position. I declined his offers with thanks and tried to edge away because the monster ship was only about twenty or thirty meters from us and could have crushed us like an eggshell. Obviously we had been picked up on radar by a picket ship of the big American–British military base where strangers were not welcome. The crew on *Gulf Shipper* was all lined up along the starboard deck above us and shouted down questions and took photographs. The galley gang was down one deck farther and busy waving. It was quite unnerving for a large ship to come so close to a small vessel at sea, and by this time I was shaking like an acute malaria victim. I was pleased to see a ship from my country, and it was kind of the captain to offer assistance, but I was even more pleased to see her pull ahead and widen the gap between us. A few minutes later the *Gulf Shipper* turned to the north with a couple of friendly toots. Years before in the Rio del la Plata we had had a disastrous encounter with an Argentine patrol vessel. We preferred to keep plenty of sea room between us and other ships.

It was a relief to be alone on the sea again.

[From the log] June 12th. 1143. One day west of Diego Garcia.

How beautiful the sea is! And how lovely this journey! We slip along at six knots before the steady trade wind day after day. The yacht rolls a little as she lifts to each swell that rumbles past us every ten seconds or so. We are on a magical slide westward across an endless, azure sea.

How easy the sailing is! How well little *Whisper* soars across the waves! To run for weeks before this constant wind is so simple and satisfying that if the world only knew, a million people would be out here trying it. This morning we scooped up two fat flying fish from the lee scuppers and put them in the frying pan for breakfast. I hammered off the armorlike husk from a green coconut to get the milk, a drink much better than wine. Neither cost anything; both were delicious. Just now an inquisitive gannet from Diego Garcia circles us warily, no doubt wondering what sort of a giant bird we are with our three white wings and long black body.

In the cockpit I feel the warm sun on my shoulders. A few minutes ago I sloshed buckets of salt water over me for my daily wash. Five miles above us feathery streaks of cirrus clouds decorate the zenith with delicate swirls of white ice crystals. Up ahead the bow wave sings as we rush along toward the firm line of the distant horizon. Some people say they can't wait for a journey to end; for me this heavenly voyage could go on forever.

On June 13th and 14th *Whisper* sailed 272 miles before thirteen-knot winds across her port quarter, and we set the clocks back another hour on our eternal race toward the setting sun. I repaired the head sink pump and overhauled a kerosene Primus burner. Then I sewed some roping back on the old genoa where it had come off. While I was on the foredeck I noticed that the hardened pin of a snap shackle at the top of a short pendant at the tack of the headsail was chafing on the headstay wire. The odds of the shackle pin being turned exactly toward the wire in front of it seemed a thousand to one, yet the cursed pin had worn heavily into three or four strands of the nineteen-strand wire, which would have to be changed in port. Margaret and I spent some hours rerouting several halyards to lessen possible chafe. With thoughts of windward work in the Red Sea ahead, we took down the spinnaker halyard entirely and substituted a three-millimeter messenger line in place of the twelve-millimeter spare main-jib halyard.

On June 15th (156 miles) there was a great gathering of porpoises at *Whisper*'s bow at dawn. We saw about thirty or forty of these friendly mammals, each three to four feet long. They were medium gray on top and light gray on the sides. Their bellies were a pinkish salmon color (although it could have been the reflected dawn light, which I doubt). There was lots of splashing and jumping and twisting and turning. I sat on the windlass at the bow and watched these energetic comics of the sea for about fifteen minutes until they suddenly vanished. Far off to port a group of small terns and noddies were busy fishing. On top of a swell beneath the birds I saw the metallic gleam of half a dozen silvery fish.

For the last few days we had begun to see jet trails high in the air running from west to east. We speculated where the planes were bound. Could they have been going from Kenya to Singapore? Who would travel on such routes?

Squalls and rain and rough seas descended on us, and on June 16th (150 miles) we handed the mainsail for twenty-two hours. In the late morning we took two heavy waves on board. We continued to make good time with a south-southeast wind of about thirty-two knots, although we had begun to wonder how far west the trade wind would last. By late in the day the swells had become long and steady, with ten-second intervals between crests. In the afternoon I was sitting at the chart table working out our position when a pie crust and mincemeat filling that Margaret was working on suddenly flew across the cabin as we heeled to a momentary sharp wind. Fortunately I managed to catch evening dessert in midair. Later Margaret was in the cockpit checking something when a flying fish hit her in the face. All this flying food was getting dangerous!

On June 17th we equaled our record run of 169 miles, an average of seven knots for twenty-four hours. During the night I heard a terrible grinding noise that I was sure was a piece of broken rigging rubbing along the hull. After waving a flashlight around I finally discovered that the water-catching bucket near the mast had gotten over the side and was hanging

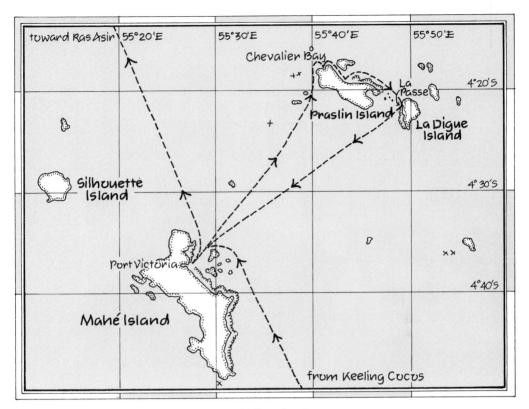

16. Seychelle Islands

from its lanyard and dragging back and forth along the forward part of the hull. By daylight the wind had eased, and the reefs and small sails disappeared. I turned on the depth sounder. Presto! We were in soundings on the extensive Seychelles Bank. Land was near. At 0630 on June 18th (141 miles at noon) we sighted the green mountains of Mahé ahead. In mid-morning Margaret announced that the chart table compass, a pile of junk made by the Maximum Company of Natick, Massachusetts, had finally given up entirely after months of malfunctioning. At 1000 we scooted along the northeast coast of Mahé with a double-reefed mainsail and small headsails, heeling to gusts while we worked out landmarks with the chart.

At 1315 we anchored at the quarantine anchorage outside Port Victoria, where we were promptly cleared. A little later—with three young soldiers wearing jungle fatigues, leather boots, and carrying Russian SLR automatic rifles in the cockpit—we followed a pilot launch to the inner harbor, where we anchored with other small vessels. We had come 2,563 miles in seventeen days and forty-five minutes, an average of 150.5 miles a day, *Whisper*'s best run ever across an ocean.

Waterfront, Port Victoria, Seychelles

The Seychelle Islands are a small group of tropical islets and shoals sprinkled lightly across a 200-mile-wide shallow bank in the northwestern corner of the Indian Ocean. The islands are about 280 miles south of the equator and 975 miles east of the African mainland. Madagascar is 600 miles to the south-southwest, and the southern tip of India is 1,500 miles to the northeast.

The four principal islands are Mahé, Praslin, La Digue, and Silhouette. Denis and Bird islands are north. Coëtivy is south, and the Amirante Isles, Alphonse, and Desroches are southwest. The population of the Seychelles is 65,000 and growing rapidly, with most of the people concentrated on Mahé, whose city of Port Victoria has 25,000 residents. The islands' total land area is 171 square miles, and usually fifteen or sixteen islands are inhabited, with some of the flyspeck coconut operations being seasonal. A tourist brochure optimistically speaks of "one hundred islands of paradise," but this total must include every half-tide rock and bird outcropping.

The main products are copra, cinnamon, vanilla, and patchouli (a perfume oil). The key industry had been tourism, but when we were there it had fallen off severely because of troubled politics and an overvalued currency. An expanding population and unemployment are growing problems.

The Seychelles were discovered by the Portuguese in 1505, and settled by the French in 1768. The islands were taken over by the British in 1815 and granted independence in 1976. In 1977, power was seized by a left-wing political thug named France René, who later set up a one-party socialist state. Since then, there has been a good deal of political unrest, with murders in the night, property confiscation, the censoring of mail, arms shipments, Cuban-style uniforms, parades with red banners, political rallies designed to bad-mouth Western countries, and a general love affair with Russia. In order to get jobs with the government, young people are obliged to attend camps and lectures where they are harangued by communist doctrinaires.

In 1981 a group of English mercenaries bungled an attempt to over-throw France René. Since that time, the president has been ringed by a bodyguard of seventy-five North Koreans and is said to employ a food taster. Prior to our visit, René—obviously paranoid about another coup attempt—had instituted a nighttime marine curfew, which meant that between 1800 and 0600 the next morning no ship or boat movements were allowed. Additionally, the only anchorage that could be used on Mahé was the main harbor in Port Victoria. While we were in the islands, two men who opposed France René were murdered. A third survived—with a fractured skull and bayonet wounds on his throat—and was under the protection of the American ambassador, David Fischer, who charged that René and his henchmen were guilty of the killings.

Unfortunately for René, only Western tourists have the money the Seychelles so desperately need, and he has been forced to ease restrictions on visitors. But the word was out, and tourist calls plummeted. Because of this, airlines canceled service to the islands. The hotel, restaurant, and taxi owners were glum.

We didn't know about the oppressive government before we arrived, but we hoped to have a reasonable visit. In any case, Margaret and I were only itinerant sailors. We were not political activists.

The Seychellois are mostly descended from Africans, Europeans, and Asians, and are a pleasant, easygoing, somewhat languorous people. Although some are black and stout, many have light-colored skins and slim figures. The main language is Creole, a local patois based on French. Practically everyone speaks French and English as well, and each news program on the radio is repeated three times, once in each language. The newspapers usually had a section in each language.

The inner harbor of Port Victoria, which offered excellent protection from the sea, had recently been dredged. The port was a good anchorage, and was convenient to the city and shopping. The cool trade wind blew across the area, and there were no mosquitoes and only a few flies. Three charter yachts were preparing to leave, and a few days after we arrived three Australian yachts sailed in. We got acquainted with Auguste Michel, a longtime English resident, who ran the very active yacht club. For a small fee we were made temporary members, which allowed us to leave our dinghy at the dock, to take water, and to have pleasant meals on the veranda. The young Seychellois who belonged to the yacht club were incredibly good at windsurfing. They had competitions several times a week, and these handsome, bronzed athletes whooshed across the harbor at high speed, maneuvering and tacking and laughing with delight. Odysseus would have liked the sight, and I could imagine one of their silhouettes on an ancient Greek vase.

Early every morning the local fishing fleet went out in small boats that had vestigial sailing rigs that hung on masts welded up from metal pipes, but in truth relied on hand-cranked diesel engines. There were always a dozen or two of the boats undergoing repairs on a nearby ramp, and when I watched the carpenters and workmen I had the feeling that the same scene had gone on for hundreds of years. In another corner of the harbor we saw several marine railways that dealt with various work boats, ferries, tugs, and yachts. In the past there had been many charter yachts in the Seychelles, but with the tourist decline some of the captains had gone to the Maldives off the southwest coast of India.

Along the waterfront were various new government buildings that were attractive and well designed. These were long and low, with exterior vertical supports of reinforced concrete that were finished in a pleasant beige color. Behind the city the granite mountains of Mahé pushed up steeply to almost a thousand meters and were swathed in tropical shrubs and low trees whose greens were heavy and dark. The island looked a little like Tahiti, although tiny in comparison.

Ashore we changed a little money (the rupee was 6.26 to the dollar), bought some fresh food, and picked up mail at the American Express office. We took a bus ride around the island and soon were rattling along country roads with a jovial gang of Seychellois. The back country was primitive, with rude houses and chickens and pigs. We walked through several tourist hotels on the southeast coast. Business was light except for a few packaged tours for German blue-collar workers who liked to sunbathe in the nude. Another day we rode south along the east coast past the new airport and a military encampment (where I noticed soldiers tilling vegetable gardens, since they apparently had nothing to do). Again the small hotels had only a few guests.

A lot of the food in the Seychelles came from South Africa, and the people from that distant country often traveled to the Seychelles for holidays because it was cheap, pleasant, tropical, and had an English tradition. The islands were one of the few places near Africa open to yachts from Durban

Southwest coast, Mahé, Seychelles

or Port Elizabeth, and while we were in Port Victoria three South African yachts arrived. We got acquainted with some of these sailors, who seemed weary of political strife but outspoken in their determination to defend their homeland to the last man. It was satisfying to meet South Africans and to hear their stories at firsthand instead of reading secondhand reports in newspapers.

I hadn't realized how black workers from nearby countries desperately compete to enter South Africa for employment. I was surprised to learn how important the products of South African farmers are to much of Africa. (One vignette: some food canned in South Africa is sent to Zimbabwe without labels; in Zimbabwe labels are stuck on that say "Product of Zimbabwe." Neither country admits to the practice, but it is substantial and of benefit to both.) I found it enlightening to talk at length with the sailors from South Africa, who asked me as many questions about my country as I asked about theirs.

A Swiss yacht named *Roi Soleil*—a Chance 37 design built in France— sailed into Port Victoria and anchored next to us. We soon got acquainted with Captain Lulu Vallotton, his wife Gigi, and their fifteen-year-old daughter Anick. This enthusiastic sailing family had spent several years sailing along the Turkish and Red Sea coasts and gave us many pointers. We heard about Russian naval bases, Ethiopian gunboats, Djibouti rip-offs, islands where political detainees were kept, Suez Canal agents, a place where the Vallottons'

Crew of *Roi Soleil* from Switzerland

yacht had been machine-gunned, experiences in Saudi Arabia, and so forth. We were told that Aden was quite satisfactory, that North Yemen was OK as long as you avoided the Russians, and that the Sudanese coast was outstanding. The Turkish coast, according to the Vallottons, was the finest anywhere.

In return we gave the Vallottons a few tips on the Pacific islands, the Caribbean, and Bali. And so the coconut wireless, as it is known, continued, a useful scheme for trading information. Of course some of the scuttlebutt is always exaggerated, but in time you get good—you hope—at sifting the spurious from the genuine. Over the years I have learned that people tend to emphasize the bad and their hardships, but not always. By talking to a handful of sailors from half a dozen vessels that have come from where you're going, you can always pick up a fair bit of knowledge of what's ahead.

We took *Whisper* twenty-five miles to the northeast to visit Praslin and La Digue islands. Praslin (pronounced PROUW-lan, with an almost inaudible final n) was a sleepy place with lovely anchorages along the north coast. Unfortunately the best bays had a constant swell, and although we spent a week at the island, the visit was unsatisfactory because the yacht rolled all the time. We sailed there with our Swiss friends in *Roi Soleil* and moved around and tried various bays, but a jerky ground swell was always with us. Chevalier Bay on the northwest corner had a superb white sand beach, but it also had nasty rollers that made trips ashore hair-raising. Once ashore, however, we enjoyed long walks and bus rides and creole fish dishes.

Just east of Praslin lay tiny La Digue, an oval-shaped island about one by two miles. The only place for *Whisper* was in a tiny dredged harbor on the west coast at La Passe, where the ferryboats came. Inside, with an anchor down and a stern line to a palm tree, we were snug and safe in calm water (at last, after a week of rolling). When we had neared La Passe we were stopped by a gunboat for a security check. I anchored, and three men—one with a machine gun—rushed alongside in a red inflatable with a big outboard. We showed our clearance and were asked all the usual questions by a cocky corporal in a beret. Meanwhile another man went below to search the yacht. Satisfied, the soldiers left. We were thanked for our cooperation. President René was nearby.

The little island was a touch out of a past century, with curious people, old houses, and narrow roads from French plantation days with ox carts, tiny stores, deserted beaches, and wooden boatbuilding. We saw men pit-sawing hardwood logs into planks, a grueling business that I thought belonged to history books. First a log was hoisted to an overhead rack, about two and a half meters above the ground. One man stood on top above the log and pulled up on the long blade of a whipsaw. A second man stood underneath

the rack and pulled the long blade down. The men had great bulging muscles, and sweat ran down their backs. It was exhausting work in the tropical heat, and to keep the sawing going, a squad of men had to be rotated to spell the sawyers every few minutes. I shuddered at the amount of effort required for the timbers of a large vessel, and I took a private vow to be forever thankful when I next switched on an electric saw.

The Seychelles had a monopoly on exotic bird life. Not only did the usual sea birds—sooty terns, tropicbirds, and lesser noddies—live on the islands in enormous numbers, but delicate fairy terns and roseate terns nested by the thousands. The islands were also home to some of the world's rarest birds: the Seychelles kestrel, the blue fruit pigeon, the scops owl, and the cave swiftlet, whose nests were discovered only in 1970. Several of the small islets had been set aside as bird sanctuaries. On La Digue Margaret and I walked out to the preserve of the paradise flycatcher. We watched quietly from a bench in the woods and saw two of these rare black birds, which were said to number only thirty pairs in the world.

We sailed back to Mahé for an outgoing clearance to Aden and the Red Sea. We weren't sure what lay ahead, so we took on a full load of fresh food and water plus extra jugs of water. When I rowed across to the harbormaster's office on the main quay, a large Russian ship was unloading weapons carriers, jeep-type vehicles, and wooden crates. A platoon of bored soldiers in rumpled uniforms was guarding boxes of small arms and ammunition that were being transshipped from the Russian vessel to a small coasting ship from Dar es Salaam in Tanzania. I was surprised that I was allowed to watch all this, but the Seychellois soldiers didn't seem to care. One of them asked me for a light for his cigarette.

"What is all this?" I asked quietly, motioning to the guns and military equipment with a nod of my head.

"It's trouble," answered the Seychellois soldier. "I wish they'd all go away. I'd rather go fishing like we used to. . . ."

Whipsawing boat timbers, La Digue, Seychelles

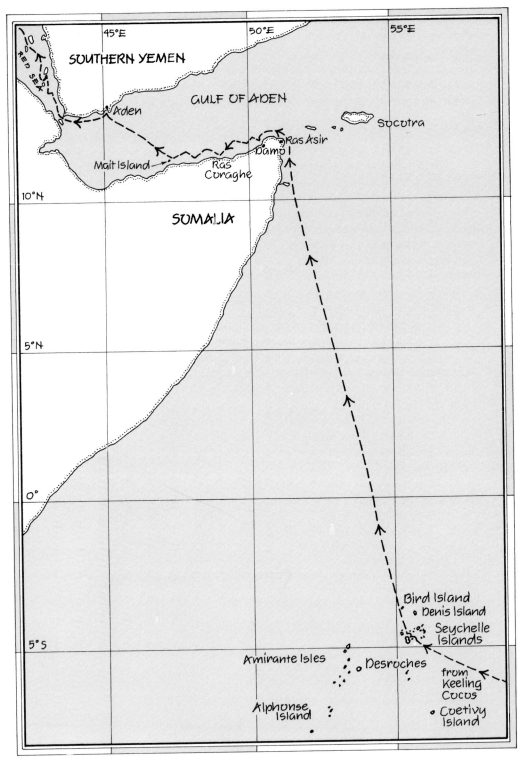

17. Seychelle Islands to Aden

. . . .

CHAPTER FIFTEEN

The Edge of Africa

*T*he distance from the Seychelles to the easternmost point of Africa, the so-called Horn of Africa—whose proper name is Ras Asir—is 1,030 miles. Our wind was fair, from the southeast at eighteen knots, and during the first three days it pushed us 369 miles to the north-northwest. The only untoward incidents were a bee that stung me while I was hoisting the sails in Port Victoria and the hazard of sailing past Bird Island on the northern edge of the Seychelle Bank at night. We managed to survive both problems.

Many of our friends had urged us to get a satellite navigation device, so in Australia we purchased a small Walker instrument that proved to be handy for getting a position fix at night or when the sky was overcast. Unfortunately the frequency of the sat-nav fixes was a good deal less than claimed. Although we occasionally got a fix in two hours, it sometimes took six or eight or ten hours to establish our position. In practice we found that we could often find out where we were faster by taking celestial observations. In addition, the amperage demands were more than the glib advertisements stated, and we soon learned to shut off the machine after it had spelled out the latitude and longitude.

The sat-nav had to be keyed with the ship's position within sixty miles. Normally this was easy, but on a passage with exceptionally strong currents and overcast skies, this requirement could be troublesome. Shortly after we bought it the device began to spew out nonsense Chinese instead of proper numbers, and it was awkward to send the instrument back and forth through customs for repairs. In spite of these drawbacks, however, we concluded that the machine was worthwhile because it gave a navigator a set of answers from a different source—information that could be important in a pinch.

We were about to leave the southeast trade wind and enter the region of the southwest monsoon. I had studied the pilot charts carefully, and I thought we could easily run northward with the fair monsoon wind. The blue current arrows showed a flow parallel to the coast; farther east the arrows ran in the opposite direction and indicated a southerly current of twelve miles per day, or half a knot.

At noon on August 6th we had some strange numbers in the navigation department. The wind had fallen light, and the log read seventy-nine miles. From the noon-to-noon fixes I calculated that we had made good only eighteen miles in the last twenty-four hours and had been set back sixty-one miles by current! This sounded like a one-degree error in arithmetic. However, we checked the sat-nav position with a noon sight (hazy sun, a lot of rolling) and were only nine miles out from the sat-nav numbers. A contrary current of 2.54 knots out at sea? Had we picked up some fishing nets? I rushed out and peered over the side.

That night we rolled a lot in a light wind and a mixed-up swell. Our run at noon the next day was 93 miles, but we showed 57 miles of adverse current. Unbelievable! A strong hand in the sea was pushing us backwards. In the last twenty-two hours we had gone north only 28 miles. We were sailing hard, but going nowhere. Would we spend the rest of our lives in this spot? In disgust I climbed into my bunk and began to read *War and Peace,* perhaps the most turgid novel ever written. The next morning, after three days of small but jerky seas, the ocean swell lengthened and stabilized from the south-southwest. At noon the log read 107. The distance between fixes was 42 miles. There had been 65 miles of current against us. A total of 183 miles of contrary current in three days!

The following morning the southwest monsoon began to blow hard. At 0900 on August 9th we were down to a deeply-reefed mainsail and the staysail; by evening it was blowing a full gale. At 1900 we hove-to for star sights (impossible), and as soon as we had stopped we knew the wind (forty knots) and the seas (ugly) were more of a problem than we had realized. I decided to let *Whisper* stay hove-to. The air blade of the steering vane was bent way over, and I got it off and below just before a squall blasted us. I retreated to my bunk and continued with *War and Peace.* We were taking some water through the stem vent and had to pump periodically, so at 0200 I took it out and screwed down a deck plate.

On the morning of August 10th I didn't know where we were. Celestial observations had been impossible for two days. The sat-nav couldn't perform because it needed a position within sixty miles. Our dead reckoning was no good because of the enormous current fluctuations. There were no radio direction-finding stations within range. The water was too deep to get any clues from soundings.

I had to find my position from scratch. I took a series of sun sights, and as the morning advanced and the sun climbed higher I got progressively better position line crosses. These suggested that we were out of the adverse current and two degrees farther north than our very doubtful dead reckoning position indicated. I fed the sat-nav with this information and soon got a fix that confirmed we had traveled 260 miles to the north during the last forty-eight hours even though we had been hove-to for seventeen hours. But what a morning! Half a dozen sights, and calculations on a wildly rolling yacht. A soaked sextant and water all over the place. Obviously we were in a powerful north-setting current. The ocean rivers around the Horn of Africa were awesome.

By the early afternoon the wind had dropped to twenty-four knots. We began to sail again.

[From the log] August 10th. 1611. We've been going along at good speed, but the wind has increased again. We took a couple of waves on board that filled the cockpit (including a tiny fish, something new). The waves pushed water through the Dorade vents, and sent a waterfall down the companionway even with one washboard in place. We took down the mainsail entirely and are now going along slowly under the staysail alone. The vane is steering OK. There are big seas and whitecaps as far as I can see. A good Force eight. Some of the waves are a little frightening. I am glad we worked out our position. I had no idea the weather could be so foul in this region, but the pilot charts show a 6 percent chance of a gale here, and 11 percent to the northeast, near Socotra Island.

By midnight the weather was shocking. The wind blew at forty-five knots plus hard squalls every ten or fifteen minutes. The sea was extremely rough, and sheets of spray rocketed across the decks. Below I felt as if I were riding a bicycle across a log jam. The little Bohndell staysail pulled us along faithfully, although I expected it to disappear in a cloud of threads any moment. I was worried that we might get rolled over, so I got out a box of special fastenings reserved for bad storms and screwed down the companionway washboards and the tops of nine lockers with heavy goods beneath.* Earlier we had screwed shut the Dorade vents (from the inside) and stuffed them with rags (on the outside). Water still dribbled through these cursed fabrications, and I swore to remove them entirely.

"The wind is whistling and screaming, and the yacht is heeled over to starboard," Margaret wrote in the logbook at 0345. "It's life at an angle

---

*We later found out that the thirteen-meter Australian sloop *Lowena*, sailed by single-hander Ken Anderson, was rolled over west of us. Ken reported a north-setting current of five knots.

below, and one's body is tense with hanging on. The vane blade snapped off in a squall a little while ago. We are jogging along, waiting for dawn so we can take a look at things."

At first light the Indian Ocean was a mass of seething rollers. We managed to get a kettle boiling on our low-slung Primus and had hot tea and a few crackers. Then we got into our bunks, because the only safe place in such weather is a deep berth with a big lee cloth. One of us got up every half hour and looked around, but we saw nothing except one or two storm petrels waltzing back and forth just above the surface of the upset sea. It was amazing how these birds always seemed to be around in terrible weather.

By 1015 the seas from the southwest looked a little more regular. I was tired of my bunk and *War and Peace,* so I began steering by hand. At noon on August 11th Margaret worked out that we had done 134 miles in the last twenty-four hours. We were 55 miles offshore and 175 miles south-southeast of Ras Asir. That evening a sliver of moon hung in the western sky. The seas were still very large, but the wind had dropped to twenty-five knots. I fitted a spare wind vane blade and by 2000 had the yacht steering herself. The squalls were still with us, and the wind blade trembled frightfully as they passed. We continued with the staysail.

The next morning the sun was an orange ball in a sky of brownish murk, a sight we were to get to know well in this desert world during the next two months. Overhead, the broken clouds of the southwest monsoon were low and heavy, without sharp edges, and tinted an ugly yellow— perhaps from particles of soil from the African mainland. I missed the fresh white trade wind clouds that I had grown to know so well.

We shaped our course to the west. Since a sat-nav fix had been taking up to half a day, I hoped for early morning observations on August 12th, but the motion, the spray flying around, and the trouble of getting a suitable horizon in six- to eight-meter seas made sights daunting. At 1214 I plotted a sun line that put us within five miles of Ras Asir, but the sight was too uncertain to rely on. The water was thirty-three fathoms deep.

At 1300 I saw a great headland looming up out of the murk to starboard. We quickly changed tacks and hoisted the mainsail. Our first view of Africa looked vaguely like one of the four drawings of Ras Asir in the pilot book. The haze was too thick to be sure. A little later we got a sat-nav fix that put us twenty-two miles from Ras Asir. We still had to sort out Ras Asir from a similar headland ten miles to the south. A low beach connects the two headlands, and over the centuries the beach has been littered with the bones of hundreds of westbound mariners who confused the false headland to the south with Ras Asir to the north and made the turn into the Gulf of Aden too soon. The various navigation books are filled with warnings that seem obvious and easy; yet as we sailed along that murky coast we saw how easy it would have been to have made that deadly mistake. I felt a great wave

Desert anchorage, Damo, Somalia

of sympathy for those captains—past and present—who had to find their way at night and in heavy weather.

At 1420 a southbound freighter appeared out of the haze. As we got near Ras Asir the wind and seas eased off. Soon I hoisted the jib (which had a dozen flying fish in its folds) and began to shake out the mainsail reefs. At 1730 we tacked around Ras Asir. Close up, the eastern tip of Africa was a steep and dreary mass of rocks topped by a decrepit lighthouse. As far as we could see, the coastline was a desert of sand and rocks unbroken by a single blade of grass or a scrub bush. The daylight was fading as we sailed another two and a half miles and anchored at a place called Damo. In the lee of Ras Asir the sea was quite smooth. The southerly wind was a steady twenty knots from the shore. We crept into eleven meters of depth, dropped an anchor and thirty-five fathoms of chain, said the hell with it, and went to sleep.

During the night when I got up to check the anchor, the wind had gotten up to forty knots from the southwest again. A southbound cargo ship from Beirut, the *Phoebus,* had anchored near us to wait out the gale before slugging southward around Ras Asir into the monsoon seas. I was glad we weren't going back.

The north coast of Somalia is a searing desert of sand and rocks and naked hills and cliffs—a no-man's-land except for a few nomads of the Mijertein tribe who live in rude hide huts and raise cattle and sheep in what seems a fifteenth-century existence. I could hardly believe that any creatures on earth could survive in such a blast furnace environment. "What do these people do for water? What do they eat?" were questions we asked whenever we saw two or three of the scarecrow-like Mijertein people watching us from shore.

It took us seven days to sail the four hundred miles between Ras Asir and Aden. Our average was a miserable fifty-seven miles a day, even though we pushed the yacht hard. The weather was either all or nothing: a dead calm and a glasslike sea, or stiff blasts of gale force winds from the west and southwest that kept us reefing and unreefing and tacking along the shore on a wet and sloppy ocean. With southwest winds we thought we could make westing close to land in smooth water, but we found that the wind tended to parallel the shore, and the blistering heat from the cliffs and rock formations along the coast caused local squalls. Once we tried to anchor, but an *offshore* wind turned into a scorching *onshore* wind, and we had to clear out of a place called Ras Coraghe in the middle of the night.

Whisper was soon covered with a thin veil of red dust. Everything was full of dust. Our white sails had become dingy. There was dust underfoot and between my toes. My hair was matted with dust, and I could feel African grit between my teeth. Sweat poured off my face, arms, back, and legs, and for the first time in my life I suffered from prickly heat.

The Somali countryside got slightly better. Occasionally we passed a rude village or an abandoned guard station. But life looked abysmal and wretched.

Late on August 19th we neared Mait Island, the recommended turning point for Aden, at forty-seven degrees east longitude on the Somali coast. We had 160 miles to go and headed northwest across the Gulf of Aden. The winds got a trifle better, and at noon, two days later, we chalked up 88 miles, our best run in these waters. We crossed the main shipping line from Suez and began to experience the hazard of ships.

[From the log] August 21th. 1320. Land ho! The craggy mountains on the Aden Peninsula are ahead and show dimly through the almost opaque murk. The haze from the southwest monsoon is like a shield of gauze. *Whisper's* decks are so hot that I've put on shoes to keep from burning the soles of my feet.

Aden, with a population of 365,000, is the capital and main resource of South Yemen, a country of 131,000 square miles, a place about the size of Nevada. The port of Aden, which is tucked behind the craggy, five-hundred-meter Shamson Mountains, has been the most important harbor between Suez and India since the time of Allah. We sailed in late on a Sunday afternoon and anchored at Steamer Point, just north of the clock tower, next to a blue French yacht named *Ralas.* Both the inner and outer harbors were filled with ships—a fleet of small local coasters and an assortment of cargo ships from all over the world. A few dhows were anchored in the shallows.

After the dismal wastes of Somalia, I liked the buzz and activity of Aden. Big ships—whose tall hulls loomed above us—continually moved in and out, blowing deep-throated signals to each other. Tugs puffed across the water and pulled barges heaped with sacks and boxes and crates. Pilot boats darted here and there. A launch filled with stevedores hurried past us, and everybody waved. On the other side of the harbor, shipboard cranes nodded and turned. Near the entrance we could see a few military vessels with missiles on deck; fourteen-passenger rowboats filled with workmen criss-crossed the area in front of the missile boats and made a strange contrast. Sometimes we got a whiff of diesel oil or the zesty aroma of spices. We saw lots of Russian flags, but there were Japanese and Australian and others as well. Ashore, a procession of trucks rumbled along the waterfront.

A small launch pulled smartly alongside us, and two uniformed customs and immigration men hopped on board, smiling as they whipped out forms and tried their few words of English. Before the inspectors left, we asked them to sign our guest book. I was fascinated when the men wrote Arabic script and formed the thin curving letters from right to left.

We met Didier and Marie-Madelaine Ganichot and their three children on *Ralas,* the sixteen-meter aluminum ketch from Argenteuil, France that was next to us. Didier and Marie-Madelaine had worked in Saudia Arabia for three years and had a good knowledge of the Arab world. They had returned to France, built a yacht large enough for the whole family, and were on their way to the islands of the Indian Ocean. Their life on board was a happy confusion of children, toys, sails, books, and a galley filled with delicious smells of bubbling sauces and simmering French soups. The Ganichots were as friendly as could be and plied us with drinks and dinner and jokes while we traded route information.

The next few days we went ashore for bus rides and walks, and a look at the port. England had controlled Aden from 1839 to 1967, and there were signs of first-class Western engineering everywhere; unfortunately, however, after years of neglect, the buildings and roads were crumbling. Several hotels had been abandoned completely, and in general Aden looked as if it had suffered a hundred days of saturation bombing. We saw piles of junk and rubble on every street and began to learn that in many Arab countries there is no such thing as rubbish or garbage collection. Unwanted items are simply discarded and stay on the spot until they rot, blow away, or are somehow pushed aside.

"In Arab countries you can never tell whether the buildings are under construction or under demolition," said our neighbor on the French yacht. In a bus depot in Khor Maksar we saw discarded ticket stubs piled up to a depth of twenty or thirty millimeters. The movements of the ticket buyers had worn paths in the old piles of stubs, which had sort of drifted underneath the seats and along the walls like snow. I had trouble believing what I saw. The Yemenese, of course, paid no attention, and after a few days I no longer noticed the stubs either.

In spite of my carping about the housekeeping, I liked the men of South Yemen. They smiled, nodded, seemed slightly mischievous, and responded at once to attention. Most spoke some English. Whenever a launch filled with stevedores passed *Whisper,* the chattering men were fascinated by Margaret, who always smiled and waved. Was she a loose woman? Not at all. Just friendly.

The Yemenese women seemed pathetic. Ashore we saw them darting around the streets with long black loose garments that covered them completely, including their heads and faces. All you could see were brown eyes and either bare feet or feet with thongs. From the back, a group of women looked like a flock of crows. Women's lib had a ways to go.

We shopped in the main settlement of Crater, a forty-five-minute bus ride from Steamer Point. The buses were crowded, but everyone was good-tempered. The men always gave a seat to any woman who was standing. We found the Arab markets enormous, noisy, often flyblown, and totally disorganized. The heat was staggering as usual, and we frequently stopped for cold drinks, which seemed as necessary as breaths of air. We were after fruit and vegetables and a few hardware fittings, but our expeditions were generally frustrated. If we could get two items on a list of six or seven we considered the day well spent. One afternoon we visited a system of ancient reservoirs, said to have been built by the Queen of Sheba, ages before Aden's modern desalinization plant was constructed.

Always the hopeful photographer, I tried a few pictures in the market and on the streets. In one place a group of Arabs got into an absolute rage at the sight of my camera. The men continued to be very angry, furious in fact, even after I had put my camera away. My best move seemed to be to disappear quickly. All throughout Arabia, taking pictures of locals was a chancy business. The only way was to prefocus inside a bag, slip a camera out, shoot, and put the camera back in the bag in one quick motion. You needed to keep moving, preferably with a friendly, well-tipped taxi driver at your heels.

The best place for shopping, we found, was at the Victory Cold Stores in Khor Maksar. All the foreigners, including the Russians and the British technicians, shopped there. We had to pay in U.S. dollars, which I found hard to understand, because Yemen was supposed to be a Russian satellite. In the

Seychelles, we had noticed that the Russians always went around in groups of two or three. Here it was the same. We tried to nod and speak to them, but they were totally unresponsive. We learned that the women—who were often quite stout—were mostly the wives of technicians and military men. Some were addicted to shoplifting for various Western goodies not found in Russia. As a consequence, the storekeepers made the Russian women check their handbags and watched them closely. The Russian women we saw were certainly not cut out to be foreign travelers.

In the port area, not far from our anchorage, we discovered the Seaman's Club, where we had a few meals. Everyone was extremely polite. It was possible to sit out on a shaded veranda, have a cool drink, and watch the passing ships. Although alcohol was supposed to be a Moslem taboo, the local sailors and stevedores came to drink beer. The place was popular, and every table was taken. The men always ordered two very large iced bottles of beer and drank and talked quietly until their drinks were gone. Then the seamen would order two more bottles and so on until they were absolutely whacko. Perhaps it was their only relaxation after the hard work on the ships. When I learned that the average life span in Yemen was forty-one years, that the per capita income was $310 a year, and that the pleasures in that hot and austere land were few and fleeting, I began to think that beer drinking after work was worth considering.

One morning I walked to the harbor office—which was desperately in need of repairs and paint—where I met Captain Ahmed Ali-Noor, the harbormaster. He was short and dark, with incredibly white teeth, and resplendent in a sparkling white uniform. He held a telephone in each hand and spoke English into one and Arabic into the other, scowling in one language and smiling in the other.

"Everyone is welcome here," said Captain Ali-Noor between phone calls, "except the South Africans with whom we are having a moment of trouble. Just now we have two hundred ships in Aden."

"What about the ship sinkings in the Red Sea from mines?" I asked. "This morning the BBC reported that seventeen explosive mines have been found. Colonel Qadhafi and Libya are suspected. Is it safe to go north?"

"I have heard something, and others have asked," answered Captain Ali-Noor, looking grave. "I think this trouble will pass. In any case," he said with a philosophic flourish, "all life is a risk. Sailors must trust the Almighty."

The next day I got a haircut from an expert Yemenese barber who spoke perfect English. "When the British were here I had three shops and thirty-seven barbers," he lamented. "Shoeshine boys, manicurists, valets, tailors— the works. Now I cut hair by myself in this tiny two-chair shop. At night I sweep the floor. The hell with independence. I want colonialism back. I wish the British were still here."

That afternoon Margaret and I walked across the marble-floored lobby of the stunning new French-run Hotel Aden. It was hard to imagine an air-conditioned, grandiose hotel in the midst of so much poverty in a stifling seaport, but sure enough, the bar was full, and bone china and sterling silver clanked in the elegant dining room.

I saw a tall, dignified man dressed in an immaculate white robe talking to the receptionist. Over the man's head and shoulders he wore a white *keffiyah,* the Arab head cloth that was held in place with two thin circlets of gold and black cord (an *agal*) that went around his forehead and temples. The man's dress and poise were stunning. Was he the son of King Feisal of Saudia Arabia? Was he Lawrence of Arabia? The robe was so perfectly white, wrinkle-free, and of such splendid material that I guessed the man must have changed it three or four times a day.

In the world of *Arabian Nights* the wealthy were the kings and princesses; the rest were rug weavers and small farmers. For every hundred thousand camel drivers there was one Scheherazade. I wonder if she wore a white robe?

Arab camel driver and friend, Aden

We sailed for the southern entrance of the Red Sea—105 miles west of Aden—on August 28th. The winds were light, but they eased the desert temperatures a little. To combat the scorching sun we wore long-sleeved shirts, shorts, sunglasses, and big sun hats. We had about eighty gallons of water on board and a good supply of fruit and vegetables. During the week in Aden we had done a whole list of small jobs on *Whisper* and had carefully checked the stitching and cloth of each sail. We were rested and the yacht was in good order. At last we had begun what we thought would be the hardest part of our trip around the world. What, we wondered, would happen on this long leg north to the Mediterranean?

. . . .

CHAPTER SIXTEEN

Sailing in the Desert

*T*he Red Sea is 1,200 miles long and 125 miles wide, a narrow ribbon of water that divides the smoldering deserts of Africa from those of Asia. This long waterway separates Egypt and Sudan from Saudia Arabia in the north, and Ethiopia from Yemen in the south. The whole inhospitable region is one of devastating heat and dryness, a place not only hard on the body, but sterile to the eye.

We had three additional problems: hostile countries, adverse winds, and heavy shipping traffic. Nevertheless, the Red Sea route is a useful shortcut from the Indian Ocean to the eastern Mediterranean. Certainly a world voyager wants to see the Suez Canal sometime in his life, and even the harshest desert has moments of beauty.

The fourteen-mile entrance to the Red Sea is guarded by Perim Island, whose small harbor and grounds were open to all until a few years ago. Now the place is a military base—a prohibited area—and in Aden we were warned to stay away or risk getting shot. To the west of Perim is the main strait of Bab-el-Mandeb, but as we neared this famous passage we could hear the rumble of big ships as they converged from the south and north. To avoid

View toward the North-East across the Red Sea
and the Gulf of Aden from space

the traffic we chose Small Strait—a little over a mile wide—between Perim Island and the Yemen mainland to the east. We had been told to keep one mile away from the island or else expect bullets, so we close-tacked along the mainland in light winds and were soon through into the Red Sea.

We began to beat northward in unsteady ten-to-fifteen-knot winds from the north-northwest. The best we could do was a heading of 12° north of west (282°) on the starboard tack, or 10° east of north-northeast (032°) on the port tack, the better tack. In the north-northwest swell we tacked through about 110°.

Our initial scheme was to sail northward in the area that reached from the shipping lanes—near the middle of the Red Sea—to the coast of Yemen. On the tack to the west we carried on until we began to see ships (often we could hear them before we could see them). We then came about and headed for the coast and sailed until we got into soundings of ten fathoms (we had good charts and the bottom slope was gradual). Near the shore we tried to identify landmarks to see if we were as far north as we hoped. We then tacked and headed for the middle, and so on. We were able to follow this plan day or night. Since we were in the confines of a north-south inland sea, our longitude was no problem. All we had to do was to cross our latitude with a depth sounding when near the coast.

In general the visibility was poor, with the usual desert murk. At sunset the haze glowed with an eerie yellow color. Overhead the night sky was clear, and the stars were bright. The desert smog seemed to be only around the horizon and some fifteen degrees above it. Often at night we heard the sweet warbling of terns as they flashed and twisted around *Whisper.* We had to watch for coasting vessels that lumbered along on courses cast in concrete as well as small open fishing boats with outboard engines that scooted around at high speed on courses shaped like question marks.

[From the log] August 30th. 1000. Two Yemenese fishermen came alongside for a look. A wooden, high-bowed, round-bottom boat about five meters long with a Yamaha outboard. When we asked about Mokha, the men motioned ahead and to starboard. The heat is staggering. Margaret is at the tiller and holding the golf umbrella to get a little shade. The cabin sole is wet with moisture.

1045. A North Yemeni fishing boat came alongside for water. Margaret passed a plastic bowl to the men. Great smiles and nods. Mokha is about five miles to starboard, dimly visible through whitish haze. Three coasting vessels are in sight.

Our first close call was the next morning when *Ocean Legend,* an enormous green and gray container ship, barreling along at fifteen knots or so, came very close. We had the right of way in a crossing situation. The ship didn't change course, however, so we took evasive action and made a major course change to port in plenty of time. Thirty seconds later *Ocean*

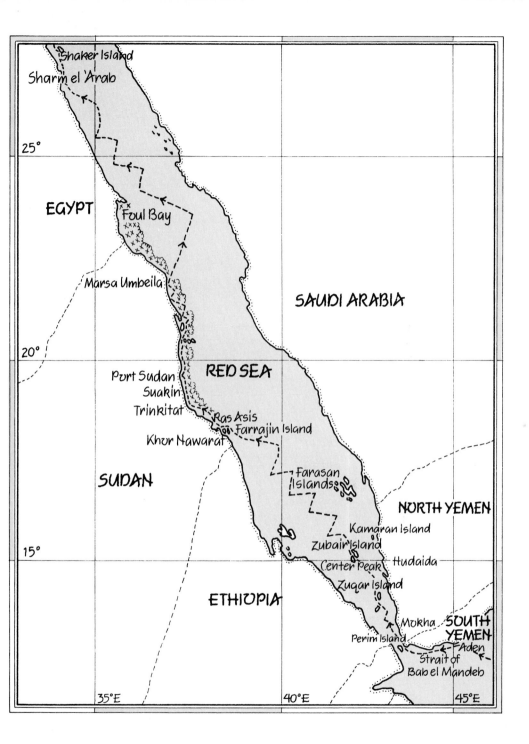

Legend swung to starboard—toward us—on our new heading. We immediately went back to our original course. It was a nasty situation. If *Ocean Legend* had hit us, it would have been like a steamroller demolishing a peanut.

We were fairly rumdum after standing close watches since Aden, so we stopped for a rest in a little bay at the southern end of barren Zuqar Island at fourteen degrees north latitude. So far we had made good eighty-four miles in the Red Sea. I had been having trouble with prickly heat again, and I was delighted to swim in the sea, although the water was tepid and seemed hardly cooler than the air. Margaret and I swam around an old wreck and looked at thousands of small fish. I was worried about going to sleep with Yemenese fishermen nearby, so I rigged two tin cans connected with a piece of thread across the companionway hatch for an alarm. I put the revolver under my pillow and went to sleep. The night was peaceful and quiet, and we woke up the next morning—September 1st—refreshed, and spent an hour in the water scrubbing the marine growth from *Whisper*'s bottom.

By 0845 we were under way and slowly headed northward against the constant north-northwest wind. We continued to tack along the coast of North Yemen. We had been warned to stay clear of the vicinity of Kamaran Island at 15°20′N. because of a Russian naval base, so the next morning, north of the city of Hudaida at 14°45′N., we headed west toward the Zubair Islands. The north-northwest wind was twelve knots at noon, twenty knots at 1400, and as we neared Center Peak and Zubair Islands, the breeze rose quickly to thirty-five knots. After some sail drill and salt spray that cooled off things,

Amado, container ship, Red Sea

we finally tacked into the lee of Center Peak Island and anchored off two abandoned lighthouses high above us. The wind whistled across the black and brown rocks on the steep volcanic slopes, which looked as if they had never seen a blade of grass nor a drop of water. I pitied the lighthouse keepers of old and wondered how they had kept their sanity and dealt with supplies and water in such a desolate location. Sigmund Freud himself would have had problems.

I was having a tough time with prickly heat, an affliction that I thought only troubled babies. The worst places were the backs of my legs and the insides of my elbows. *The International Medical Guide for Ships* advised plenty of cold showers and calamine lotion. All I could do was to spray my skin with fresh water from an atomizer bottle and rub on calamine. The problem was that five minutes after the treatment I was sweating again and back to square one. Sometimes I hung over the side of the yacht on a line as we went along. I knew the best cure: get out of the Red Sea!

For the next six days we struggled northward in light winds, medium winds, and one gale. The wind always blew from the north-northwest, except during twenty hours of calms. When we got to the latitude of Saudia Arabia and the Farasan Islands we began to head west because we had no entry papers and no wish to encounter Saudi patrol boats. We still had about a hundred miles of the Ethiopean border to pass and kept well out to sea because I had heard reports of particularly barbaric treatment of small vessels along the Ethiopian coast. We had one grisly account on board:

"When I last went through the Red Sea," wrote Peter Tangvald, a longtime cruising sailor who has spent his life in distant places, "I anchored in Djibouti next to two yachts that arrived a few days before me. Both looked like wrecks. In each case the yacht had been rammed amidships by a patrol boat in Ethiopian territorial waters. The patrol boat then backed off, circled around, and rammed the small boat from the other side before speeding away. Both incidents happened out of sight of land.

"The two yachts were not in company but a couple of days apart," continued Tangvald. "In one case, the collision resulted in a crew member getting a badly broken arm with the bones sticking out. The yacht sent up a distress signal, but the patrol boat did not return. Both yachts had open holes in their topsides, partially torn-off chainplates, and some broken spars. The two vessels made port under power after plugging the holes with mattresses and canvas and pumping most of the way. No doubt the Ethiopian officials consider such a technique an efficient and simple method of keeping yachts out of their territorial waters, and trust that the news will get around."[8]

[From the log] September 5th. 0745. I am discouraged at our slow progress. Indeed progress is the wrong word. A turtle or snail would be insulted to be aboard *Whisper* on this run. It's all so pitiful and frustrating. We are sailing ever so slowly in light headwinds in a persistent swell from the direction of the wind. The swell is larger than the light wind would indicate, and tends to stop us unless we sail a little freer, which in turn means our distance made good is worse. Terrible! I wish my mother had taught me patience.

The next night we had our second close call. At 1940 we were sailing well on the westerly tack about two miles east of the shipping lanes. *Whisper*'s masthead running light was burning brightly. Five ships were in sight, all crossing several miles ahead. Suddenly a southbound ship made an abrupt ninety-degree turn and headed directly toward us. Had our radar reflector been picked up on radar? I watched the red and green lights of the ship get closer and closer. There was little we could do because the ship approached at relatively high speed and seemed to be zeroing in on us. As fast as I turned, the ship turned. I finally gave up, and, with the tiller between my legs and a white flare ready in my hand, waited to see what our adversary would do. At the last minute the large cargo ship changed her course a little and slid up alongside us, *ten or fifteen meters away.* An officer in a white uniform on the starboard wing switched on a huge searchlight. All at once a flood of white brilliance poured down on me. I was totally blinded and quite speechless at such idiocy. Then the man switched off the light, and the ship glided away. The vessel was French and apparently looking for someone. The episode scared the hell out of me.

On the afternoon of September 10th we picked up the barren coast of Sudan. Hooray! We were safely north of Ethiopia and away from the problems of Yemen and Saudia Arabia. Henceforth our course was in Sudanese and Egyptian waters, countries where tourists and yachts were welcome. We tacked along the coast, now in shallow water heavy with coral. We had hoped to reach an anchorage behind Farrajin Island, a place called Khor Nawarat, which was mentioned in Henri de Monfreid's *Adventures of a Red Sea Smuggler.* However, the wind was light, and darkness overtook us when we were one mile offshore. The depth was four meters. Coral patches were all around. We anchored and waited for morning.

Now our sailing pattern changed completely. For the next 260 miles we sailed northward inside the reefs along the coast of Sudan, west of the great coral structure that parallels the coast from 5 to 20 miles offshore. The route is at least seven fathoms deep (often more), totally out of the north-northwest swell, and is free of traffic except for a few small local boats. We found plenty of calm and peaceful anchorages just off the brow of the desert. Often we saw pink flamingos wading in brine pools and Arab dhows in the distance. We fought the heat by swimming each morning and evening.

Open air market, Port Sudan

We were back to coral pilotage and daylight sailing on a route that seemed to date from year one. Navigation was simple. There was a large stone beacon about every ten or twenty miles, so we followed a compass course from one beacon to the next, taking back bearings as we sailed away from a beacon. About the time the beacon behind us slipped out of sight we began to see the next one, and so on.

[From my journal] September 13th. Yesterday we left Ras Asis and headed northwest. The wind began to rise, and in a little while we were racing along close-hauled with a freshening west wind. Soon we close-reefed the mainsail. A little later we handed it entirely and hoisted the trysail when the wind got up to thirty-five knots. The sun was dim, and dust flew everywhere. An honest-to-God sandstorm. My first ever. Since we were going along a weather shore, I kept heading up so I wouldn't lose the land. Our progress was marvelous. However, trying to see into a howling sandstorm was a business. Sunglasses were no good because of the salt spray. The wind was hot, and I drank cup after cup of water. Around noon the wind began to ease, and by 1300 we were in a dead calm. Nothing! Then a light north-northeast wind—old faithful—came up.

We had read in the pilot book about the old port of Trinkitat. Our chart showed a road, a railroad, and a telegraph line. When we rounded South Point and headed in, however, we saw only a desolate wilderness of sand dunes, one tumbled-down shack, a harbor encumbered with coral, and no people at all. Obviously time had bypassed Trinkitat and the description in the Admiralty pilot book.

On September 14th we sailed into Port Sudan, a startling change after the quiet reefs and the solemn desert. Port Sudan is a bustling place, and the only sea link that Sudan—the largest country in Africa—has with the outside world. The cargo docks had eight or ten ships loading and unloading while another thirty or so waited outside. We anchored in a side inlet among a hodgepodge of coasting vessels and a few tired-looking yachts. We had planned to stop for only a day to get water and fresh food, but the officials whisked our passports away, and then announced that because of a religious holiday we could not clear for seven days.

We saw a brown and dusty city of 135,000 people on the edge of the Sahara Desert, a place busy with trucks, railroads, ships' agents, banks, freight companies, import services, small shops, stalls, a central market, and taxis that scrambled up and down the flat dirt roads. "Change money!" "Change money!" "Best rate here!" cried the money peddlers as they flocked around us like children running for ice cream.

Many men in the city wore the traditional long white robe of the Sudanese and a headdress that appeared to be made of a bedsheet rolled into

Local ferry, near Port Sudan

a slim tube and wound spirally around the head to make a kind of cone-shaped cap. Camels, goats, and donkeys roamed up and down the streets. Big noisy crows—like black punctuation marks crying for attention—hopped about everywhere. Most of the buildings were flimsy four- or five-story apartments with outside walkways and white-curtained windows. Central electricity was sporadic, so each building had its own small diesel generator puffing away outside. Plenty of good water, we were told, came from deep wells to the west. Unfortunately—as we had seen in Aden—the rubbish was simply thrown into the streets. Mounds of garbage, bottles, cans, dead cats, plastic junk, and piles of trash were everywhere. The dogs and goats and roving camels ate some of the stuff. The public health aspects boggled the mind. No wonder the average life span was forty-four years!

The heat was unreal. The daily temperature usually got up to 50°C.—122°F.—and protection from the sun seemed to be the most important thing in life. *Whisper*'s big awning was a godsend, and going without a hat was unthinkable. In walking along the streets we tacked from one shady patch to another: a dark wall here, a pool of black beneath a scraggly tree, an oasis in the lee of a store. Anything to keep out of the sun. I often looked at local poor women squatting along a street, bathing their faces with a few drops of treasured water from a small bottle that each carried with her. My heart went out to them.

A domestic scene in the old Red Sea port of Suakin during the
nineteenth century. In this sketch of a cook and her two young helpers
it all looks romantic., but one wonders about the difficulty of getting
drinking water, firewood, and fresh food. Plus the ghastly heat of
Sudan. Yet the port flourished for a century.

Whisper was anchored about a quarter of a mile from the main highway. There was a good stopping place at the side of the road, and buses from the interior pulled off so the overheated passengers could have a dip in the sea. It was marvelous to see the relief and pleasure on the faces of the weary travelers and to hear their laughter and shouts of pleasure ring across the water as they waded into the sea, modestly holding up their long robes about them as they went in. The sight and colors of twenty or thirty animated women in their loose black, white, brown, yellow, orange, and pink wraps made a fine sight. The scene seemed right out of the Bible.

We discovered that the main nerve center of Port Sudan was the coffee shop at the Palace Hotel, which had rows of heavy-duty air conditioners plus rotating fans. We had been told to try a Sudanese specialty called *karkade* (pronounced KAR-kah-day), which was tea made from the dried reddish flowers of the hibiscus plant. We drank this cold, with ice, and slightly sweetened. The karkade was delicious, and we were soon hooked.

The coffee shop was always filled with businessmen, government hacks, nervous travelers, and James Bond types who sat with cold drinks in the cool air and discussed the price of cottonseed oil, the civil war in Ethiopia, and the worrying problem of explosive mines laid in the Red Sea by a Libyan ship. Already, it was rumored, two cargo ships had been sunk. Would moderate Egypt and extremist Libya go to war? Would the Suez Canal be closed? Would our trip up the Red Sea be for nothing? We had to get through the canal quickly, before it was closed! We chafed at the delay in Port Sudan.

The central market was large and noisy, and limited mostly to purple onions, tomatoes, eggplant, bananas, and grapefruit. The giant grapefruit were excellent, and we bought two dozen. Although full of seeds (once I counted fifty-five), the yellow grapefruit were succulent and tasty and perfect for the sea because they kept well and were juicy and refreshing. Again we tried a few photographs and again we were rebuffed, generally by someone who jumped in front of the camera or held his hand over the lens. Fortunately the reactions in Sudan were restrained and not as violent as in Aden. We were learning that you had to be quick to get anything on film in the Arab world.

We met a British engineer, Bob Southin, who ran the local cottonseed oil plant, and his friend Jan Van Asselt, a Dutch engineer who looked after an oil refinery. Both had taken jobs in Sudan as desperation moves, and both clearly enjoyed an evening whisky. It was extremely bad news for them when the Sudanese government accepted a big loan from Saudi Arabia with the proviso that henceforth Sudan would allow no alcohol of any kind. Since *Whisper* was U.S. territory, however, I asked Bob and Jan whether they would like to come for a drink. *"Would we!"* they chorused.

One day we took a thirty-five-mile bus trip south to Suakin, an old Red Sea harbor that was Sudan's trading center and gateway to the outside world a century ago, before Port Sudan was built. It was a lively trip on the bus, which was jammed with locals together with three Rachaida women who got out at their tribal tent camp halfway to Suakin. The Rachaida women, who were quite fearless and outspoken, dressed differently from the Sudanese and wore heavy flowing garments of a silvery hue, with lots of jangling silver and gold jewelry. Their head veils were studded with bits of silver. One of them was a girl about fourteen or fifteen who was extremely attractive and in whose hazel-colored eyes I kept losing myself. The Rachaidas had dual Sudanese–Saudi Arabian citizenship, raised camels, sheep, and goats, and had long been involved in smuggling between the two countries.

The bus fare was the equivalent of $1.48. Most people gave the conductor $1.50 and let the change go. Not the Rachaida women, who went to work on the poor man. In loud and screaming tones they told the startled conductor and all aboard the bus that the man collecting the fares was a liar and a cheat and a scoundrel who went around taking money from defenseless women. The conductor was a disgrace to Sudan, to Allah, to all humanity, and certainly should be punished. He was thoroughly disgusting, and if the men from her tribe had been on the bus he would have been beaten and thrashed and been made to answer in full. The women verbally ripped the poor conductor up one side and down the other, cut him across the middle, and stabbed him in the stomach in the most venomous and screeching manner. All of this was in machine-gun Arabic.

I didn't understand one word. But I understood the message and intent perfectly. The abashed conductor tried to pass back the trifling change and even offered to let the women ride free as recompense for his error. This tactic failed completely, because the enraged women threw the money in his face and fulminated louder than ever, their rawhide voices shrill and threatening.

"Useless insect. Lover of Satan. Cheater of children." The conductor squirmed nervously. He looked as if he were about to jump out of a window. I bet he had never been taught about this problem in conductors' school. Finally the bus stopped at the Rachaida camp. The women got out, shaking their jangling arms at the terrified conductor and glaring at him with an intensity that would have drilled holes in diamonds. From outside the bus the women continued, gesturing and raving. It was only when the bus started up and sped out of earshot that the conductor and all the passengers breathed a collective sigh of relief.

We passed the tents of the Rachaida camp, staked out on the scorching, flat desert. A fifty-five-gallon drum of water hauled from Port Sudan stood at each tent. The heat was brutal. There was no shade. The Rachaidas strode about purposefully, some riding camels and some shepherding small brown and white goats. Tough people!

Camel and Suakin ruins, Sudan

The old city of Suakin was a tumble-down ruin of trading rooms and houses made of coral blocks topped with ornate wooden balconies and delicately designed windows and shutters that had once sheltered mercantile princes, their harems, and their servants. Long controlled by the Turks and then the Egyptians, trade had flourished in such things as slaves, ivory, gold, senna, coffee, hashish, hides, cotton, sesame oil, candles, and ostrich feathers. It was hard to believe that every three months for a hundred years or more, trading caravans of up to one thousand camels had left Suakin for the interior of Africa. Now the collapsing city was merely a Sudanese park where people came to walk and wonder and enjoy the astonishing blue of the Red Sea.[9]

When we got back to Port Sudan we saw a modern version of an Arab dhow anchored next to us. The vessel was about thirty meters long and had a colossal hull with very high freeboard. Schooner-rigged, with a large engine below, she appeared to be brand-new and was nicely painted in gleaming white, with a broad blue stripe along her side plus yellow trim. Part of the crew were busy touching up the paint; others were fishing over the side. I couldn't read her Arabic name. Little did we know that *Whisper* and the big white dhow were to race all the way to Suez.

. . . .

CHAPTER SEVENTEEN

Sudan to Suez

On September 22nd we finally got our Port Sudan clearance from the poky officials and headed north up the inside passage in the reefs. We found that as we sailed north, the north-northwest winds got stronger. Close-tacking in the channels was a slow business. Sometimes a better scheme was to slip outside the reef on a long port tack, make some northing, and then head back to the coast while it was still light enough to pick our way through the coral and find an anchorage for the night. The anchorages were remote and quiet, and we were able to swim each night and morning and to look at the reef fish. Generally we saw no people at all. Sometimes we couldn't get back through the reef in the afternoon. Then we tacked through the night, and favored the port tack to keep us away from the reefs in the darkness.

At 0700 on September 30th we were near the Sudan-Egyptian border at twenty-two degrees north latitude. The wind was thirty knots from the usual direction, and the wind-driven current was about one knot. We were heeled to twenty degrees or so, and bashing into head seas with a four-second period between swells. With all the crashing and banging I sometimes wondered whether the vessel would fall to pieces from the violent blows when she fell off a wave in the short irregular seas. The yacht was closed up below because of water flying around, and it was stifling in the cabin. My prickly heat was not too good. We decided to tack for the coast to have a rest. Maybe the headwinds would ease off.

At noon we could see the coast through the haze, but were uncertain of our latitude. The sat-nav gave us a spurious position (it said we were on land), so we hove-to while I took two sun sights. With our position in hand we headed west through the reefs that I knew would be easy to spot because the seas would be breaking violently. The wind had freshened to thirty-five knots, and *Whisper* was soon reaching along at seven knots. Margaret steered while I directed the yacht from aloft. I had a death grip on the mast, and I kept my legs wrapped around the spreaders so I wouldn't get thrown off when the boat rolled. With Polaroid sunglasses and the sun overhead I could see perfectly. The scene was spectacular, and of all my sailing through the years this was my most exciting moment.

A mile ahead I saw three enormous patches of yellow, brown, and pink coral that pushed up from the deep blue of the sea like giant fists of stone. Each islet measured perhaps three-eighths of a mile across; the surfaces were pancake flat and just above the level of the water. Waves from the north were exploding on the windward side of the islets with raging force and shooting water high into the air. I had absolute confidence in my pilotage in the good light and decided to go between two of the islets. However, I had to direct Margaret by hand signals because the noise from the wind and the thundering breakers made it impossible to shout down steering instructions. My view of the coral, the colors, the stampeding seas, and our intricate course ahead was wildly exciting. If a person ever wanted high adventure, this was it.

I yelled down and pointed. "Look! Look at that! Look at the colors!" I shouted. Margaret couldn't hear me and immediately steered where I pointed. "Oh no! Get back on course!" (Never mind. I'll tell her later.) The gale force seas were crashing to destruction on the unyielding coral, a flint-edged murdering ground where a ship or a human would have been pulverized in an instant. Even from half a mile away I could feel the thundering impact of the seas as they hit the coral after a run of 350 miles of open water.

The wind blew my hair, the yacht rolled, and sun glinted on the water. The colors and the action were marvelous. I wished all my friends could have been with me to have shared that moment.

We turned one way and then another and soon were in smooth water behind the main coastal reef. A little later we took a compass bearing on a prominent wreck noted on Admiralty chart 138 and used it to find the narrow entrance to Marsa Umbeila, an isolated notch in the bleak desert where not a person nor a trace of man could be seen. We handed the jib and luffed up to the weather shore under the mainsail. Then we dropped our anchor and chain. Safe again. But what an afternoon!

An hour later I heard a noise and looked up. The big white dhow that we had seen in Port Sudan steamed in and dropped a big fisherman anchor. Everyone smiled and waved. The men on the dhow began to fish over the side. We all shook our fists at the wind.

The wind rose to forty knots during the night, but by dawn had dropped to half that strength. We got under way at once. As we tacked northward, however, the wind increased by the minute and was soon back up to forty knots. The Red Sea was a contrary horror. We returned to Marsa Umbeila, anchored next to the white dhow, and spent the day working on the sails. The following day the wind continued the same. Would it ever ease? Would we be in Marsa Umbeila forever? Would our bones be found on the yacht? The trip up the Red Sea was endless.

We put the dinghy in the water and managed to pull over to the dhow. The mate put a rope ladder over the side, and we climbed up the high topsides. The grizzled captain gave us a little tour. He knew about ten words of English, and we knew five words of Arabic. With that and sign language we learned that the ship was fifteen years old and displaced three hundred tons. She was carvel-planked, heavily framed, and powered with a 175-horsepower Caterpillar engine from Detroit. Fifty-five-gallon drums served as water tanks. In the bow she had a fisherman storm anchor that must have weighed two hundred kilos. Except for the captain's cabin there was no crew accommodation; the men must have slept on deck because the vessel was simply an empty load-carrying shell. The reason we had seen all the fishing was that there was hardly any food on board. The five men had to fish in order to eat. The captain showed us his chart and how he navigated. We soon

The Arab dhow that accompanied us from Port Sudan to Suez

realized that he went from point to point and never dared get out of sight of land. He was on his way to Suez for cargo and thoroughly fed up with the headwinds.

On October 3rd the voice of the wind was so strong that it woke me in the night. In the morning Margaret made bread while I set a second anchor. When the Arab crew on the dhow saw me putting out the extra anchor they got very agitated and ran around their decks pointing and gesticulating. "What does he know that we don't?" they seemed to be saying.

After watching the desert landscape for four days and taking short walks we noticed that a few people lived behind the first range of hills, where there were some stunted trees and green shrubs. Sometimes in the blue of dawn or in the pink of dusk we could see a man driving a herd of goats or a few camels. Once a family in bright-colored Sudanese dress came to the sea to bathe. Another time a tiny blue boat appeared with two Sudanese fishermen who camped on the shore for several hours. The men changed their rough garb for the traditional long garments, and strode off into the desert with vigorous, robust steps. I marveled at the skill it took to live in such an environment.

Finally, on the fifth day—October 4th—the wind decreased. We got under way at 0714 and began a long offshore tack. North of the Egyptian border the coast is a mass of coral and rocks for 120 miles, so we stayed well out and tacked back and forth and adjusted our sail area to the strength of the headwind. In twenty knots of wind with one reef and the number three jib, *Whisper* sailed fifty-five degrees off the wind at five knots. We logged 110–115 miles per day and made good about 75 miles toward our goal.

In four days we sailed 446 miles, made good 299 miles, and saw hundreds of big ships. On the fifth day in lighter winds we slipped into a wild-looking Egyptian anchorage called Sharm el'Arab at twenty-seven degrees north latitude. The weather and water were cooler. My prickly heat had begun to vanish, and I wore a T-shirt for the first time in more than a year. I couldn't wait to get farther north. Already we had been in the Red Sea almost two months. Would this marathon ever end?

Now we passed through the Strait of Gubal—with a wrecked ship here and there—and entered the Gulf of Suez. We avoided the south end of Shaker Island because of reports of trigger-happy soldiers, and tacked between Egypt and the Sinai Peninsula. From the center of the Gulf of Suez—fifteen to twenty-five miles wide—we could see Africa to our left and Asia to our right. We crossed the shipping lanes often and spent a lot of time taking compass bearings of ships to check whether our course was safe. Some of the ships were enormous, ill-proportioned, and must have been unwieldy to handle. Typical was a blue vessel of the Maersk line whose deck had *sixty* giant containers (twelve rows piled five high). How the officers ever conned the ship from the aft bridge was a mystery.

Sharm el'Arab, Red Sea

[From my journal] October 20th. This morning we almost finished the voyage as well as our lives while crossing the shipping lanes. *Capella* of Singapore, a big ugly ship piled high with containers, was on an almost parallel, slightly converging course with us. It was 0630 with good daylight and the early sun was flat on *Whisper* from *Capella*'s view. I presumed she would ease off a hair, since we were hard on the wind, and heeled to twenty-five degrees. But no! She didn't give a millimeter and almost thundered into us. At the last minute I threw the helm over and changed course.

A cap to this shameful performance was that the two men on the bridge rushed out on the starboard wing and waved merrily at us as we rolled in the spinoff from the bow wave not more than ten or fifteen meters away. I wished I had had a hand grenade. This was our third close call in the Red Sea. The last, I hope.

The usual headwind blew from twenty to forty knots day after day, night after night, hour after hour. Sometimes the wind died for a little while, but before we knew it, the whitecaps would be up again. One day we watched a southbound yacht, running at hull speed with only a tiny jib flying, disappear to the south. I felt envious.

We began to smell oil, to see oil rigs, and workboats and buoys and cables. We sailed past enormous platforms that stood on spindly legs miles from land. These giant tables in the sea sparkled with hundreds of lights—

some white, some yellow, a few red—and were set with noisy machinery that towered high in the air and sent up pipes spouting smoky yellow fire that flickered like candles in a draft of air. There were German cranes on barges, French helicopters whirling overhead with crates underneath on slings, and snorting American tugboats that carried squads of men who wore helmets and looked like soldiers going into battle. On the headlands we saw boxlike barracks for the oil workers together with strings of harsh electric lights that looked strangely out of place on the soft brown desert.

The scope of the oil drilling was impressive. There seemed to be a great race to suck the oil from beneath the land in the shortest possible time. The scene was a war with the earth; the army in front of me was determined to win, no matter what the cost. It's amazing what men will do to tap the riches of the earth. "How long will the oil last?" I wondered. "How long will the wreckage of the machinery clutter up the landscape?"

A little after dawn on October 17th *Whisper* and the big white dhow left an anchorage called Mersa Zeitiya. According to waterline length, the dhow should have made at least twice the daily run of *Whisper,* but the Arab vessel was hopeless going to windward. We went out under sail, while the dhow motored along the coast. Invariably we met at the next anchorage, which astonished the Arab crew. How could the foreigners in their little sailboat match the dhow with the big engine? Unbelievable.

That day we headed north toward a town named Tor on the Sinai Peninsula. At lunchtime we reached Tor and tacked west for Egypt. The wind increased to gale force. When we neared the anchorage of Ras Shukheir late in the afternoon, I used my binoculars to scan the cliffs ahead. Sure enough, there was the big white dhow south of the port, smashing into head seas and plunging up and down about thirty degrees and making maybe two knots while its smoking engine tried to drive the ungainly hull into the wind. The gulf was nasty, and many small and medium-sized ships gave up trying to make Suez and anchored, generally with two anchors. We got to shelter before the dhow, anchored and tidied up, and sat on deck to watch her enter. She came rushing in, headed up next to us, and *both* the regular and storm anchors went over. The captain and crew all sat down on deck and held their heads, too tired to start fishing. It had been a long day.

Out in the strait I saw a southbound coasting vessel hoist a large red square sail, which immediately billowed out and began to pull hard. I had never seen a modern ship hoist a sail before.

We arrived in Suez Bay on October 21st, on the twenty-ninth day from Port Sudan. The 764-mile passage had been our pokiest ever, and one we would never forget. The irksome head seas had vanished, and the weather became soft and easy. The desert murk was gone. The sky was high and very blue. We had finally broken loose from the Red Sea weather pattern. Our last view of the big white dhow was in Suez Bay when we crossed tacks.

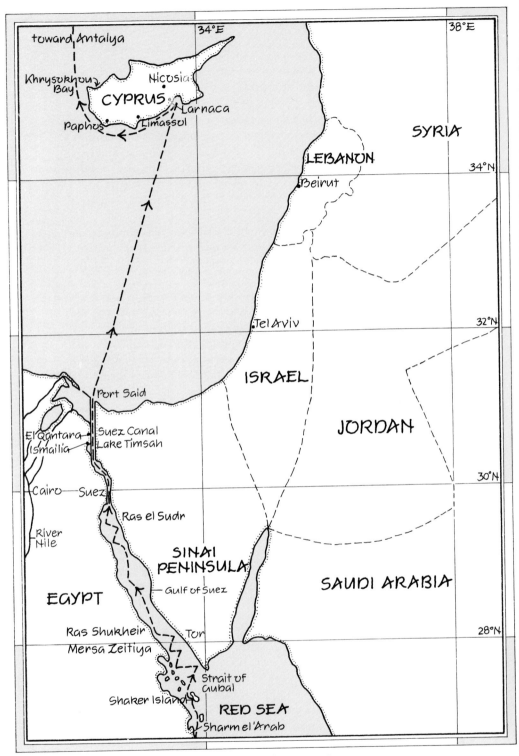

19. Northern Red Sea to Cyprus

We were surprised to see a big sail up on the dhow. Everybody waved and smiled and pointed to the sail. I felt a real kinship with those Arab sailors.

While I was basking in the glory of pleasant sailing and picking my way though a hundred anchored ships, a trim launch flying an enormous Egyptian flag pulled alongside. A man jumped aboard *Whisper*. I thought he was an official of some kind until he removed his shoes. I was suspicious at once because *officials never remove their shoes.*

"Who are you?" I asked the slim, well-dressed man.

"I am the Prince of the Red Sea," he replied with an arrogant toss of his head. "You need me to be your agent for the transit of the canal and . . ."

"How much will it cost?" I said.

"For you, it's a mere trifle," replied the Prince, grandly gesturing toward me with the palm of his right hand upward.

Just then another launch pulled up on the other side of *Whisper*. "Hello, captain," shouted a smiling man in a white suit. "I need to talk with you."

"Who are you?"

"Moses."

"Moses?"

"I want to help you, captain. I have mail for you. I will wait for you at the yacht club."

Meanwhile the Prince of the Red Sea stood at my side while I steered. He talked nonstop, and claimed that harbormaster fees for transits had increased from U.S. $5 to $80.

"You are such a nice man, captain, that I will charge you only $350," he purred unctuously.

I kept shaking my head. The prince reduced his quotation to $300, then $250, and finally to $180, which he said was less than the fees he would have to pay for us.

I couldn't understand how an agent could negotiate downward from fixed fees. If he had to pay all those fees to the canal authority, what would *he* get? Obviously an agent had to profit at some level. When I asked the Prince these questions he immediately began to talk about how trustworthy he was, how honorable, nice, etc. He rambled on and produced an envelope with some old and very worn letters of recommendation. When I looked at one of the letters I saw that someone had written in bold pencil at the bottom: "Do not employ this man under any circumstances."

I had the feeling that I had read this whole scenario in a book somewhere.

We soon got to the entrance of the Suez Canal and tied up at the little yacht club. I told the Prince that I would think about his offer. "With my vast experience and my superior knowledge I may be able to get your clearance in two or three days," he said as he left.

Moses appeared and swept Margaret and me to the veranda of the yacht club, where he clapped his hands to summon a terrified bar boy who brought us two warm Seven-Ups.

"Actually my name is Ibrahim Said," said Moses. "I was formerly the chief agent with the famous Moses of the Red Sea, formerly the best agent. My prices are the cheapest and I can supply the best. . . ."

Ibrahim quoted us his prices. I told him that I was anxious to go through the canal at once, and that if he could arrange for our transit the next day I would hire him. We also needed diesel fuel and fresh food. The breakdown according to Ibrahim was as follows:

doctor	$6
insurance	15
immigration	10
customs	10
harbormaster and light dues	80
ship and two crew	45
official stamp	4
total	$170

If these were the charges, I could only assume that the agent got a percentage from each agency. In any case, it was not my worry.

Ibrahim called a taxi and we went to a money changer, where we traded some U.S. dollars for Egyptian pounds. He then took us to a series of small Egyptian markets that were bursting with the most wonderful produce from the valley of the Nile. After two months in the sterile desert we couldn't wait to buy the succulent, bright red tomatoes, giant dates as sweet as honey, limes full of juice, sweet oranges, and bunches of purple and red grapes. We bought sugar, flour, butter, and a kilo of pungent Egyptian coffee. Our bags of groceries included smelly cheeses from France, fresh eggs, halva, and loaves of crusty bread. Back at the yacht club we got a freshwater hose on board and had an orgy of washing and rinsing and filling the water tanks.

The scheming of some of the Egyptians was incredible. There were six or eight yachts in transit at the yacht club. The charge was six dollars a day for use of the facilities and the water hose. Late in the afternoon a man came around in a rowboat to collect the money. There was a knock on the hull and the man said: "Yacht club, six dollars please." We paid him. Then he went to the next yacht, knocked on the hull, and said: "Yacht club, six dollars please." And so on down the line. Unfortunately it turned out that the man in the rowboat was not from the yacht club at all. He was a crewman from a passing ship. . . .

That night we collapsed into bed thinking how lucky we were to have made Suez. I reflected on the contrasts of world voyaging: one day misery and the next day luxury.

The following morning things moved fast. At 0600 Ibrahim brought down forty-nine liters of diesel fuel. At 0700 a tug pulled alongside with an inspector who wanted to see *Whisper*'s engine run. At 0800 another inspector arrived to check the bilge pumps and fire extinguishers. At 0900 Ibrahim came with a sheaf of papers for me to sign. At 1000 the pilot climbed on board, and we were off under power as required, our little one-cylinder Farymann diesel running sweetly and pushing us at five knots.

The Suez Canal is eighty-eight miles long and is merely a flat ditch of water through the Egyptian desert, a far different prospect from the Panama Canal. From thirty to forty ships make the trip each way each day. There are no locks, and our transit was quick and simple. Small vessels generally go in two daylight stages and spend one night halfway along at Ismailia on Lake Timsah, where the pilots are changed. Our first pilot was a serious young Egyptian in traditional dress who spoke only Arabic. He steered *Whisper* expertly and seemed to know what he was doing. Since we couldn't talk, I went below to deal with a couple of jobs. A little later I felt the yacht turn oddly, so I looked in the cockpit. The pilot was gone, and *Whisper* was lurching toward a passing container ship. I grabbed the tiller and got back on course. Where was the pilot? Up on the foredeck kneeling on his prayer mat facing east and saying his prayers. I didn't mind the prayers and the ritual washing that used up my buckets of fresh water, but I wished the pilot had made some sign to me that he was giving up steering.

We got to Lake Timsah at dusk, put the pilot ashore, and anchored for the night. The next morning the second pilot climbed on board at 0630 and we started north. Ibrahim Ibrahim Amudda was certainly different from the first pilot. He wore Western clothes, carried his lunch in a brown bag, and said that he was part Egyptian, part Greek, and part Italian. Instead of the lean Arabic visage of the first pilot, Ibrahim's face was flat and his nose large. He spoke English nonstop and started crying for money as soon as he got on board.

"Do you have my present?" were his favorite words. "I'm doing so much for you," he yelped.

"Rubbish," I answered. "You're paid by the canal company. This is your job. Just steer us to Port Said."

"Oh don't forget my present. I'm so poor. . . ."

As we continued along the canal we kept being passed by convoys of loaded oil tankers. Some went south. Some went north. Why couldn't the oil have been unloaded at a convenient storage point along the way, which would have stopped the useless shipping of oil back and forth? Logic,

"I'm doing so much for you."

however, is often superfluous. We hurried along the bleak canal until we stopped for a traffic problem at El Qantara, where a group of American tourists swarmed around us on the west bank. Our American flag was up, of course, and we were asked about our trip around the world.

"I'm Mabel Glonk from Bucyrus, Ohio," said one lady. "Are you really an American or are you make-believe?"

By 1600 we were into the heavy traffic of Port Said. Ships, launches, tugs, ferries, tour boats, fishermen, rowboats, and tankers crowded us on every side. We stopped for a moment to deliver papers filled out in Arabic to immigration and customs. We stopped a second time to drop the pilot.

"Do you have my present?" he whined. I had been told to tip the pilot four U.S. dollars, but I had one ten-pound Egyptian note left, which I gave him.

"It's so small for all the things I have done for you," he complained.

"If I gave you one million dollars you would ask for two," I said. "If you don't like my present, give it back to me."

"Oh no! It's OK! Thank you very much." The pilot stepped ashore and disappeared in the crowded city.

Margaret and I had no desire to be cheapskates, but we had talked to people on many yachts about Suez and the Egyptians, and we knew that foreign sailors had to take a hard line because everyone connected with the canal had his hand out.

For example, when the American yacht *Hornet* was ready to leave Port Said, Jeri Huber went to Egyptian customs to pick up the ship's passports. Her husband Dale was desperately sick and unable to leave the yacht. The customs man, sensing an opportunity for a fifty-dollar bill or more, got the passports but asked for the captain. Jeri said that he was sick and unable to come ashore. Jeri refused to give the customs man a bribe, and the two of them began to argue. Finally Jeri grabbed the passports and started to leave. The Egyptian customs man pulled out his gun.

"Give me the passports or I'll shoot," he said.

Jeri had no choice but to surrender them. But as she handed back the passports she said:

"Now I know why you lost the war with Israel!"

"I sentence you to seven days in jail!" cried the furious official.

Jeri then lost her temper and made an unmistakable gesture that can only be called unflattering.

"I sentence you to fourteen days in jail!" shrieked the official.

Later the passports were picked up by the captain of a French yacht after the tempers of Mrs. Huber and the customs man had cooled down.

"The mentality of the Egyptians is fantastic," said Lulu Vallotton from the Swiss yacht *Roi Soleil*. "The money-grubbing, lying, scheming, and cheating is unbelievable.

"When my yacht *Roi Soleil* entered Egypt a doctor came on board to issue a quarantine certificate. The man was nicely dressed in a suit with a shirt and tie, and he carried a briefcase. After looking around, the doctor wrote out a certificate, handed it to me, and asked for fifty U.S. dollars.

"When I looked at the certificate, it said that it was free. Free practique! Why should I pay anything? I offered the doctor one dollar. He started to object and we got into a terrific argument. The Egyptian doctor said he would put me in jail, he said he would confiscate the yacht, he said that bad things might happen to my wife and daughter. He made all sorts of threats.

"I said that I would get the Swiss ambassador to have the doctor's license revoked—if he was a doctor. I talked about international law. About inter-country courtesy. I said all kinds of crazy things without any basis in fact, just to keep talking and not to cave in to the Egyptian's demands. In the end—and this shows the hollowness of the whole structure—he settled for a dollar and a half and we shook hands when he left!

"When you deal with Egyptian officials you need to act like Hitler," said Lulu. "They cry about low pay, their big families, how rich you are, and they go into a big sympathy act so you will feel sorry for them and give them money. They never talk about the high canal tolls that we pay. Why should I get involved with their problems? I have my own."

As we headed north out of the Port Said shipping traffic I hoisted *Whisper*'s sails. An official launch came alongside and I passed across our outgoing clearance. Ahead we saw the calm blue of the Mediterranean.

Three days later we arrived in Cyprus after a lovely sail on easy seas with light winds. The gritty sands of Arabia were behind us.

. . . .

CHAPTER EIGHTEEN

The Divided Island

*C*yprus is a pleasant, fertile island 120 miles long and 40 miles wide tucked away in the northeastern corner of the Mediterranean. The island—shaped like an elephant's head with the trunk facing northeast—lies just 40 miles south of the Turkish coast and 60 miles west of Syria. A shaft of morning sunlight on Cyprus also shimmers on Beirut (90 miles), Tel Aviv (170), and Cairo (290). The mountainous island (peaks up to 1,952 meters) is dotted with forts and castles and relics from a long line of small-time kings and power brokers, and a catalog of onetime rulers includes not only the Phoenicians, Assyrians, and Egyptians, but the Persians, Romans, and Venetians as well. Many of the Crusaders (eleventh to fourteenth centuries) passed through Cyprus, and most recently (until 1960) the English were in charge.

Even today the island is caught up in a cross fire between the Greeks and the Turks, and United Nations troops patrol a nervous border that has split the 650,000 residents into two separate countries. Yet Cyprus has somehow held on to its sanity, and we found an oasis of calm in a Mideastern world that was torn apart by wars, terrorism, and bloodshed.

Margaret and I sailed *Whisper* into the marina at Larnaca on the warm and sunny south coast, where there were 210 yachts jammed together on floats and shoreside docks. Everything was quite new, but built to marginal standards. Friends had told us not to write ahead to reserve a winter berth, but to simply appear, and that space would somehow be found for us. We did just that, and the friendly Greek Cypriots told us to "wait one minute" while they shoved and pushed and switched around half a dozen boats until there was enough room to squeeze in *Whisper*. The side docks were full, and most finger piers had yachts on their right and left sides, plus another vessel tied stern-to at the end and held off with lines and fenders. Since we were late arrivals, we were warped to the end of a finger pier, where we carried out two anchors and made fast with a maze of breast, stern, and spring lines. It was a marginal arrangement; nevertheless, we were snug behind a massive breakwater that seemed secure against all winter storms.

The marina was fenced, watched over by a sleepy security guard, and slightly isolated from tourists; yet the facility lay only a few steps from the main street of Larnaca (population 28,000). We had fresh water three days a week, and the 210-volt shore power was dependable once we had bought special blue plugs. Our marina charges were a modest forty U.S. dollars a month, and there was a large haulout facility and storage yard nearby. The showers and toilets and laundry machines were housed in a special building called the ablution block. Unfortunately the condition of these facilities—known on the docks as the pollution block—generally ranged from terrible to ghastly (I soon learned to heat water on *Whisper*'s stove and take sponge baths). Nothing ever worked quite right at the marina in spite of the smiling management, but the place was satisfactory in the Greek manner, and we spent a pleasant interlude in Larnaca.

On our first night in Larnaca we celebrated and ate out. The dinner was dreadful, with greasy food and bitter wine, and we resolved to have all future meals aboard *Whisper*. The next morning we discovered Larnaca's wonderful central market in a covered building at the far end of town. Suddenly we were in a fairyland of food where the sellers shouted greetings (in Greek) and offered us samples of fresh figs and sweet juicy grapes. We saw boxes of scrubbed potatoes, carrots pulled that morning, crispy leaf lettuce, and crunchy apples that sent out a spray of juice when you bit into one. Margaret bought day-old eggs, farm-fresh cabbages, two lovely white cauliflowers, and a glossy purple eggplant. We got firm yellow lemons and melons that were lovely to sniff. In another corner of the market we were offered every cut of beef and pork and chicken by butchers in long bloody aprons. I bought a string bag of almonds from a Greek woman with the sweetest smile, who was so pleased to make a sale. We began to realize that the Greek Cypriots delighted in being a nation of small shopkeepers. We staggered back to the yacht with our shopping bags overflowing with food for a week or more that had cost perhaps ten dollars.

The marina was more of a destination than a transit stop, because many of the yachts had been there since the place had opened in 1980. Though about one-third of the boats had people living aboard, the docks were peaceful and quiet and it was a good place for repairs. Most of the vessels had been sailing on the Mediterranean and were from England, Germany, and France plus a few from the United States, Canada, Holland, and elsewhere. There were a number of small, frail-looking catamarans from England that had crossed to the Mediterranean by way of the French canals and had then day-hopped from port to port until they reached Cyprus. The crews seemed mostly elderly and retired ("robustness" was not a word to be used). Evidently these people traveled together in little groups and the crews became great friends. They often ate together, and on many mornings we heard their breakfast bell at 0900.

Half a dozen sailing yachts had arrived from the Red Sea. We were anxious to hear about their experiences.

Bill Barbena was a retired U.S. Air Force fighter pilot, an ex-colonel who had bought a Cheoy Lee 38 in Hong Kong and was trying to sail the vessel to the United States by himself. He was suave, handsome, and enthusiastic, but his sailing skills were poor and his yachting friends had helped him through one disaster after another. Asleep in the Strait of Gubal, Bill had piled into a reef and holed his vessel. He got help from a nearby oil rig service ship that luckily had scuba divers on board who patched his hull. He was rebuilding the bottom of his vessel in the Larnaca boatyard.

In Darwin we had met Australian Ken Anderson on *Lowena,* a forty-foot ocean racer. Ken was also a singlehander and had completed the Red Sea passage unscathed, although he had accidentally been struck by a North Yemenese gunboat and had twice hit sandbanks while asleep. Down the dock from us was *Arafura,* a ten-meter, hard-chine steel sloop owned by Jean-Claude Alain, a French merchant ship officer who had sailed most of the way around the world and had made the Red Sea passage without any trouble. (Jean-Claude was a demon amateur classical violinist, and we often heard him playing when we walked down the docks.)

In general—but not always—the clever sailors had managed the Red Sea with little trouble. But if your sailing act wasn't together and you had bad habits, you were in trouble. Pieter and Karen Boersma on *Chenoa,* a beautifully built forty-two-foot ferrocement ketch, had no problems at all. Yet Billy Budd and his wife and two dogs on *Olive Marie* had continual adventures. Pieter Boersma knew Billy well and told me this story:

Billy always motored downwind because to sail meant rolling, which his wife hated. Billy would be thoroughly juiced up while his wife was eased down on big doses of Valium. Their anchoring was pandemonium: a large sweeping turn through the anchorage, dropping the anchor, and then a lot of screaming and shouting and dog barking as they let out chain and backed down and dragged. *Olive Marie* was perpetually in trouble and forever sending out Mayday signals. In Australia *Olive Marie* had problems and was towed into Darwin and billed for $3,000. In the Red Sea, Billy started to sink again and radioed for help. A cargo ship appeared to windward, swung out a boom, and picked up *Olive Marie* on two slings. Billy relaxed and figured that a ride on a big ship was the best way to do the cursed Red Sea. However, some hours later he noticed that the sun was setting across the starboard side of the ship. "Jesus, the ship is going south, not north," he said. The cargo ship went to Djibouti in the Gulf of Aden, where *Olive Marie* was unloaded. Billy Budd had to face the Red Sea all over again.

Whisper needed a major refit and improvements to her coachroof. Cyprus was an ideal place. The weather was good, and as the boats got switched around I managed to get alongside a finger float, where I had easy access on and off the yacht and a place to work. One morning I took a bent and twisted twenty-kilo CQR anchor away for repairs. Someone had suggested Antonio in an alley next to Barclay's Bank on Hermes Street. I got a taxi, which roared off to the north despite my entreaties to go south. At length, after a stop and "One moment, please," we reversed directions.

Antonio was an energetic Armenian, aged sixty-three, who spoke a kind of violent English which he emphasized with continual swordlike thrusts of his arms and hands. He ran a tiny machine shop that specialized in small repairs (next door was a welder whom Antonio would summon by pounding on the wall). Antonio was thin, with a somewhat pinched face, a genial fellow who was pleasant and full of advice. When I entered the shop he was seated with several friends, one English who spoke no Greek, and one Greek who spoke no English. As soon as Antonio saw my anchor he jumped to his feet and began to stab the air with his right hand.

"Yes! Yes! I mean no! no! I can't do it. What you need is a blacksmith. A forge. An expert. You need Psaris. Do you know the bypass road?"

"I know nothing. I only arrived yesterday."

The thin Englishman in one of the chairs spoke up. "I will take you to Psaris in my car." The man left to fetch his vehicle, and while he was gone I had a few words with Antonio, who thought he could do several other small jobs for me. He ordered me a coffee while he jabbed the air with gestures.

"Full sugar? Medium sugar? Light sugar? No sugar?" he said.

The Englishman appeared with a small truck, and we drove off to the blacksmith. Tom Denne had lived on Cyprus for years, but he didn't speak a single word of Greek.

"Why should I?" he said. "If I spoke Greek, there would be no cause for the Greeks to speak English. By the time I learn Greek I will probably be elsewhere, so why begin at all?"

After stopping for directions several times we found the blacksmith shop. Psaris, who was shoveling charcoal into his forge, examined the pretzel-like anchor.

"OK. OK," he said. "I can fix it in five minutes."

"Five minutes? In five minutes?"

"OK. OK. Four minutes if you're in a hurry. I'll do it in four minutes. I mean four days. I get the words upside down. Come back at the end of the week."

"What about galvanizing the anchor and the ship's chain?"

"Ah," said Psaris, waving a sooty finger. "Not in Larnaca. You must go to the zinc place in the mountains on the way to Nicosia. I will give you directions and you can go in the express taxi."

One day I got acquainted with Costas Christopoulou, a tall, heavy-browed, gray-haired man with thick lips and an engaging, upbeat, super-friendly manner who ran a newspaper store and stationery shop. His English was poor and delivered in somber, priestlike tones, but his manner embraced you, and he was so eager to talk that he would let customers waving cash wait while he discussed the weather and politics with you in a manner so personal that you felt you were the only human being in the world. The shop was heaped with piles of envelopes, boxes of typing paper, last week's newspapers, and *last year's* news magazines. (After buying a paper with the current day and month but *a year old,* I learned to check the full date.) You could scarcely get in or out of the front door because of racks of dusty paperbacks, shelves jammed with artists' paints, and tables so loaded with balloons, crepe paper, and children's toys that half of the stock had fallen on the floor. Costas wanted to give me a card with his name in English letters, but he was unable to find one in the rubble on his desk. Disorder was everywhere (Costas' cash register was in his pocket), and you shouldered your way to the counter past tipsy paperback stands and knee-high piles of still-unopened newspapers fresh from the airport. How Costas ever found anything in the confusion of the counters and tables was a mystery. Yet he moved around his store like a gazelle, and neatly sidestepped all the confusion like a young Fred Astaire dancing at the edge of a stage.

"Tomorrow we'll have a coffee together," he shouted as I began to leave and unwittingly knocked over a tottering display of detective novels near the door. I began to pick up the books, but Costas waved me out. "If the people want something, they can bend over."

Our neighbors on the dock were Emrys and Ingrid Thomas, two expert sailors who lived on *Naim,* a sleek, forty-six-foot wooden cutter that was built in Alexandria. Emrys was a robust Welshman, and Ingrid was a charming, blond Swedish woman. Both had the most pleasant temperaments and were always full of smiles and good humor. When Emrys laughed I could hear him a hundred meters down the dock, a high-pitched, ringing laugh that filled me with hope and buoyancy, even when I was depressed. He had been in business with an Egyptian partner in Cairo with the usual result. "A disaster," said Emrys, who looked serious for a moment.

Emrys was a demon woodworker whose winter boat projects included building a refrigerator and making a complex folding door of exotic inlaid hardwoods. Meanwhile Ingrid painted away, kept up *Naim*'s large varnished bulwarks, and perfected her cooking. The Thomases had a small house in the Turkish zone near Kyrenia on the other side of Cyprus, but they liked to live on *Naim* and, I suspect, enjoyed meeting all the sailors who came to Larnaca.

As the weeks turned into months Margaret and I made good progress with the coachroof project. I closed up the leaky forward vents that had long been a problem and improved the areas around the mast step and companionway. It was a big job because I had to remove the handrails, the staysail tracks (whose bolts I found stretched), the stove chimney (which needed replacing), the spray dodger bases, the boom gallows, and the entire main hatch assembly. I used a disc grinder to take off layers of old paint and filler. We added fiberglass to the low places and put two layers of fiberglass mat over the entire coachroof to strengthen it.

To fill the small hollows in the coachroof, I used a mixture of talcum powder and polyester resin, which I scraped across the coachroof with a bent straightedge. This scheme worked well, but I used a good deal of talcum powder. The only powder I could buy was for babies and came in small plastic jars from the local drugstore. When I bought the first jar, the lady clerk thanked me for the purchase. The next day I bought two more jars, and when I paid, the lady made some pleasant remarks about my family and babies. When I bought three more jars on the third day the woman got upset and nervous. I muttered something about special problems and tried to smile, but when I appeared again and took four jars she lost her temper and began to scold me in Greek. God only knows what she said, but it was obviously not nice. I had to find another drugstore.

On bright days we sanded and painted and began to replace the coachroof fittings, overhauling each thing as we went along. While the coachroof paint was drying I reconstructed the bottom of the fiberglass dinghy. On rainy days I checked over the mast and standing rigging and halyards. When the coachroof was finished we began on the deck. To do a proper job we removed the bulwarks, mooring cleats, and steering vane. I was surprised to find that most of the eight-millimeter stainless steel bolts that held the vane gear to the transom broke with the first touch of a wrench. Inspection showed old cracks in the bolts. While I ground off all the old nonskid paint, Margaret scrubbed *Whisper*'s dirty sails and marked places that needed attention. We lugged the sails to a woman in the marina who was an expert at sewing and repairs.

[From my journal] December 21st. Last evening we went for a drink with the sail repair lady—Liz Purkis—and her husband George, who own a steel yacht named *Quo Vadis.* Unfortunately the vessel piled on to a reef about thirty miles from

Port Sudan in the Red Sea. George and Liz had poor charts and appear to have been tired and unsure of their position. In any case, the vessel was holed and partially filled, and one night when the owners were away for a few hours, the yacht was boarded and stripped by Sudanese sailors. The couple managed to get a Sudanese vessel to tow *Quo Vadis* off the reef, and after some frantic patching— including the use of cement and sheep fat, which George says is an extraordinary combination—the Purkises struggled north to Suez and Larnaca, where the yacht has been hauled out for the last six months.

George hired a local welder for £1,250 Cyprus ($2,312) to repair the hull. Unfortunately the welder turned out to be an incompetent good-for-nothing, and George was finally obliged to fire the man after paying him £1,100. George says that he will pay the other £150 only after the welder produces bona fide invoices for materials. The welder has countered with a claim for £750 and has put a writ on *Quo Vadis*. George has hired an attorney, but the episode has thoroughly demoralized the poor captain of *Quo Vadis*.

George is English and a sheep farmer who lived in Australia for eight years. He seems a tremendously sincere person. He has a large beard and often speaks in the present tense about things that have happened in the past, which is confusing. He told us that all his resources are gone but that he and Liz are progressing with the repairs. George's former wife died of cancer at age twenty-six. He and Liz have been married for eighteen months, which he says—wreck excepted—have been the happiest of his life. Meanwhile Liz sews sails to bankroll the repairs. . . .

We became great friends with Joe and Bonnie Darlington, two Americans who were on *Tortoise,* a Golden Hind 32, a Maurice Griffiths shoal-draft, hard-chine sloop built in England. Bonnie was a sweet thing from the Arkansas hills. Joe was a retired New York jazz musician who had lost an eye in an accident and wore a black patch. Though he looked a little like a pirate, he was the most gentle soul you ever met, and he wouldn't have forced a fly to walk the plank. Joe was more an artist than a nautical mechanic, so Bonnie did the carpentry and technical repairs on *Tortoise.* They were newcomers to sailing but were learning fast.

I had grave doubts about the rig on *Tortoise* because her standing rigging was fairly light wire with *single* Nicropress wire end fittings. The stays were not tensioned properly, the rig was loose and floppy, and the windward performance must have been abysmal. I offered to re-rig *Tortoise* at no cost, but Joe had asked advice from everyone and had collected half a dozen opinions and was quite confused. Someone had told him that if the wire was tensioned, the mast would break (yet every other yacht in the marina had a properly tensioned headstay and shrouds). I set to work on the rig, but Joe got increasingly nervous and asked me to stop. *Tortoise* continued on as she was and eventually crossed the Atlantic—in fair weather—which made me think that my advice must have been wrong. Sometimes God rests on the shoulders of the innocent. . . .

Margaret and I alternated work on *Whisper* with a bit of traveling around Cyprus. Little by little we began to learn about the people and the troublesome political situation.

If you look at a regional map it seems reasonable that Cyprus should belong to Turkey, since Cyprus is only a few miles off the Turkish coast while Greece and the Greek isles are hundreds of miles away. However, Cyprus has a vocal Greek majority (80 percent, while the Turks total only 18 percent), and union with Greece has long been a goal of some of the Greek Cypriots. Union with Greece, as might be expected, has been firmly opposed by the minority Turks. When the British pulled out in 1960 and Cyprus became an independent republic, all was peaceful on the surface. In 1974, however, a group of officers from the Greek army seized the government and attempted to steer Cyprus toward Greece. Turkey responded by invading the island and taking over the northeast portion, about 40 percent of the land. Greece mobilized its forces but did nothing. There was a good deal of cruelty and killing of innocents by each side, and both the Greeks and Turks had bloody hands. Gradually the violence lessened. In 1975 the Turkish Cypriots voted to form an independent state, and in 1983 they declared their land to be the Turkish Republic of Northern Cyprus. The border between the two sides has been patrolled by United Nations forces since 1974, and an uneasy peace continues, with each side taking a few pot shots at the other from time to time.

Margaret and I were at Larnaca on the south coast in the Greek Cypriot zone, where the industrious Greeks had all sorts of shops and businesses going full blast. The Larnaca airport was jammed with international flights, and after ten years of peace and lots of promotion, the tourists—as well as a lot of refugees from Lebanon—had returned in force. Though the island had poor medical service and was short of cultural events and libraries, the south coast had dozens of large and small hotels, hundreds of tourist apartments, and we saw new roads and building projects all along the coast. A second major airfield was under construction near the western end of the island, and we noticed sightseeing buses at many of the old ruins. The cities of Limassol, Paphos, and Nicosia also had tourist developments, and there was a fledgling winter sports program in the mountains.

People had begun to buy small cars; Larnaca had half a dozen driving schools, and it was a common sight to see a car bumping along and a patient teacher talking to a serious-faced pupil who was trying to master the gearshift lever. I learned that there was a local mafia to whom the shopkeepers paid protection money. We often used the highly organized express taxi system (you went with five or six people to a common distant destination), which had new Mercedes-Benz cars with excellent drivers. I could not understand the operation, because the fares were ridiculously low and in no way could have paid for the fine cars, fuel, and drivers.

Goatherder, Cyprus

Though the prosperous Greek Cypriots were busy with their stores and services, they always found time to bad-mouth the Turks, especially to foreigners. The Cypriots were great chest thumpers, but I often felt that their words were hollow. "We're going to have to fight again," was a common boast, but the Greeks knew in their heart of hearts that with their poorly trained army of eight thousand they didn't have a chance against the better armed and trained Turkish force of twenty thousand. The Greeks kept the border mostly closed and inflicted all sorts of petty obstacles on trade. The Turks were less aggressive commercially and had weak currency, not much business, and little tourism (although the prettiest part of the island was on the north side). Rauf Denktash, the Turkish leader, seemed willing to compromise—or at least talk—but the stubborn Greek Cypriot politicians refused to give a millimeter, and the pathetic stalemate continued. It seemed to me—a casual outsider—that only a new generation of Greek Cypriots would have the wisdom to be less emotional and more practical.

One weekend the Darlingtons and Margaret and I hired a car and went for a drive in the western foothills. In a few hours we were far from tourists and poked along a rural countryside that was covered with vineyards. The soil was rocky, but generations of grape growers had scraped the rocks from the fields and built high stone walls that ran for miles. I winced when I

thought of the efforts such walls must have taken. Sometimes we passed
women herding goats or carrying bundles of faggots. We drove through
small villages where some of the men wore high boots and black native dress
and sported impressive handlebar mustaches. Often we saw a group of old
men sitting on a bench in the sun and talking quietly.

We had heard about the Baths of Aphrodite, so we drove to Khrysok-
hou Bay at the remote northwest corner of Cyprus and bounced over a
mountain road into a peaceful and serene valley. The baths were a disappoint-
ment (a single pool fed by a spring), but the countryside was open and green
and pleasant. We stopped for lunch at a restaurant that overlooked the bay
and had the most marvelous views of the water and distant cliffs. We met
the owner, Nestor Neophytou (who had gone to college in the United
States), and picked our meal from a catch the fishermen had just brought in.
We had an excellent lunch of grilled gray mullet *(kephalos)* and sat a hundred
meters above the surging ocean while we speculated on the ancient Greeks
and drank glasses of Bellapais wine. I felt like booking a table for life.

On March 10th, with *Whisper*'s deck work completed, we moved to
the haul-out facility. The big marine Travelift hoisted the yacht out of the
water, and we were soon scrubbed and blocked up. I wanted to paint the
topsides and bottom and to deal with the engine shaft, which made a terrible
clanking noise at certain revolutions. Farymann, the manufacturer, had suggested installing a bearing at the front end of the propeller shaft, so I had
a conference with Antonio at the machine shop.

"Yes! Yes! I mean no! no! I can't do it," said Antonio, stabbing the
air with his hand as usual. "That's heavy stuff. You must go to Zohrab
Karaoghlanian. He fixes buses and repairs Caterpillar tractors. He's got the
big machines and is a specialist in shaft and propeller problems."

Zohrab was a short, intense man who wore greasy clothes and worked
all by himself in an enormous old building filled with giant lathes and
milling machines and hydraulic presses. Zohrab was so quiet that at first I
thought he didn't understand me. "Maybe he doesn't speak English," I said
to myself. . . .

Zohrab paced the floor. Back and forth. Finally he turned to me and
began to speak like a college professor. "We must make an analysis," he said.
"We must look at the problem from every side. You must take out the
propeller shaft, the present bearing, the stuffing box, the engine coupling—
everything—and bring the parts here. The propeller too. All the big and little
pieces—keys, screws, bolts—*everything!* We will assemble them here on the
floor and see where we are. Talking and diagrams never solve anything. If
you have a nervous shaft we can remedy it, but first we must find out what
is rattling and what is best to do."

Zohrab sounded sensible to me, so I did exactly what he suggested. Soon
I was making two or three trips a day to his cavernous machine shop, where

I often found him in a dark corner machining a giant bearing for a truck or straightening a bent propeller from a local coasting vessel. Once or twice I gave him a hand with a big job.

We had coffee together. Another day we had lunch. Once we took a little walk. Zohrab came down to see *Whisper* and met Margaret. I liked the old man and enjoyed our visits. One afternoon Zohrab waved me into his little office. He motioned me toward a chair, took off his glasses, and began to talk.

"I work by myself because my sons have gone to America," he confided. "They wanted to earn the big money. But right here in Larnaca I can earn all I need. I had planned that the boys would take over the business. But now I am all alone. I'm too old and soon I'll be gone. Yet I have all this," he said, motioning vaguely toward the machines. "You understand what I am doing and I can teach you how to run things. Why don't you stay? One day it can all be yours."

I sucked in my breath because old Zohrab, the Armenian machinist, was unburdening his heart to me. "It's a kind offer," I said, groping for the words, "and I appreciate it. How I wish I could say yes. But in spite of my interest in this place and my affection for you, I'm a sailor and a wanderer. I'd stay with you a year or two, but then I'd get bored and want to go off somewhere. Your offer is generous. Too generous. I don't deserve it, and to be kind to you and honest to myself I must say no."

[From my journal] February 13th. Last Thursday Len Hobbs, a nearby boat owner (who is sixty-three and a pilot with Jordanian Airways), drank half a bottle of Johnny Walker Black Label and got very drunk. He became sloppy and went aboard *Safari,* where he boasted of his Swiss bank account, his houses, and his swimming pools. His audience—Douglas and June Orchard of *Ocean Gypsy,* Pieter and Karen Boersma of *Chenoa,* and Arthur and Margi Benteng of *Safari*—were soon disgusted with him. June Orchard offered to get him some food and coffee. Unsteady Len, while on his way to *Ocean Gypsy,* fell off *Safari*'s gangplank and into the water when his knees suddenly buckled.

Len went straight to the bottom. He evidently surfaced under the dock and struck his head and then sank a second time. Arthur stripped off his clothes and jumped in. It was 2200, however, and dark. Arthur yelled for a flashlight and dove again. He found Len and dragged him to the surface. The group got a line around the unconscious pilot and dragged him up on the dock. Meanwhile someone called an ambulance. Len wasn't breathing at first, but the people on the dock managed to clear him of blood, water, and vomit, and with a little pumping Len began to breathe. The ambulance crew hauled him off to the hospital, where he stayed for three days. Yesterday a most chastened Len Hobbs appeared on the dock and quietly went to his yacht, where he has been keeping a low profile. Since Arthur is quite broke and saved Len's life, I told Len to give Arthur some money. Len told me that he would give Arthur a hundred dollars.

We continued to work in the boatyard. By now Margaret and I had set up rickety scaffolding around *Whisper,* and we spent a week filling and sanding the topsides. Ingrid Thomas told me about a local chandlery that had a sale on one-pot polyurethane paint made by a famous British company that had gone bankrupt. When I investigated I found that all the paint had been sold except for black—a color that no one wanted except me—and that the paint cans were rusty and dented. I bought the paint for a ridiculous price, and the next day Margaret and I rolled and brushed on the first of three gleaming coats. Zohrab had the new bearing made for the engine shaft, and I soon installed the whole assembly. I completed a number of small joinery jobs. The sails were back on board. The work on the yacht was about finished. We were scheduled to go back into the water.

One lovely April day we were rolling on bottom paint when I heard a strange, hollow-sounding noise overhead. Everyone in the boatyard looked up to see a great flight of flamingos. We watched two or three hundred birds slowly wheeling across the deep blue of the afternoon sky in an enormous V formation. It was a breathtaking sight. Though the birds were several hundred meters up in the air, we could plainly hear their gooselike honks and see their long necks stretched ahead and their stalklike feet trailing behind. The birds were headed north, chasing the sun, following the call of spring.

It was time for us to move on.

. . . .

CHAPTER NINETEEN

Old Coastlines

*W*e sailed for Alanya, Turkey, on May 1st. Our target was two hundred miles away, and we skirted the south and west sides of Cyprus and headed north toward the mainland. The winds were from the east, of trifling strength, and we glided along on a blue and peaceful Mediterranean. It was marvelous to get to sea again after months of boat work and shoreside living. *Whisper* was in good order, and the various small jobs we had done made life aboard easier and more pleasant.

On our third morning at sea we looked at a distant black headland beneath the Taurus Mountains, a row of snowy peaks with heights up to 2,400 meters. We worked shoreward toward a large bay open to the south, and gradually through a mask of haze I began to see a few misty lines and boxes—dreamlike and vague—that strengthened into the buildings and houses and minarets of a real city.

At noon we anchored near a long jetty. I took the dinghy and went ashore to a customs kiosk at the head of the mole, where an official gave me a cup of sweet tea and sent me to the police (immigration) and to the doctor (health). The main language was Turkish, of course, but I was surprised to learn that the next language was German. I heard a few words of English and absolutely no French or Spanish. At each office I was asked for crew lists, which I wrote and stamped (I had been told to get an official-looking stamp for use in Turkey). At the police station I sat down at a typewriter to tap out an additional crew list and was amazed to find a completely unfamiliar

Turkish keyboard, which reduced me to the most basic hunt and peck typing. All the officials were pleasant and courteous, including a police captain who was fairly drunk. I finished up with the customs man, whose usual questions included a new one about scuba equipment because the Turks keep a sharp eye on people who dive for antiquities and take them out of the country.

"We welcome you, captain," said the customs man, who struggled to read a card with English words in phonetic Turkish. "Please stay as our guest." Pronouncing the words was hard for the guard, and he smiled with relief when he was finished. I smiled too.

So far our formal entry into Turkey had been easy. I changed a fifty-dollar traveler's check at a bank where I got 341 Turkish lira for each dollar. Though most of the tourism efforts were aimed at Germans, the shopkeepers were intrigued with the English language and amused themselves by trying a few words. I went back to the yacht, and we moved *Whisper* to the inner harbor, which was more convenient and free from swell. Margaret and I relaxed in the ship's cockpit. We looked up at the houses of Alanya and at a great medieval wall that climbed up the steep headland that rose above the harbor immediately to the west. The buildings of the city fanned out toward the north, and I could see five minarets and one large domed mosque. The minarets looked exactly like the French Ariadne rockets that in our space age blast satellites into orbit; both had business in the heavens.

I counted forty-six fishing boats in the little harbor, which was full of shouts and hammering and the staccato bang-bang of one-cylinder diesel engines as the vessels hurried in and out, a red Turkish flag fluttering at each transom. The boats were carvel-planked double-enders six to eight meters long, nicely painted in white with red and blue trim, and in good condition. All were fitted with a stump mast suitable for a lateen yard, but I saw no sailing rigs. A dozen boats were hauled out for repairs, and four new ones were under construction. The men seemed a good deal more industrious than

Fisherman and nets, Alanya

their Cyprus counterparts (were there more fish?) and when not at sea were busy with their nets. The fishermen moved their boats around the harbor with long oars whose shafts—looms—had extra thicknesses of wood near the handles, which perhaps served as counterweights for the long blades. The boat names used a strange combination of letters. *Firat, Sevil,* and *Cenk* were the names of three near us.

On the second morning Margaret and I walked up to a museum in the five-story octagonal Red Tower that rose above the harbor. The Red Tower was built of pink-colored stone by Sultan Alauddin Kayjubad in 1225 to protect the nearby dockyard, and we looked at a dusty collection of bows and arrows, chain mail, and tapestry looms. We puffed up two additional flights of steep stone steps to the top for a view of the harbor, the walls of the old city, and an expanding new Alanya with hotels and apartments (the population was 25,000, up from 5,000 of thirty years ago). We could see that except for fishing boats, *Whisper* was the only vessel in the harbor.

We continued our walk up the steep hill to the castle on the heights that overlooked Alanya and the coast. I thought of taking a taxi via a long roundabout road but Margaret overruled me, so we started up the walking route through the town and heights above. A little way along we passed several very old houses built of stones held in place with horizontal wooden beams. We were unsure of the route to the castle, so we asked a group of people who were at a gate in the city wall. Five women going to their houses agreed to guide us. Margaret walked with the women, who were small and slim and light on their feet; two wore baggy trousers, three had dresses, and all wore head scarves. The friendly women walked arm in arm with Margaret as we passed small houses and climbed the steep lanes and twisty trails. Margaret didn't have a single word in common with the ladies, but they all had a great time in sign language, pointing and laughing, especially when the women's friends shouted from their houses as we passed.

"Are you working for the tourist bureau?"

"Who is your new friend?"

"Are you speaking English now?"

We made our way upwards along the steep hill above the city and the sea, and stopped for a brief rest at the house of one of our guides. After a moment a bottle of scent appeared, the first of many bottles we were to see during our stay in Turkey. The custom is for a host to pass around a bottle of scent—eau de cologne—from which everyone rubs a few drops on his hands and face to refresh himself. Everyone in our little group perfumed himself—ugh—and then I took a group photograph of Margaret and her new friends. A thirteen-year-old girl was sent to show us the rest of the way.

View from the castle, Alanya

She walked with us until she pointed out the final switchback. We soon scrambled up the last bit of trail, where we met the road leading to the top. We passed a massive gate amid almond and carob trees, which gradually thinned out to cactus plants with sweet fruits. By noon we were at the castle. Around us were giant walls, battlements, old stone foundations, and the ruins of a Byzantine church. I marveled at the construction of the castle and its walls and wondered how the stones were cut and moved to such steep heights. Either slavery was successful or the ancients were clever engineers. Probably both.

From the topmost point of the castle we looked far up a wild coast-line—to the west-northwest—where steep mountains of gray and brown tumbled into a sea brushed with azure and turquoise. To the southeast the foreground of our picture began at the bottom with the serrated walls of the castle; the image moved up to a slim minaret and dome-shaped mosque backed by a crescent of beach and shoreside buildings; the top of the scene ended with a background of bluish mountains frosted with snow.

We stopped for a cool drink at a little shaded place in the castle and then took a taxi partway down the mountain to *centrum,* where we had lunch and a walk among the downtown shops. I made a note to photograph a shoeshine man whose stand was made of solid, brightly polished brass.

Five times each day we heard the wailing call of the muezzin (pro-nounced myoo-EZZ-in), the Islam crier who calls the faithful to prayer from a minaret. Alanya had five or six minarets dotted around the city, and pre-cisely at the same moment, lights suddenly blazed from the needlelike towers, the loudspeakers were switched on, and the air reverberated with shrill, wailing calls to the faithful. Each muezzin must have worn a digital watch.

The next day we looked around the nearby ancient dockyard, a series of five arcaded chambers fifty-five meters long that dated from the days of the Seljuks in 1226. Once squads of shipwrights, soldiers, and slaves had swarmed over the area when fighting galleys were built and serviced and stored. Now we walked below the stone arches and silent chambers by ourselves and tried to imagine the old days. In the last century, according to Captain Denham, three-masted sailing xebecs were constructed in the dockyard.[10]

Whenever we passed a rug shop in Alanya (or elsewhere in Turkey) we stopped and looked at the beautiful hand-loomed rugs displayed in the windows. The window lights were generally kept off to save electricity, but when the proprietor spotted a live prospect the lights would flash on and he would dance out to deliver his sales pitch in German. "Nichts, danke schön," I would reply, speaking my three words of German.

One evening we were invited to the summer house of George McGhee and his wife. George was formerly a U.S. ambassador to Turkey and liked the country so much that he bought and restored an old historic house high

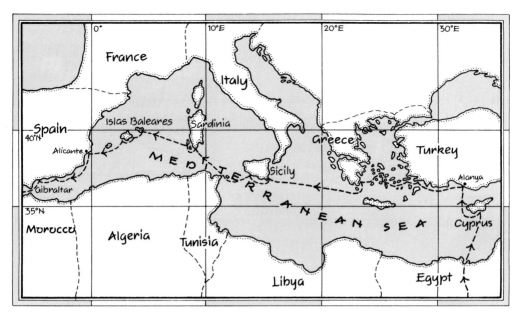

20. The Mediterranean

on the hill toward the castle. The house was full of tall rooms with fine
paneling and heavy wall carvings of dark cedar, and had been turned into
a sort of museum with a collection of Greek columns, old doors (1697), and
so on. Even a tiny swimming pool and a marble desk. The house was pleasant,
but made me think of the jumble of a museum storeroom. We sat on
uncomfortable low divans in the harem room and looked out at a splendid
view to the east (*Whisper* was far below). We met two prominent Turkish
lawyers, one of whom spoke excellent English. Ahmet Tokus, a charming
fellow, had been a member of parliament and matter-of-factly told us about
being imprisoned for two and a half years for political reasons ("It gave me
a chance to learn German and to do some reading").

The next day Margaret spied a pretty cotton dress hanging outside a
tailor's shop. When we stopped to look at it the tailor came out and began
to extol the fine cotton fabric, the nice design, good workmanship, etc.
Margaret held the dress around her. It was much too large. OK for a portly
figure but not for her slim body. Margaret shook her head. The tailor looked
glum.

"For big woman," he gestured, shaking his head. He would wait until
someone bought it. Then he would sew up another.

"Why don't you make me a smaller one?" she gestured at the puzzled
tailor. "Yes, yes, like this one, only smaller. I'll come back tomorrow," she
said, motioning to her watch and going round and round with a forefinger.
The tailor looked puzzled, then his blank face slowly brightened. He smiled
and agreed.

"You had better measure me now," said Margaret, grabbing hold and jiggling the end of the tailor's tape around his neck. The tailor recoiled slightly. He was obviously not used to such an aggressive customer, but he agreed and measured Margaret carefully and wrote down the figures. I asked the tailor his name. He whipped out a business card that read Tevfik Uslu.

"Tevfik," I said, "how much is the dress going to cost?"

He calculated on the back of a piece of paper and wrote 2,200 lira, about U.S. $6. We looked up the word for "tomorrow" in our dictionary.

"Yarin?" I said.

The tailor nodded.

When we neared the shop the following afternoon Tevfik rushed out waving the dress and beaming. Margaret went into the shop and tried it on. The fit was perfect. We paid Tevfik and left after much handshaking and many smiles.

The next morning I got the ship's clearance from the harbormaster, whose office was in the middle of town but so hard to find that I had to get a policeman to lead me. Finally I spotted the sign "Liman Baskanligi" in a small office building and made my way up the steps to the Central Marine Authority. After I showed *Whisper*'s papers, my clearance from Cyprus, produced a crew list, and bought a few tax stamps, he gave me a formal document that was valid for all Turkish ports.

21. Turkey

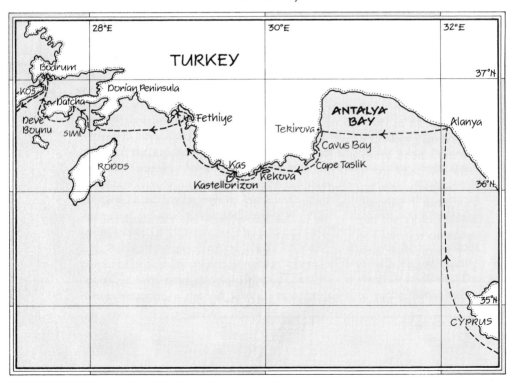

We had done a bag of laundry and bought a few fresh stores, including some wonderful Turkish honey. I tried to photograph a man outside a music store who was singing and playing an enormous Turkish guitar. When I got near, however, he stopped playing and tried to sell me the guitar. I could not make him understand that I merely wanted to photograph him playing and singing. We all had a lot of laughs. But I got no picture.

Alanya had been a good stop. We liked the Turks, and they were curious about us. We found the country sprinkled with the relics of a dozen different centuries and peoples, something we were to see again and again along the coast. The region had been overrun by wave after wave of foreigners—Greeks, Lydians, Romans, Seljuks, Armenians, Venetians, Genoese, Lusignans, and others. Some of the races were strange to me and had names that I could scarcely pronounce. Each of the invaders had left a different archeological fingerprint, and a visitor finally ran up against the unanswerable question: Who was the invader? Who was the native? And when the soldier took a native wife, to whom did the child owe his allegiance? Now as we sailed westward along the coast we were to see traces of all these peoples in mixed-up, confused ruins.

On May 4th we hoisted our sails in the shadow of Alanya's castle and headed for the old Roman settlement of Tekirova on the west side of Antalya Bay. The southwest wind was light—it sometimes stopped altogether—and the seventy-mile trip to the west took twenty-eight hours. I began to understand the advantages of galleys in these waters.

Several small land birds flew on board. They were purplish with a white breast, a long V-shaped tail, and a rust-colored bib around the throat and face. The birds were quite tame, did a lot of noisy twittering, and hopped all over the yacht. They eventually went below into the cabin. Margaret got out the bird books and decided that we had been invaded by barn swallows.

From various descriptions I thought that Tekirova (once called Phaselis and described by Strabo as "a noteworthy city with three harbors and a lake") was good-sized, but in reality the place was quite small, and its headland peninsula measured only three hundred meters in length. I had a detailed chart, but I didn't pay enough attention to the scale, and I spent two hours searching for a peninsula and cliffs much larger than the real thing. At first we anchored at the northeast side near the old boat harbor, but the bottom was stony, we swung close to rocks and old moles, and there was some swell. We moved to the southwest anchorage, which was better. The next morning we went ashore.

We climbed up a low headland above the east end of a gravel beach and did a lot of scrambling over tumbled-down walls before we located the main street of the Roman town. We passed fallen stone pillars and stepped across old foundations. The area was a bit hazardous, and I was afraid of falling into a cistern or an old well. We found a small amphitheater, the ruins of a temple, and the ancient city gate which led into the main street, where we saw a collection of collapsed arches and building foundations, some with Greek inscriptions. Nearby was a raised Roman aqueduct partially hidden in a pine forest. The circular boat harbor was mostly silted up. I wondered what sort of vessels had used the place. Had they been built there? What sizes had they been? Since the best anchorage and main gate were on the other side of the town, I speculated that larger vessels might have used the same southwest anchorage that we did. Perhaps fishing boats had worked from the smaller harbor.

This was my first encounter with such an old untouched city. I kept thinking that I would bump into a man in a toga or hear laughter around a corner, but the place was absolutely deserted, soundless, and a bit spooky. Why had Tekirova been abandoned? War? Malaria? New trade patterns? Another frontier? A changing civilization? Certainly the place was too well built to have been a temporary settlement. The ruins were full of riddles. I began to understand the fascination of archeology.[11]

That afternoon we pushed on to Cavus Bay, fifteen miles to the south, where we found a sandy beach and a good anchorage next to a solitary British yacht from Lowestoft named *Moon & Stars,* a name I liked. Her owners, Roy and Vivienne Tremaine, came over to ask about Alanya. The Tremaines had wintered at Kusadasi, farther west, where fifty-five people had been on various yachts and where each foreigner had been required to renew his passport every ninety days, which meant leaving and reentering Turkey. Later we all went ashore and had a simple meal of omelets and fish at a little taverna on the beach. We ate at one table, and four fishermen ate at the next. When they left we all stood and shook hands and traded smiles. They wished us good sailing. We wished the fishermen big catches.

After dinner we had a drink of Samos brandy aboard *Moon & Stars* and learned a little about the Tremaines. Roy was forty-five, a computer engineer who had worked in East Africa where he had met Vivienne. They had returned to England and built a house with their own hands but decided it was not the life for them and sold out. They had become fascinated with sailing and bought a partially constructed Sadler 32 sloop which they finished themselves (and did a good job). Vivienne was young, enthusiastic, and keen to cross the Atlantic ("Imagine doing that in your own boat!"). It was a pleasant evening.

Early the next morning I cranked up the anchor, winched up the sails, and we sailed out of Antalya Bay with a sixteen-knot wind from the south. By 0825 we had rounded Cape Taslik and headed west at a good clip. Cape Taslik (also known as Cape Gelidonya) is the place where George Bass led a University of Pennsylvania expedition that dove on a Bronze Age wreck in 1960. The old Syrian trading vessel—which ranged as far south as Egypt, west to Crete, and along the coast of Asia Minor—sank about 1200 B.C. while

Castle walls and sea, Kekova

carrying a load of copper ingots from Cyprus. Most of the vessel was destroyed by shipworms long ago, but fragmentary wooden pieces showed that the ship was built of cypress planks shaped with an adze and edge-fastened with wooden pegs—a construction scheme described by Homer. Internal framing was put in later. This 3,200-year-old wreck is the oldest ever found.[12]

When we got past the Cape Taslik lighthouse and away from big Antalya Bay to the east, our wind faded away. An hour later a light northwest wind commenced, and we made our way west along the coast a mile or two offshore, past the town of Finike. A Turkish coasting vessel chugged by us going east, and by 1100 we had picked up a sea breeze from the south-southeast. We set the running rig by easing the mainsail to star-board and holding a headsail out to port with a spinnaker pole.

By 1500 we were sailing nicely in the wide channel between the four-mile-long island of Kekova and the mainland. We had a storybook castle to starboard, and ancient stone walls and foundations along the shore of the island to port. We anchored at the northwest corner of the island at a place called Xera Cove, but it was small and we didn't have swinging room, so we ran a stern line ashore. Not a soul was in sight. All around the cove the old shoreside foundations and walls lay a meter or two underwater, which

Turkish ferry girl, Kekova

showed that the island—or at least the cove—had dropped in height during the last thousand years. It was hot, the island was dry, and we enjoyed a swim in the deep blue Mediterranean.

The next day we sailed across to the mainland, where there was a little settlement of houses with red tile roofs below the castle. Kekova was a remote part of Turkey and did not appear to be connected to the main road system at all. We went ashore and took a short walk up to the castle for the view. Bright red poppies grew everywhere. We met a few women tending goats or weaving among the lower walls of the castle. Even in summer the women were always fully dressed in long skirts and petticoats, often with a long-sleeved blouse, a short-sleeved jumper, and a head scarf. Sometimes they wore loose trousers, a skirt, a blouse, and an apron. The peasant women were clean and tidy, and their clothes were always fresh and neat.

In the afternoon we sailed to a small inner bay behind the castle to the northwest and anchored near a few houses. At once a man and boy came out in a rowing boat and asked us to honor them by having dinner at their restaurant. We had the feeling that they desperately needed our business, so we did as requested and had a modest meal of potatoes and fish at a tiny quayside place. Dotted around the countryside were Lycian stone burial vaults—large, formally carved rectangular stone boxes with steeply arched tops, incised on each side with formal decorations. The Lycian civilization must have been quite advanced to have had the time and money to have buried its dead so elegantly.

The next day we sailed back to Xera Cove on Kekova Island and went ashore for a hike to look at ruins at the west end of the island. We returned to Xera Cove, where we had a quiet lunch in the shadow of an old Byzantine church that was in the last stage of collapse. In the afternoon a local boatman brought a wealthy Turkish couple from Istanbul across for a swim. The woman was extremely attractive, and when she was ready to swim she stepped out of a wrap to reveal slim legs, a narrow waist, and a pair of rising beauties fit for a king—all accented by the briefest of bikini swimsuits. It was a standard of Moslem undress I had not seen in Turkey. The boatman—clad in a long-sleeved shirt and trousers and a cap—pretended to be busy with his outboard motor, but when I caught his eye and discreetly nodded toward the woman and winked, his eyes twinkled, he gave a little gasp, and his white teeth sparkled with a smile of perfect understanding.

On May 16th we pushed westward another twenty miles and slipped into Kas, in the shadow of Asas Mountain, where we dropped an anchor, ran a line ashore, and pulled alongside half a dozen other yachts. Kas had a tiny harbor built around an ancient Greek mole that had been built up and extended. We saw more tourists and activity in the setting of a delightful waterfront village.

Peasant women, Kekova

Unfortunately our stay was not delightful. I went to the customs office with the papers from Alanya. Nothing was right. "Where is your paper from customs?" I was asked again and again. I explained that I got none from customs and had only followed directions (crew lists, visits to the police, doctor, harbormaster, tax stamps, and so forth). My English was translated by the local schoolmaster, who had been specially summoned (by now I was in a smoke-filled room with four worried men and a nervous secretary).

"Why not telephone Alanya?" I suggested. The chief, a small, slow-moving man with a star on the arm of his uniform (henceforth known as Star-arm), did not like telephones but agreed to call at my expense (680 lira). He reported that the Alanya customs people were out on a ship. Star-arm distrusted telephones and refused to call a second time.

The next day I was summoned ashore to the customs office. "Why don't you sail back to Alanya for the paper?" said Star-arm in a brilliant burst of logic. "Otherwise we'll have to fine you."

Plainly the men did not believe my story. Yet I *had* seen customs. How else could I have been sent to the police and doctor, whose documents I had given to the customs people? What about the clearance from the Alanya harbormaster? I was queried about the difference in dates between the visit to the harbormaster (May 9th) and my passport stamp (May 4th).

"In Turkey you must visit all the offices the first day," said Star-arm.

It seemed that different parts of Turkey had different rules. I resented the Kas men's not believing me. I was told (in another smoke-filled meeting with more cups of sweet tea) that I could be fined forty thousand lira.

"If you pay the forty thousand you can claim a refund from Ankara if you can prove your innocence," said Star-arm. He said that since I was a bad person, they were going to search the yacht. One of the men went aboard *Whisper* and spent hours looking for anything illegal. The customs man got wildly excited about a CO_2 fire extinguisher that he was sure was a scuba-diving tank. He spent a long time putting seals on the guns and counting *Whisper*'s bullets. The totals were carefully written in my passport, which, like Margaret's, had been confiscated.

I was fined ten thousand lira (twenty-nine dollars) for not having the mythical customs paper. I could have gotten the U.S. embassy involved, but it didn't seem worth the trouble. I had tried to remain law-abiding. I could have slipped Star-arm a ten- or twenty-dollar bill, but I think that if he had wanted money for himself he wouldn't have involved the whole office and the schoolteacher. At least I don't think so. Would he have arrested me for trying to bribe him? I thought he was just dull enough to try it. Maybe he was looking for a second star on his sleeve, which required perfect paperwork or a jailed transgressor.

I wondered why Star-arm simply didn't issue me a customs paper if it was so important. It was obvious that I wasn't smuggling anything. I was merely a sailor who had gone afoul of paperwork demands. I don't know what Star-arm's wages, those of his associates, his secretary, the schoolmaster, and the tea bill totaled, but they must have amounted to more than the twenty-nine-dollar fine. Star-arm's narrow view of the world was certainly different from mine. . . .

I had had enough of Star-arm and the smoke-filled Turkish offices. When he issued me the papers he claimed were necessary, we sailed immediately. The Greek island of Kastellorizon was only four miles away.

. . . .

CHAPTER TWENTY

The Isolated Island

Suddenly we were in a different country. Or were we? Tiny Kastellorizon is the southernmost of the Greek Dodecanese (which means twelve) Islands. Despite the name, there are some twenty small islands in this southeast Aegean group (Kálimnos, Sími, Kós, and so on). Kastellorizon was long under Turkish rule and was once the capital of the entire adjacent Turkish province on the mainland. At that time the island had a population of 20,000, a big firewood-trading business with Egypt and Syria, three hundred sailing vessels, and enough shipping to justify European consuls. However, the Turkish-Italian war of 1912—which gave control of the Dodecanese Islands to Italy—ended the island's relationship with Turkey and its general seafaring position. At about the same time, sailing ships were being put out of business by steam. During World War I, according to one source, the British bought what was left of the ragtag Kastellorizon fleet for use in the Dardanelles campaign and paid the islanders in gold sovereigns. With the ships gone and business finished, Kastellorizon's importance collapsed.

In World War II the Italians—who patrolled with high-speed torpedo boats from well-fortified bases—occasionally scrapped with the British from Lebanon and Cyprus, and Italian and German air reconnaissance from Ródos was troublesome to the English. When the Italians surrendered in 1943, British forces occupied some of the islands. However, the Germans took over the Italians' role and, in a series of sharp clashes and bombing raids (two

British destroyers were sunk at Léros in one), forced the British out of some of their new bases. The Greek residents suffered greatly during World War II and barely kept ahead of starvation. Life didn't get back to normal until 1947, when control of the Dodecanese was given to Athens because most of the residents were Greek.

When we sailed into Kastellorizon we saw an isolated orphan. It was far from the Greek islands to the north, and only help from Athens kept the child alive. A free ferry ran from Ródos (sixty-nine miles), and the government had built a new tourist hotel (mostly empty). The Greeks were working to improve the desalinization plant (fresh water was a problem), and supplies arrived on the weekly navy barge (the green hills and inexpensive food of Turkey were nearby, but things had to come from Greece). Pride exacted a terrible price.

The island itself is three miles long and one mile wide, an arid and rocky place with heights up to 250 meters. The attraction is the harbor on the northeast side. As I said earlier, Kastellorizon was once a thriving trading center. I have an old photograph taken about 1910 or so that shows fifty large and small sailing ships in the port, and hundreds of two-story houses, each with a high formal front with six tall, arched windows and a tiled roof peaked in the middle. The houses ringed the U-shaped harbor right down to the waterside road and then ranged up the slope behind in close rows five to ten houses deep. The town has an elaborate church built with Corinthian columns brought from afar, and a large schoolhouse that is scarcely used today. In July 1944, when British forces controlled the place, a serious fire broke out and gutted many of the houses. During the same era a great deal of damage was done by German planes in a bombardment of exceptional severity.

To sum up: Havoc from the Turkish-Italian war and two world wars, the loss of trade, and poverty drove most of the people away. In seventy-five years a bustling population of 20,000 plummeted to only 180 people. Many had migrated to Australia and elsewhere. From a distance the houses looked attractive, but when you walked around the port you soon realized that most of them were mere shells. It was a skeleton city with a ghost population.[13]

Yet we had a marvelous time. We eased in under a small jib and dropped a stern anchor two boat lengths from the quayside and tied *Whisper's* bow to the harbor wall. Seven other yachts were similarly moored. While I was adjusting the lines I heard a reedy voice say hello. It was Frank Rosenow, an artist friend from Sweden who was next to us in *Moth,* a nine-meter sloop designed by Pelle Petersen. Frank was sailing with two girls, and in company with another Swedish yacht whose captain, Per Albihn, had three more Swedes as crew.

It was Per's birthday, so we had a grand party at a little Greek restaurant on the quayside with many bottles of wine, salad, octopus, fried potatoes,

Grandmother knitting

meat, a whole baked fish, coffee, and brandy. I sat between two Swedish girls. Rita was very pretty, about thirty-two, with a slim figure. She dressed well and used a trace of blue eye shadow, which accented her eyes. She had made a study of Karen Blixen for a teaching degree but had been unable to get a job. She bragged that she was constantly falling in and out of love, and most of her life seemed to have been spent studying bedroom ceilings. She yammered on and on about this boyfriend and that fellow, a marriage, trouble with this man who was no good, etc. After ten minutes I had had enough, but it went on for the whole evening. My other companion, Lotta Dale, was a large, sturdy woman who was good-natured, pleasant, and not such a talker. Lotta was an artist and promised to show me her drawing book. The food and wine kept coming, and we toasted Per and his birthday. Some Greek sailors from the supply barge were at the table next to us. They had emptied several bottles of ouzo, which had set their heads on fire, and they were enjoying traditional dances and going round and round with one another. After each dance they had another drink and then smashed their little glasses on the paving stones while the restaurant proprietor kept tally on a blackboard. Finally the cook marched in with a birthday cake, and we all stood and sang good wishes for our Swedish friend.

Rita said that her current boyfriend—who was away—was an expert windsurfer and had recently sailed from Kastellorizon to Kas, a distance of four miles. This was quite a feat on a tiny windsurfer, and the fellow reckoned that he would be in all the Turkish newspapers. He made the newspapers all right, but the story was not as he expected. He was arrested and thrown in jail when he arrived in Kas because he had no ship's papers for the windsurfer. The Swedish sailor finally got a call through to his embassy and was released, but there had been a lot of trouble. "The customs man in Kas was unreasonable," said Rita. *"He was a small fellow who walked slowly and had a star on the sleeve of his uniform. . . ."*

The next day a whole gang from the waterfront sailed around to the south side of Kastellorizon where there was a wonderful blue grotto. It was a large, high-domed cave whose entrance was only a meter or so above the level of the sea. We swam or took a dinghy inside and suddenly were in an enormous room with strange acoustics, and water the color of transparent blue ink, a miraculous blue that I'd not seen before.

That evening a French yacht came into the harbor with a woman on board who had dislocated her shoulder and was in great pain. The woman had been on deck and had stepped through an open hatch. There was a doctor on Kastellorizon, but he had no suitable drugs. The woman's shoulder muscles had tightened, and all the doctor could do was to twist and turn the poor woman's arm and cause her even more anguish. I must say the woman had grit, because she never uttered a sound while the doctor worked on her, though it was obvious that her shoulder hurt like hell.

I hurried around to all the yachts to see if any doctors had come in. "Try the French one over there," I was told. "There are three doctors on board." I rushed over to the yacht. Unfortunately one doctor was a dentist. The second was a psychologist. The third was a professor of zoology. Nevertheless, they came up with an injectable muscle relaxant.

In the meantime someone in the village had summoned the local healing woman, an old crone, a wisp of a thing with wrinkled and parched skin, with most of her teeth gone, and dressed in typical widow's black. She walked and moved swiftly with kind of birdlike grace.

At once she stroked the Frenchwoman's brow, uttered some words in Greek, and produced two bottles from her bag. One had ouzo, the Greek national drink, an anise-flavored liqueur. The second bottle held ordinary olive oil. The healing woman mixed the two in a bowl, dipped her hands in the mixture, and began to massage the woman's shoulder. While this was going on, the doctor injected the muscle relaxant from the French yacht. The old woman's hands were strong, and although the patient cringed with pain and felt every finger, the French woman knew the Greek healing woman was trying to help her. After fifteen minutes of massage (and a terrible mess from the oil and ouzo), the healing woman nodded to the doctor, who took over and used his expertise (now that the muscles were relaxed) to snap the arm back into its socket. Meanwhile the little woman in black had disappeared. The ordeal was suddenly over. The little crowd breathed a collective sigh of relief!

On May 20th we sailed for Fethiye, fifty-five miles to the northwest. We were back in Turkish waters, but had proper papers (we hoped). In any case, since Fethiye Bay was twelve miles across and had dozens of isolated anchorages, we didn't think we'd see any officials. We anchored in a protected cove at Tersane Island and soon were ashore looking at old ruins. Again we saw the local peasants who were dignified and respectful and who paid little attention to us. They kept to themselves and generally engaged in trifling farm chores or tended a few goats. Sometimes the local farmers lived in ancient buildings (or parts thereof) that had been turned into small and miserable dwellings. In no way were these people comparable to the races of old who had been advanced enough to have constructed elegant buildings, fine streets, important harbors, and ornate tombs. People with literature, fleets of ships, armies, and highly developed political structures. I wondered whether it was possible for a race to become too highly developed, so far advanced that it created its own destruction. Maybe the peasants we were seeing had the best life after all. I wondered. . . . My travels were turning me into a keyhole philosopher.

One afternoon—in company with Frank Rosenow and Lotta Dale on *Moth,* which had also gone north—we sailed to a small cove on the east side of Skopea Bay on the northeast side of Hurma Mountain where there was a natural spring we had read about. We had begun to see more yachts and had even heard about fleets of charter vessels. As Frank and I sailed in, playing light puffs of wind and using every trick to keep going, I saw a mast. Then another mast. Imagine my surprise when I rounded a point of land and saw ten identical new ten-meter fiberglass charter yachts precisely lined up in a row, all the sterns facing outward from a beach. At the end was an eleventh boat (probably the leader) with her bow outward, but exactly in line and parallel to the others. A big cookout was underway on the beach, and we could hear sounds of music.

Frank and I sailed to the other side of the bay—where in fact the spring was—and anchored by ourselves. Our little cove was lovely. The hills were heavily wooded with two-leaved pines, and climbed steeply above a rocky beach whose northwest side was covered with oleander bushes in full bloom. Never have I been in an anchorage where I could see hundreds of clusters of pink flowers that must have extended for forty meters. At the south end of the little anchorage was the spring—a good place to fill our water tanks.

Moth tied alongside *Whisper* for the night. We were all tired from a day of wind and sun and had a scratch supper of wine, cheese, nuts, and bread. While the four of us sat in *Whisper*'s cockpit eating, we suddenly heard a marvelous flute sound through the trees. The melody was plaintive, in a minor key, and seemed magical, almost unbelievable. We listened, our breathing stopped to catch every note. At first we couldn't tell where the flute was. A little later two boys hove into view, each blowing on a small pipe. The effect from the pink flowers, the dark pines, the high rocky walls (some with ancient tombs), the still water, and the cool air was enchanting.

After visiting four anchorages in Fethiye Bay and saying goodbye to *Moth,* we headed for Loryma, fifty-five miles to the west.

[From my journal] May 22nd. 0950. Off Kurtoglu Point. I am always amazed at how novice sailors hug coastlines. It's almost as if they feel safer with one foot on land. I can see three charter boats inshore right off the cliffs where the wind is sure to be fluky or nonexistent and there's a good chance of rocks. All three are in great danger if their engines quit. Sailing so close to land—unless there's a reason for it—is foolish. Not only are the boat drivers burdened with noise, fumes, and the cost of expensive fuel, but they have lost the pleasure and delight of sailing. We are two or three miles offshore and going along nicely with full sail and a light wind from the south.

At 1100 Ródos (ΠΟΔΟΣ) was clearly visible on the port bow, twenty-eight miles away, a big island with high mountains. The sky was hazy, but we had superb visibility, and in the early afternoon we watched a distant oil tanker creep eastward and saw a few yachts in the distance. We could clearly make out two rows of mountains on Ródos. Our headland destination lay on the horizon far ahead, a dark insect recumbent on the

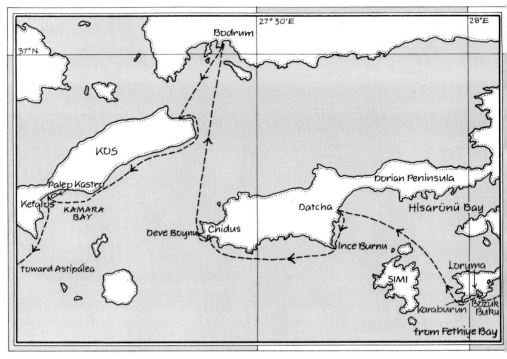

22. Loryma to Kos

water. At 1500 we set our running rig before a southeast wind. The sky had become dark gray, and we heard the rumbling of ships' engines in the south. At 1630 the wind died and then came suddenly from the northeast at sixteen knots. We scooted along with whitecaps behind us, passed several small islands, and by 1800, near the mouth of Bozuk Buku in gusty winds, dropped our genoa and headed into the bay. The headland was guarded by grandiose stone walls, and ruins lay all around us. Closer to the anchorage we handed the mainsail, rounded up under the staysail, and anchored in six fathoms with twenty-five fathoms of chain in a spacious anchorage with four other yachts. Just before dark a small boat came out and three swarthy men offered to sell us honey, fish, and sweet herbs for tea.

The bay was large and open and beautiful, with scattered scrub trees, and the sail from Fethiye had been wildly exciting. Somehow the presence of Ródos and the great Turkish headlands gave me a feeling of bigness and space. Just above us were the ruins of Loryma, and on a ridge to the north were the remains of a fortress. Ancient Phoenix was only four miles away. We spent a day walking among the wildflowers around the colossal entrance walls (how did they ever move those huge blocks of stone, cut them slightly convex, smooth the edges so perfectly, and fit the blocks with such precision?). We thought about the day almost 2,400 years earlier when ninety triremes of the Athenians and Persians (led by Conon and Pharnabazus) had

defeated eighty-five triremes of the Spartans (led by Peisander). The history
of the place was so complex that I reckoned I'd need a year of reading to
sort it out.

I wondered about the general conduct of war in the old days. So many
fortified places could have been easily bypassed, isolated by siege, and left
to languish. Maybe the idea was to meet and take the enemy, not to bypass
him and capture the land.

One problem with sailing in this area was that every prominent place
had three or four names. The next day, for example, we sailed around
Karaburun, which was also known as Cape Alupo, Kinossima, or Alobi
Burnu. The names on small-scale Admiralty chart 1604 were completely
different from the names on large-scale Admiralty chart 236, which covered
some of the same places. The authors of the various pilot books could have
made life simpler for sailors by cross-referencing the confusing names. Even
the authors of the Admiralty pilot books got rattled at times, judging by the
bulky corrections.

We sailed north and east past the big Greek island of Simi into Hisarönü
Bay, an enormous, peaceful area with at least twenty-five sheltered harbors.
We stopped for supplies at Datcha, anchored behind Ince Burnu until a fresh
headwind died away, and sailed sixteen miles west to Deve Boynu (often
called Cape Krio), the easternmost headland of the great Dorian Peninsula.

Immediately behind the lighthouse hill was the site of ancient Cnidus,
which had a small harbor on each side of the headland. We sailed between
ancient moles into the southeast harbor, where we dropped a stern anchor
on a bottom of hard rock and carried a long bow line to a tree on the western
shore. There were a dozen yachts and tourist launches in the little harbor;
all depended on the prevailing northwest wind and bow lines ashore to hold
them in place. We went on land for a scramble up the hills and made a tour
of the ruins. I showed my sailing papers to the local policeman, who endorsed
them and produced the usual bottle of scent. We all rubbed a few drops on
our hands and nodded and smiled.

Cnidus was the ancient Greek city of Caria. It was one of the cities of
the Dorian Hexapolis and sought to retain its independence but fell (in 540
B.C.) under Persian rule. It had a large trade, particularly in wine, and was
noted for its medical school. One of the most famous statues of the ancient
world, a nude Aphrodite by Praxiteles, was displayed in Cnidus.

A Greek author of late antiquity [writes Gören Schildt] . . . together with two
companions . . . went ashore to see the renowned work of art while their ship waited
for a favorable wind. . . . The little chapel was open at the front, so that the visitors
could see the goddess, who, unlike all older cult images of her, was portrayed naked
at the moment she laid aside her mantle to step down into the ritual bath. At this
sight the three men so lost their self-control that one of the author's friends, who
was known to abhor the very sight of women, stood as though struck by lightning,

Roman ruins, Ephesus

while the other ran forward and, deaf to the protests of the temple servant, flung his arms round the lovely goddess and kissed her over and over again. . . . Quite overwhelmed, and hotly debating the goddess's merits, the three friends could not tear themselves away from her until the captain of their ship threatened to sail without them.[14]

Cnidus retained its importance in Roman times and is mentioned twice in the Bible. It's unfortunate that the abandoned city has long been a quarry for everyone from castle-building knights to harbor engineers. The city was still in reasonable condition two hundred years ago, but the stone plundering accelerated, and Cnidus has been largely carted away piece by piece.

During the last few days we had begun to see Turkish tourist yachts—often called *caïques* (pronounced cah-EEKS)—which were all roughly the same: a fifteen-meter heavy displacement hull with lots of beam, high free-board, and exaggerated sheer; a large varnished coachroof, doghouse, and windshield complex; a hefty six-cylinder diesel engine; toothpick-sized varnished spars and bowsprit; a cut-down ketch rig; vestigial sails; a huge awning, generally fixed, which precluded use of the mizzen; and finally, an enormous varnished gangplank that stuck out over the stern like a goat's tail.

The Turkish yachts never sailed, but motored at high speed and towed a large dinghy. Usually there were three men in the crew: the captain, who was in charge of motoring and dealing with a heavy fisherman anchor and chain, a man who varnished and cooked, and a boy. The caïques were popular with European tourists, and the business was highly developed. The captains were friendly and competent, but ran a motorboat operation and had no concept of sailing maneuvers. On our last night at Cnidus, two caïques moored near us.

[From my log] May 29th. Early last evening a group of French tourists on a big caïque had a terrific party. They pulled one cork after another, and soon the whole vessel was alive with six or eight couples madly dancing and shouting and twisting and jumping to blaring recorded music while the crewmen clapped their hands to the rhythm. The Turkish captain began to flash the bright deck lights off and on disco style. First we saw gyrating dancers. Then complete blackness. Then the dancers again. During the blackness the dancers moved a little so that when the lights flashed on, the positions of the dancers' arms and legs and heads had changed slightly. The next effect was a series of staccato, jerky images—like an old-time motion picture. A kind of frieze that was sensual and frenzied. It was fun to see a group of people having such a good time. I wonder what the ancient Greeks would have thought if they'd watched this happening in their harbor? Lights they'd never seen and music they'd never heard. I suppose the Greeks had similar revelries.

Our last stop in Turkey was the modern city of Bodrum, once called Helicarnassus, which was twenty-four miles north of Cnidus. The closer we sailed to Bodrum the more Turkish yachts we saw. When we passed the great castle on the east bluff above the entrance to the port we looked at rows and rows of caïques with bluff bows and varnished spars. Instead of the triremes of old, it was caïques. Tourism was certainly more profitable than war. Why fight your enemies? Entertain them and get their money!

After we anchored in the busy bay I rowed ashore with my papers. As soon as the customs man (one star) looked at my documents he began to mutter in Turkish and shake his head. He was obviously swearing. A few minutes later a second customs man (two stars) appeared. He read over the papers and began to swear and shake his head. The Bodrum officials said that the actions of the men at Alanya and Kas were all wrong.

"We will have to inspect the ship," said Two-star.

I was told to take *Whisper* to the Bodrum marina, which turned out to be a small, neat, well-designed complex with modern yachts from all over the world. The two customs men looked over the yacht (especially the seals on the weapons, the ship's documents, and our passports) and said that I would have to buy a green transit card for ten U.S. dollars. I did this and it was duly stamped and signed.

"Hello," said the man in the office. "Now you are ready to enter Turkey."

"Goodbye," I said. "Now I am ready to leave Turkey."

. . . .

CHAPTER TWENTY-ONE

Tourist Dodging in Greece

*F*rom Bodrum to the big Greek island of Kos is only eleven miles, but at last we had begun to head west. More than twenty years earlier I had sailed into the harbor of Kos on another vessel. At that time I was only learning to sail, and I had watched a small white yacht named *Dorothea* come gracefully into the small harbor and tack back and forth. Her captain, Peter Tangvald, looked the place over and decided where he wanted to anchor and tie ashore. Peter then dropped his headsails, steered slowly toward the shore under his mainsail alone, and, when he was about three boat lengths from shore, tossed over a stern anchor. *Dorothea* slowly moved toward the quay, and when close enough, Simonne, Peter's crew, heaved a line ashore which a fisherman made fast. Simonne and Peter then adjusted the bow and anchor lines until the vessel was secure but close enough to the quay so that the two sailors could step on shore. Voilà! It was a miracle to handle a small vessel with such expertise. I vowed to learn to do it myself and one day to return to Kos and see if I could duplicate Peter's technique.

Now almost a quarter of a century later, I steered *Whisper* past the thirteenth-century castle of the Knights of St. John at the harbor entrance. The simple Greek harbor that I remembered from long before seemed full of large and small vessels. Fortunately no big ferries or tourist ships were

Windmill grinding corn, Kefalos, Kos

coming or going. We dropped the genoa and continued with the staysail and main. We then tacked in the middle of the harbor to look things over and handed the mainsail. Finally, we glided toward the south quay under half the staysail. I dropped a stern anchor and kept half a turn of the warp around a cleat while I steered. Just before we got to the quay I belayed the anchor line, which dug in the anchor and stopped us only a meter or two from the stone wall. Margaret tossed a bow line to someone who made fast to a bollard on shore. Marvelous! I had satisfied my wish and had given some entertainment to a little crowd on shore who were sure we would come to grief, but who smiled approvingly after we had made it.

Our entering formalities were easy. Yachts were common in Greece, brought money and tourists, and were welcome. I cleared into Greece and got a paper that was good for all ports and merely required an endorsement at each stop.

The island of Kos is twenty-four miles long and five miles wide. Most of the tourist action is in the harbor and surrounding town which has the same name. On the earlier visit I had seen two yachts and a lot of local fishing boats, some of which had used cotton sails. The port was quiet and sleepy, and children played along the edges. A little boatyard and primitive marine ways operated in the shadow of the great castle. Fishing nets were everywhere. There was still a lot of talk about World War II, and we met a Greek who had flown a Spitfire against the Germans.

Now it was all different. I counted thirty-three yachts, twenty-four fishing boats (with diesel engines), two fifteen-meter navy tenders, and half a dozen good-sized ferryboats. A cargo freighter was unloading in the entrance to the port, and a large cruise ship lay anchored just outside with its tenders running back and forth to shore. Masses of blond tourists were everywhere. What I remembered as quaint quayside restaurants had become vast drinking establishments with hundreds of chairs and tables set in long rows. Platoons of waiters served the tourists, who came mostly from Germany and Sweden. The newspaper stands featured *Der Spiegel* and *Rheinischer Merkur* from Germany, and the *Skånska Dagbladet* and *Nordvastra Skånes Tidningar* from Sweden. The prices of everything were high.

The people were on holiday, and the place appeared to be a vast mating ground. Drinking and dancing seemed much more important than looking at Greek ruins, a moldering castle, or an ancient medical school. Who wanted to meet a local family or learn a few words of Greek or visit a Greek artist or potter? A new generation cared nothing about wars of the past. I felt old and tired and cynical.

The next morning we fled to the countryside. We rented bicycles and went off for a day of cycling along the open roads on the east and south coasts. We returned after a wonderful day of fresh air and peddling. The

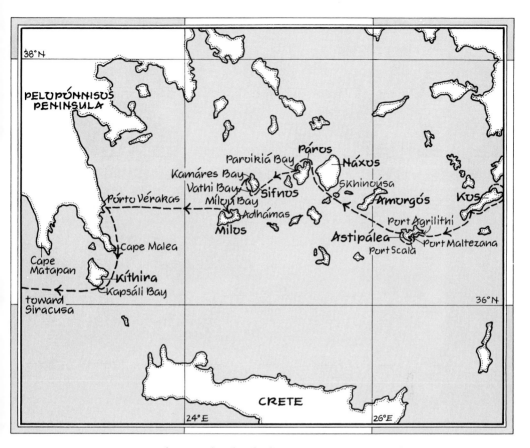

On the map:

38°N

PELOPÓNNISOS PENINSULA

Paroikiá Bay
Páros
Kamáres Bay
Náxos
Vathi Bay
Skhinoúsa
Milon Bay
Sifnos
Pórto Vérakas
Amorgós
Kos
Adhámas
Port Agrilithi
Milos
Astipálea
Port Maltezana
Cape Malea
Port Scala
Cape Matapan
Kíthira
Kapsáli Bay
toward Siracusa

36°N

24°E   26°E

CRETE

23. The Greek islands (Kos to Cape Matapan)

following day we cycled out to the Asklepeion, the ancient healing center, based on the work of Hippocrates, the founder of modern medicine. The ruins were originally Greek, but were added to by the Romans and partially restored by the Italians. The site was beautiful, with a view over the port to the harbor.[15]

When we returned to *Whisper* I was horrified to find newly arrived Turkish tourist yachts jammed against both sides of our vessel. The Turkish captains had laid their anchor cables across ours, and it looked as if someone had simply moved us—anchor and all—to a less desirable place. A north wind was coming up, and with a slack anchor cable, trouble looked likely. We immediately put our dinghy in the water and laid out a second anchor, but the wind continued to rise and we began to feel a swell that rolled in through the recently widened port entrance. In a little while the Turkish caïques were pressing hard against *Whisper*'s hull. We pulled ourselves off the quay a little to get clear. The meltemi—the vigorous summer wind that

Children, Kos Harbor

blows from the north, generally each day about noon—continued to increase, and all sixty-five vessels in the harbor had a miserable night of anchoring, re-anchoring, and fending off each other.

At first light the next morning we got out of Kos Harbor and sailed south around the east end of the island and then west along the south coast in the lee of the high land. The water was smooth, but squalls knifed down the green slopes of the mountains. With a second reef in the mainsail and the staysail we had a brisk sail westward for twenty miles. We anchored in white sand in Kamara Bay just west of tiny Paleo Kastro Island. The little islet had a tiny white church with a blue door and a blue bell at one side. On the mainland to the north we saw the usual ancient ruins.

Ashore to the west of us was a Club Mediterranée hotel where there was a big sports program that included dinghy sailing and windsurfing—even in the thirty-knot wind that was blowing. There were twenty to thirty windsurfers tearing around at terrific speeds. One fellow got out of control and crashed into us. Fortunately he did no damage to himself or *Whisper*. The speed of the expert windsurfers was surprising. They had bendy masts, streamers at the mastheads, fancy windows in the sails, and violent colors (one was a two-tone purple that would have excited a king). Some of the wind-surfers were not so expert, and the rescue boats were busy saving those who were blowing out of sight downwind. The rescue boats also collected upside-down dinghies whose skippers were exhausted. All of the rescued sailors seemed quite pleased to get ashore.

The next morning I noticed a windmill merrily spinning away on a high point far above us in the distance. I wanted to have a look at it, so we went ashore and walked several miles up a steep roadway to the village of Kefalos at the top of the mountain ridge at the western end of Kos. The isolated village was small and pleasant. At its northern end we found a big stone tower surmounted by a windmill with twelve triangular sails. The power of the wind turned a central axle which drove a wooden gear train and a set of large millstones that made flour from corn and grain.

The miller poured sacks of grain into a chute above the millstones; later he carried away sacks of flour. The miller—who was a kind of sailor, I guess—paid close attention to the wind. He reefed the windmill sails by taking a turn or two or three on the spokes that ran between the axle and the rim of the great sail wheel. It was all clever, cheap, dependable, and picturesque. There weren't many tourists at the end of the island, but all who saw the windmill stopped for a look and took a couple of photographs.

For our second Greek island we picked Astipálea, thirty-three miles to the west-southwest. From a distance the place looked high, dry, and barren. We found an excellent harbor at a place called Port Agrilithi. The anchorage was a deep, fingerlike bay, well protected and snug, and surrounded with steep, rocky hills. The only signs of life were two goatherders and many black and white and brown goats (tails high) with tinkling bells that echoed across the hills. After the strain of Kos, we had a good rest.

In the Greek isles it's common to find tiny isolated churches or chapels on remote hillsides or way out at the end of headlands. Often the little churches are built by a family to honor the memory of a child. A man who has become wealthy in a big city may pay for a chapel to remember his parents. Or it can be a memorial to someone lost at sea. The tiny buildings usually have arched or domed roofs (often blue) and are always whitewashed before Easter. There was a nice chapel above Port Agrilithi—the sole building—so we went ashore to have a look at it. On the way back we walked up to the two goatherders and spoke to them, but they were extremely shy and got very rattled when Margaret tried to talk to them.

We stopped briefly at Port Maltezana and then sailed a few miles farther to Port Scala, population 1,000, the main settlement on Astipálea. Port Scala was a pretty place with a small, U-shaped harbor and streets with cube-shaped white houses that climbed above the deep blue water on three sides. The doors of the houses were often painted blue, brown, or yellow. On the south side the houses continued up and up a steep hill to a crumbling Venetian castle that had been built by the Quirini family who ruled the island from 1207 to 1522. The Turks then took over and held the place until 1912 when Italy took charge which explains the Italian names on the chart. The island had no airfield; a ferry came twice a week.

Port Scala was a sleepy place and we liked it. *Whisper* was the only yacht. We sat under an awning in a little café, drank coffee, and watched a second vessel, the gleaming motor yacht *Blue Albacor,* come in, anchor, and run two stern lines ashore. I saw that the enormous thirty-two-meter white yacht flew the burgee of the Royal Cruising Club, an organization to which I belong. Since our burgee was flying also, it wasn't long until we were invited aboard to meet Colonel Louis Franck and his wife Evelyn. Unfortunately Colonel Franck was elderly and not well. He had had five operations during the preceding three months. He was a gutsy type, however, and in spite of his ill health was enjoying his cruise immensely.

Colonel Franck, who was Belgian and lived in Gstaad, Switzerland, was looked after by a crew of five. His people were fond of their chief and were doing all they could to see that he enjoyed his summer trip. Once aboard, Margaret and I told our hosts about our passage up the Red Sea which particularly interested them. Colonel Franck said that he had sailed 140,000 miles in small vessels. Like a true gentleman, he asked me what I needed for *Whisper.* I mentioned a few small things, and Colonel Franck summoned his captain who found what I wanted. Meanwhile Mrs. Franck loaded Margaret down with all sorts of luxury provisions. Finally (with our heads full of fine brandy fumes), we were taken back to *Whisper.* When I got up the next

Men launching boat, Port Scala

morning and looked out, *Blue Albacor* was gone (they had planned to leave at 0200). Had the night been a dream?

We tramped around Port Scala and climbed hundreds of steps to the old Venetian castle which still had the family coat of arms at the entrance. Some of the rooms had crumbling ceilings of inlaid hardwoods. There was a tale that the defenders of the castle had once repelled assailants by throwing down beehives full of "previously maddened bees." (What does one do to a bee to make it "previously maddened"?)

After lunch Margaret and I sat in the shade of a tree above Port Scala's little dock while we watched the fishermen working on their yellow nets. Suddenly a woman with a green shopping bag stopped and began to speak English with a Boston accent.

"I'm Maggie Bromell," she said. "My husband and I have a little place up the hill. We watched you sail in on the black boat. Why don't you come up at five?"

In the late afternoon we puffed up the hundreds of steps again to the tiny hillside home of Bill and Maggie Bromell, who had spent the last nineteen summers in Astipálea. Bill was a retired diplomat, very bright, and a lifelong model airplane builder. The Bromell house was high above the harbor, and we looked almost directly down on *Whisper*. Their house was intriguing: a deck with a wonderful view, small rooms with high ceilings, a decrepit kitchen, and a different style of building upstairs and down. Bill was constructing ship models for museums. He was building an 1835 Maine pinky schooner from plans drawn by Maine artist Sam Manning who had done the maps for one of my books!

"We like it on Astipálea," said Bill over dinner. "It's a hard place to get to and isn't drowned in tourists. We have learned a little Greek and know some of the locals. Not as brothers, but as acquaintances. We have a measure of peace, of simple village life. Of course the Greeks are frustrating as hell at times. Slow, impractical, and ornery. Then they turn around and suddenly become generous, accommodating, and sentimental.

"Everything balances out," he said, running his finger around the rim of his coffee cup. "We're pleased to have this place. It probably sounds silly, but somehow when we're here we're anchored in reality."

We left Astipálea on June 10th and sailed to the northwest toward Páros. Near the big island of Amorgós dark clouds formed over the mountains, and the wind began to blow freshly from the direction of our target. Just south of Náxos we took refuge in a little harbor on the west side of tiny Skhinoúsa Island. From the bay we watched a procession of donkeys, horses, sheep, and goats on their way to a farm for the night. The farmer had a high-walled enclosure for the sheep and goats. There was no gate. The herder simply took the wall apart at one spot, shooed the animals inside the enclosure for the night, and then quickly built up the stones again.

On Páros the little settlement of Paroikiá—which we remembered from years before as a peaceful hamlet with a single dock—was now a swinging village with buses roaring along the quayside, car rental agencies, fast-food tavernas, and discos. Fortunately the wonderful blue-domed church with the red-flowered shrubs in front was unchanged. The bay itself was churned up by giant ferries rushing past each other and a succession of incredibly ugly large motor sailers from Athens.

I was sick for a few days with a fever and chills. I was convinced that I had malaria until a blood test showed that I was OK. It more likely had something to do with the grass that came out of the water pipe when we filled the water jugs.

We had to plan our sailing life around the vigorous meltemi wind that appeared each day around noon. If the meltemi got too strong, we had to think of alternate anchorages. Sometimes we had to push against south-flowing current set up by the fresh north wind. The sailing became more demanding, and we had to be careful in the anchorages.

On Sífnos we stopped at Vathí Bay on the southwest coast. The circular bay was small, snug, and remote. We anchored on the north side and walked to a pottery shop at a place called Tsópos. The walk was about a mile or so around the beach to the southeast, and we were halfway back to the yacht when Margaret looked out at *Whisper*.

"We're dragging," she said.

"Nonsense," I said. "You . . . my God, you're right!"

I began to run down the beach toward the yacht and our dinghy, but it was a long way, and *Whisper* was drifting southward almost opposite us. Just then a little fishing boat putted by. Never have two sailors shouted or waved harder. Margaret and I both waded into the water up to our chests while we screamed and yelled at the fisherman, who got the idea at once and hurried over to us. We pulled ourselves aboard the fishing boat in a twinkling and rushed out to *Whisper*. As we neared the yacht I gave all the money in my pocket to the fisherman, and we scrambled on board. Margaret started the engine and steered away from the nearby rocks while I hauled up our two anchors at a record pace.

At first I thought our problem had simply been grass growing on the sandy bottom, grass that had kept the twenty-kilo plow and the fifteen-kilo Danforth from digging in. When I jumped into the water with a face mask and had Margaret drag the yacht astern with the engine, I saw the real problem: a thin veneer of sand and grass roots over soft mud. Only when we got out our Luke thirty-kilo storm fisherman anchor—whose flukes were long and sharp—and re-anchored did we stop moving. It had been a close call. It took hours for me to calm down. I did not feel too friendly toward the crews of three other yachts who had sat and watched *Whisper* drag away from her anchorage.

Greek mother and child

The next bay north on Sífnos was Kamáres Bay, which was crowded with tourists and traffic. We took a motor scooter and rode up the hills to the main settlement of Apollonía and Kástro as we had done years before. In Kástro a wrinkled old woman stopped us in the street and urged us to eat at her grandson's restaurant. We agreed, and soon sat in a tiny place with four tables (we were the only patrons for a time). We had the most wonderful view of white buildings and the blue sea far below. The young owner of the restaurant could offer us only three things to eat, and he struggled hard with a few English words to tell us what we could have.

In a little while—his white teeth gleaming from his dark face as he smiled—he brought our lunch, and served us devotedly. The food was meager, but the young man's spirit was not. He tried so hard to please that his ordinary food became more desirable. The badly cooked lamb chop somehow tasted better, and the ordinary wine changed into vintage stuff.

Had I fallen under the Greek spell? When I left I wondered what to say. I didn't want to praise him too highly because the fellow needed some cooking lessons. Yet with his spirit and determination he could not fail to be a success. The best I could do was to leave him the change, grip his hand smartly, and trade smiles. . . .

We stopped at Mílos, a dusty, volcanic island. Here the meltemi blew so hard that we sought shelter in Mílou Bay tucked up close to Adhámas on the northern shore. Five large fishing boats motored into the harbor and anchored around us. They were handsome, double-ended Greek caïques with low freeboard, lots of sheer, outboard rudders, and hydraulic power blocks for the nets. The boats were nicely painted in white, blue, and yellow. Their radios were turned up with a lot of jarring music from Athens. On one of the boats someone was hammering and making a terrific racket. A few friends of the sailors came to the beach opposite the fishing boats and shouted across. Soon ten people were carrying on four separate conversations. It was funny, because with the wind and all the noise and the conflicting conversations, the people had to shout louder and louder to be heard. I thought it must be some kind of perpetual motion scheme to make more and more noise. Soon even the participants were laughing at the shouting and were enjoying themselves. The Greeks *love* noise.

In all we visited six islands in the Aegean. All were crowned with ruins. All were good places for walks. All had fine scenery and flowers. All had little villages whose buildings were like white sugar cubes stacked up diagonally as they climbed the slopes above the blue water or rose above a far valley to make a distant, dreamlike village. We saw outside staircases in unlikely places and often walked beneath lovely arches. The flagstones on the streets and walks were sometimes outlined in white. Every now and then we would see a doorway done in marble with carvings of flowers and clusters of grapes. Sometimes there was an old marble fountain.

Everything had a patina of time. The edges were softened by centuries of patient use. All the Greek islands had sunshine and a wonderful dreamy light, a kind of diamond, crystalline brilliance that made the reds seem redder, the whites crack with hardness, and the blues bluer than belief. The quality of light is a definite thing in the Aegean, and writers have always talked about it.

On June 25th we headed for the mainland, sixty-seven miles to the west. We made a brief stop at Pórto Yérakas in the Pelopónnisos Peninsula. The port had good shelter, but the tiny village baked in the sun and was the poorest we'd seen in Greece. Then in a thirty-knot easterly wind we sailed south past Cape Malea (Akra Maléas) to Kapsáli Bay on Kíthira Island. Kapsáli was an old bastion of the Venetians with a castle and a tidy village at the top of a steep-sided mountain above the bay. Few tourists came to the area.

After a long day of blustery sailing we were ready for a powerful meal. Tom Kaye, the captain of a yacht named *T'morn,* claimed that the first beat-up taverna along the beach had the best food and lowest prices in Greece, an unlikely combination. The proprietor was Maniolis, a tall, thin, nonstop talker whose left-hand fingers had been blown off years before when he had been out dynamiting fish. Maniolis didn't waste time on preliminaries but led us directly to the kitchen to inspect eight or nine dishes bubbling in copper pots on a big black stove.

Everything was hot and fresh, with spicy smells and delicious-looking toppings. The cook, proud of her work, spooned out little samples of savory lamb with rice, macaroni with meat and cheese, stuffed tomatoes, eggplant and minced meat, fish soup, chicken with herbs, and so on. The aromas were so good that it was hard to choose, but we asked for a little of this and a bit of that—and, oh well, a spoonful of the moussaká. The meal was first class, and afterward we slept the sleep of the dead.

The next morning we sailed for Italy.

CHAPTER TWENTY-TWO

The Mysteries of Siracusa

*E*xperts told us that it was impossible to sail the 430 miles from Kíthera to the Italian island of Sicily because of contrary winds, no winds, or terrible storms. I rather doubted all these harbor stories, because the sailors of old had certainly used the wind. And if they had, we could certainly sail with our sleek hull and good sails.

Late in the afternoon of June 28th, with a meltemi blowing from the north and warnings of thirty-to-forty-knot winds, we started out with a reef in the mainsail and small headsails. Just outside Kapsáli Harbor, however, the wind suddenly fell away to nothing. Three hours later two passing ships threw us a light breeze from the south. We shook out the reef, put up a larger jib, and headed west.

A little before midnight Margaret watched two satellites scratch thin white tracks high across the black sky. When I took over from her I saw a ship to port. Later the light of a distant ship winked to starboard, although when the light went black on a regular basis, I timed it (thirty seconds) and found that I was looking at the occulting light on Kávo Matapás (Cape Matapan). The next day and night we paralleled a main east-west shipping lane and counted twenty-four ships in as many hours. Most of the big vessels changed course a little to keep away from us, but a red bulk carrier from

Building entrance, Siracusa

Istanbul, the *Topkapis,* seemed determined to chop us in two. We tacked away until she passed. I noticed that most of the eastbound ships were laden and low in the water while the westbound cargo ships were empty, sometimes with the top of the propeller churning a trail of white froth.

West of the southern tip of the Greek mainland we crossed the old track made by the thirty-five-thousand-ton Italian battleship *Vittorio Veneto* during the Battle of Matapan in World War II. It happened on March 28, 1941. Italy was trying to invade Greece, which had appealed to England for help. Churchill, the British prime minister, decided to send sixty-eight thousand troops from North Africa. However, the British were afraid that their troop transports would be sunk by the powerful Italian fleet, which by all logic should have controlled the Mediterranean. Unfortunately for the Italians, their initiative had been whittled away by a hopeless command structure and a series of humiliating raids by the British navy.

Three old British battleships, one new aircraft carrier, four cruisers, and twelve decrepit destroyers set out to match a crack Italian armada of one new battleship, six heavy cruisers, two light cruisers, and seventeen destroyers. On paper Admiral Angelo Iachino's superior Italian fleet should have whipped Admiral Andrew Cunningham's creaky British squadron. However, the new Italian ships had hulls of clay because they lacked air cover and the advantages of proper aerial reconnaissance. Iachino had only begun to experiment with radar, and—incredibly—none of his ships were able to use their guns at night.

At 0812 that morning, five of the Italian cruisers traded salvos with the four British cruisers, but there were no hits and the outgunned British retired under smoke screens. At 1059 the *Vittorio Veneto* fired salvos from her fifteen-inch guns at the four British cruisers, which again escaped under cover of smoke. In the afternoon one of the planes from the aircraft carrier *Formidable* launched a torpedo that exploded at the stern of the Italian battleship. This caused her speed to drop from thirty to nineteen knots. A little later another plane sent a torpedo into one of the Italian cruisers. Six Italian ships were sent back to assist the disabled cruiser.

That night the British fleet detected the Italian cruiser division by radar and got to within three miles without being detected. At 2227 the British suddenly opened fire on the astonished Italians. Great orange flashes from the three British battleships knifed into the inky night as salvo after salvo blasted out from twenty-four fifteen-inch guns and forty smaller weapons. At the point-blank range of 3,800 yards the shelling practically blew the hapless Italian ships out of the water. Three heavy cruisers and two destroyers erupted into raging infernos of orange flames.

"You could see whole turrets being blown sky-high," wrote Admiral Cunningham. "Great lumps of metal flew through the air. The ships turned into flaming torches."

The stunned Italians hadn't even had their guns loaded. The new Italian battleship escaped in the confusion and limped home with the rest of the fleet. Never again during World War II did the British lose control of the Mediterranean shipping lanes.[16]

In our sailing trip around the world we'd retraced an ancient naval engagement with triremes in Turkey. Now we'd been over the tracks of a modern naval battle. At first the issues over which the battles had been fought and on which men had died were complicated and abstruse. After I thought about the causes of the conflicts for a time, however, they became understandable: against extremes in government, greed, and personal power. Certainly our little sailing voyage was trifling and insignificant compared with these great battles. I hoped, however, that my thinking about the causes of these battles was sound and not too simplistic.

We pushed *Whisper* westward. Twice on the way to Italy we were becalmed for three hours, but generally we had a northwest wind that

24. Sicily to Sardinia

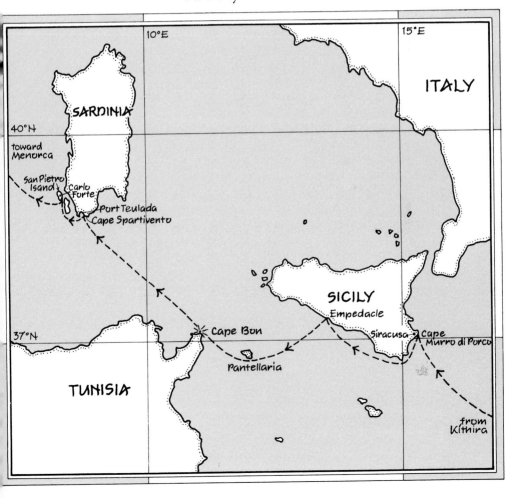

averaged about twelve knots. Then our big genoa pulled us steadily across calm seas. When it breezed up we tucked a reef in the mainsail and changed to a smaller jib, but a few hours later we were usually putting up more sail again.

On July 2nd we retrieved an orange-colored plastic float and line that had "SUB" in large black letters on the side. I immediately thought of a stricken submarine. However, the line was floating free and we saw nothing. That night the wind increased to twenty-two knots from the west-southwest, but in the lee of the southern tip of Sicily, the swell eased. We noticed a number of searchlights flashing around at sea south of us. At 0245 Margaret picked up the Siracusa light on Murro di Porco. An hour later she called me to help her avoid two large fishing boats that were busy handling nets. The wind died, and at dawn the skyline of Siracusa lay before us.

At first we tried to enter Porto Piccolo for small vessels. Not only was it terribly polluted, but it was shallow and crowded. We sailed around to the main harbor where there was more room and deeper water and tied up at the westernmost part of Ortygia Island with half a dozen other yachts. We were in the heart of the city.

Ashore we found a modern Italian city of 100,000 people that was built on layers and layers of settlements that began with the Greeks 2,500 years ago. Siracusa grew to be the largest fortified city in the world and at one time had a population five or six times that of today (just to protect its commerce the city had three hundred warships). Everybody in the Mediterranean has controlled Siracusa. First the Athenians, Carthaginians, and Romans. Then the barbarians, Visigoths, and Vandals. Byzantine domination lasted three centuries. The Arabs sacked the city in 878; later the Normans, then the Spanish, and finally the French took over. It wasn't until 1861 that modern Italy came into being.

Margaret and I tramped through a medieval city with narrow lanes and overhanging balconies that were bright with showy clusters of white and pink oleanders. We looked at three-story stone buildings, Renaissance palaces, baroque facades, and open sunny squares. We saw a cathedral whose walls were supported by enormous Doric columns from a Greek temple. The city was adorned with religious statues, ornate carvings, elaborate doorways, scrolled ironwork, and neatly fenced-off Greek ruins. We saw city offices, outdoor cafés, and well-dressed people going to work. Smart shops abutted decrepit houses. The stink of drains and garbage sometimes mixed with the aroma of coffee from a smart restaurant or the zesty smell of barbecuing lamb from a street vendor. Children rushed past us shouting as they played, and we noticed the frustration of people as they hunted for parking spaces for their small cars.

Some of the Italian buildings were too garish for my taste. I had the feeling that there must have been a design competition and that the judges decided to throw in everything which resulted in an orgy of overbuilding, overdecorating, and over-ornateness. Yet it was intriguing to look at such vitality. Sometimes among a confusion of spires, statuary, columns, and gates I would see the most delicate stone arch or a bit of intricate woodwork that was simply lovely.

[From my journal] July 6th. This morning we walked through the local street market, the best city market I have seen. For a quarter of a mile on the north side of Ortygia Island we passed stand after stand of food: small dark-red tomatoes, brilliant green lettuces, and mounds of zesty Italian cheeses. There were piles of striped cantaloupes, heaps of dark-green broccoli, and crate after crate of peaches (large, fuzzy, and sweet smelling). The butchers had great hunks of beefsteak, veal, and pork ready to be cut, and as the eager meat cutters sharpened their knives they cried: "Come in! Come in! We have the best for you!" The fishmongers sliced steaks from giant tuna whose cross sections were as big around as a soccer ball. We saw wriggly eels, flatfish of all kinds, small panfish, red mullet, and glistening silver and blue tuna (small, one-third of a meter, you took the whole fish). We inspected long white trays of fresh oysters, new mussels, delicate whelks, tiny periwinkles, and clams. We bought jumbo eggs, bread almost too hot to touch, a slice of fresh red snapper, fruit, vegetables—our bags were soon full.

Hundreds of people jostled courteously at the market while the vendors' cries pierced the air. A purchase was quick. The sellers wanted action. The broccoli man took my 1,000-lire note for one bundle (cost 333), but instead of giving me change he pushed two more bundles in my bag and said, "Grazie, molte grazie." I smiled at his tactics and bravado. The orange seller claimed to be short of change and also made up the difference with more oranges. The quality, variety, and freshness of the food was surprising. Italian was the language, but the sellers wrote the numbers on a piece of paper so you knew what to pay. I felt the sellers were honest, and they scrupulously weighed each item. It was fun to shop.

Back at the dock we began to get acquainted with the other yachts, which hailed from France, Germany, Malta, the United States, England, and of course Italy. One or two small vessels arrived or left every day. The docking arrangement—typical of the Mediterranean—was to put an anchor out at one end of the yacht and take a line ashore from the other end. The anchor held the yacht off at right angles to the shore, and the line to the shore kept the other end only a meter or two from the land, which made it easy for the crew to get on and off. This scheme is usual in the Mediterranean, but dealing with the anchor(s) and shore lines is tricky for a beginner to execute in a calm, and not so easy for an expert in a crosswind.

Our Siracusa docking was satisfactory until a southerly wind blew up. Then we found it best to clear out and go to the other side of the harbor and anchor until the wind changed. Most captains tried to hold on during poor conditions, but their vessels often suffered damage from bashing into the massive stone quays or into another yacht when an anchor dragged. There was lots of free advice (some not good) and various small dramas (and frayed tempers) with lines and anchors. There was always a crowd on shore watching the show.

Unlike some countries we'd visited, Italy had lots of artistic activity. I often heard men singing snatches of opera, and their voices were good. They sang for the enjoyment of singing, and it was pleasant to hear them. We'd seen placards in town for a free concert on July 4th, so we walked over to the Piazza Duomo where chairs were being set out and a stage arranged in front of the cathedral.

Unfortunately there were cars parked all over the piazza (in spite of notices), and the police were busy hauling them away. Many of the Siracusa streets were too narrow for normal tow trucks, so the police had built a special narrow, cranelike vehicle with four overhead arms. The auto crane would creep up behind a car, its four arms would come down over the vehicle, and the arms would lock around the wheels. The car would then be lifted into the air and whisked away, to be ransomed after a heavy fine. The auto crane caused the greatest anguish to the Italian drivers who would come out of a restaurant or office to see their cars being taken away—or worse—gone entirely! Then a drama of screaming and anguish would begin that was grand opera at its best (the driver of the auto crane was threatened with death four or five times a day). The action around the auto crane was often so violent that it was always accompanied by four or five very tall special policemen in full uniform (with guns).

Finally Piazza Duomo was cleared. The tuxedoed musicians began to arrive with their instruments, and soon the Autonomo Orchestra Sinfonica Siciliana under the direction of Roberto Abbado was playing Mendelssohn. In such a setting—in front of the venerable church, the Greek columns, the Renaissance stone buildings, and the old piazza—the music was wonderful, and the hundreds of spectators listened rapturously to every nuance of the beautifully played notes. A cluster of black heads peered out from every overhead window, the surrounding cafés had been booked ahead of time, the office staffs slipped out to listen, and even the children were attentive. When the violinist Eugene Sarbu played Ciakoski, the audience fairly swooned with delight. Never did an orchestra have a better audience.

We had gotten acquainted with a slim Sicilian named Antonio X____, who was about thirty-five and intrigued by *Whisper* and our various adventures. We soon learned that he had a mysterious side and a strange power over people.

One day Antonio was on board when we were taking fresh water from a hose that led to the quayside water system. The official rates for fresh water in Siracusa were seven hundred lire for a hose for an hour in the morning or one thousand lire an hour for water in the afternoon. The water man came around from time to time in a little three-wheeled car, and you saw him about the water. He always shaded the time, however. If you used the hose for one hour he claimed payment for two hours. If you used morning water he wanted afternoon time, and so on. The sums involved were trifling, but the man's ways were aggravating. The water man had the special key to open the water pipes, however, so he had the upper hand.

One morning a German captain who was leaving got into an argument with the water man and refused to pay his inflated demands. The German paid what he thought was correct, let his lines go, and started to recover his anchor. The water man immediately summoned a policeman, who beckoned to the German to come back. The German refused, so the policeman got out his gun and began to wave it around. The German returned and settled the argument, but all the other sailors watched the exhibition with distaste.

Now a few days later, I was using a freshwater hose. The water man was nearby, swaggering around on the quay. I explained to Antonio about the trouble with the water man.

"Why didn't you tell me before?" said Antonio. "I'll have a word with him."

Antonio went ashore and began to talk to the water man. After a few words the water man's face turned absolutely white. The swagger disappeared. He dropped his special keys down on the pavement, jumped into his three-wheeled car, and drove away in a cloud of blue oil smoke. We never saw him again. I wondered what Antonio could have said to the water man, but I didn't ask.

The next day Antonio was on *Whisper* again when a big fishing boat motored past us. The boat had often gone by, and the crew had paid absolutely no attention to us.

"Would you like to have some fresh shrimp?" asked Antonio.

"Oh yes," said Margaret.

Antonio waved at the fishing boat, which immediately stopped. He shouted something to the captain. A bucket of shrimp was quickly passed across at the end of a boat hook.

Whisper had a leaky water tank pipe, so the next day Antonio took me out in his car to look for plumbing parts. When we got to a big shopping center there were absolutely no parking spaces. Cars were double-parking or leaving without stopping. Antonio beckoned to a parking attendant, who shrugged and lazily shook his head. Antonio waved the attendant closer and said something to him. All at once the man jerked upright. He began to nod his head vigorously, and he quickly ran down the line of cars. A car started up and backed out, and we were waved into the place with gestures that suggested we had angels on our shoulders.

Finally, on July 8th we went to the Bolshoi Ballet, which was performing on the outskirts of Siracusa. We had never seen the Russian Bolshoi troupe nor been in the Greek theater. Antonio and three sailors from another yacht and Margaret and I went together. When we got to the box office Antonio offered to buy the tickets, so I gave him twenty thousand lire (twelve dollars) for Margaret and me. Antonio got the money from the other three people and went up to the ticket window. I noticed that he bought just five tickets, which seemed strange.

When we got to the entrance barrier a uniformed guard let our party of six through the gate. He took the five tickets that Antonio offered and then counted our party again. One ticket short. Antonio leaned over and said something to the guard, who suddenly stiffened as if he had been stabbed with an ice pick. The guard's head began to shake violently, and with a feeble gesture he waved us through.

What had Antonio said to these poor men?

The ancient Greek theater was a huge, fifteen-thousand-seat outdoor arena that had been in use for twenty-five centuries. It was an ideal theater, but the weather had to be good, and it was best to take cushions because the seats were stone.

The Bolshoi group was marvelous. The stars were Vladimir Vassiliev and Ekaterina Maximova. In all there were five men and six women plus an extremely skilled pianist named Pavel Sal'nikov. Though the troupe was limited in numbers, their mastery of ballet was certainly not limited. The dancers jumped, twisted, spun, leaped, pirouetted, and did all sorts of clever and unexpected steps as they told stories through dance with music. The first part of the program was a classical review. The second half was based on the tango and was a rich, modern, fast-paced fantasy with black tights, white and black checked shirtwaists, and swirling, dreamlike sequences. At the end the five thousand Italians in the audience rose as one and cheered and applauded until, after a dozen curtain calls, the dancers were obliged to do an encore. Meanwhile, a full moon beamed down on the old theater. The ancient Greeks would have been envious of our evening.

When we left Siracusa, Antonio came down to see us off. We shook hands, he let go our lines, and I began to crank up the anchor. Our Sicilian acquaintance stood on shore and watched us. I watched him beckon to a policeman in a way that suggested a man who was used to gesturing and being obeyed. I don't know what Antonio represented, but it was powerful and gave me an ominous feeling. I half expected the policeman to rush away on an errand of some kind, but the two men stood talking quietly as we made sail and began to move away.

. . . .

CHAPTER TWENTY-THREE

A Summer Storm in Spain

*W*e sailed south around the corner of Sicily and tacked into a northwest wind. We were in a main shipping lane that paralleled the coast, and generally had lights or a plume of smoke in sight from an eastbound merchant ship, an oil tanker, or a bulk carrier. Plus the usual fishing boats. The wind was directly against us, and our progress was poky and slow. We hoped for a change in the wind direction, so we stopped one night at Empedacle (where the ancient mooring bollards were chiseled out of granite). We continued westward, but an eighteen-knot west-northwest wind drove us a little south, and when the wind rose to thirty-five knots from the northwest—a wind unheard of in July—we sought shelter behind the Italian island of Pantelleria (pan-tal-la-REE-a). I had thought of going into the main port on the northwest side of the island. However, both Captain Denham and the Admiralty pilot book stated that the place was dangerous in bad weather from the north. I knew we would be better off at sea.

[From my journal] July 17th. 2015. We finally got to the southeast coast of Pantelleria a little past noon, where together with a seagoing tug and six fishing trawlers we found a lee. The eight-fathom anchorage is deep, and I needed a long cable. I was worried about hooking my main anchor in volcanic rock, so I dropped a ten-kilo Danforth, a fathom of chain, and a long nylon line. I used the line from the reel on *Whisper*'s aft deck and anchored temporarily from the stern for a few minutes while I led the line forward to the bow. Just as I was carrying the line forward, a squall struck the yacht. All at once there was a big load on the line, and I was almost yanked over the side. It was a bad moment until I got a couple of turns around a stanchion base. I was stupid not to have carried extra line forward and made it fast *before* I released the cable at the stern. I don't think I'll forget this lesson because it'll take a while for the rope burns to heal.

We have been nicely anchored all day about four boat lengths from the shore, which is very steep, of lava, and terraced in narrow fields bright with green vine leaves. Above us are several houses and various huts. We are in smooth water with occasional squalls and have dried out the yacht and cleaned ourselves and slept. The barometer continues to hover around 1013.

The next day the wind eased, and we got under way for Sardinia. The continent of Africa was now quite near. We had to weather Tunisia's Cape Bon, fifty-two miles to the west-northwest. From somewhere on land came the persistent smell of drying fish as we continued on a close-hauled course into a northwest wind. Finally, in the middle of the afternoon Margaret shouted: "Africa exists! Land ahead!"

We had a foul tidal stream and perhaps some current against us, and it took until midnight before we tacked past the light on Cape Bon. There were ships all around us, but we were in no danger and gradually sailed into the open sea. The night was bright with a waning moon, and we loafed along in light headwinds. Since Sicily, the nights had been damp, and the decks and coachroof ran with moisture. We were aware of enormous offshore tuna nets, fishing boats, and lights.

Margaret and I stood watch and watch, and we continued to see lots of shipping, which now included ferries and cruise ships. One old cruise ship that chugged past the next morning looked as if she had been clipped from a 1920 magazine advertisement. I almost expected to see people in full dress waltzing on the promenade deck. Were you there, Fred Astaire?

Whisper had the bad smell of wet wool and moldy oatmeal in the cabin. I can tolerate with many things at sea, but I do not like wet clothing and damp food. Everything in the starboard saloon lockers was wet, not from a leak from the outside, but from a leaking freshwater tank on the inside. We had been fighting this problem ever since Cyprus. First I had changed the delivery and breather pipes from the tank. Then the plumbing fittings at each end of the lines. I had removed and rebedded the tank shutoff valve. I did the same with the tank clean-out plate and added four additional fastenings. Not only did the leak continue, however, it got worse. We made a landfall just west of Cape Spartivento on the southern tip of Sardinia and ducked into a little place called Port Teulada, where we anchored and pumped out the cursed forward tank. (We had a second freshwater tank in the bilge, but this move cut our capacity from 320 liters to 160.) We emptied all the starboard lockers and mopped out the water. *Whisper*'s lifelines turned into enormous laundry lines with shirts and sweaters and towels and sheets

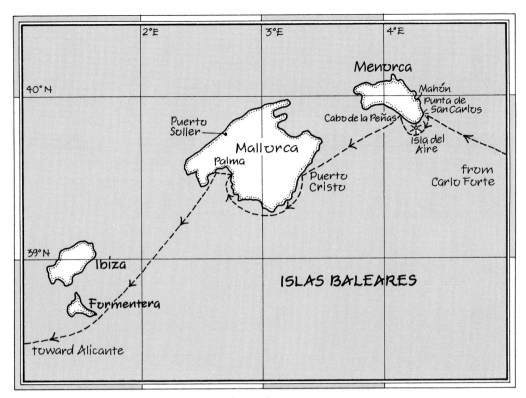

25. Islas Baleares

drying under the warm Italian sun. When the fishermen motored past they saw a strange boat well camouflaged with clothes. The old sailors understood, because leaks are usual. What is not usual is to drown from within!

The weather was idyllic, and the next morning everything was dry and soon put away. We sailed another thirty-two miles to the southwest corner of Sardinia, where we stopped at Carlo Forte on the tiny island of San Pietro, a place recommended by Emrys and Ingrid Thomas, our friends in Cyprus. Carlo Forte was a sleepy, well-sheltered port, with a roomy area to drop an anchor and a wide quay to tie up to. There were a dozen or so other yachts, mostly French. The lineup changed every day, and we always had a new boat show around us.

The little town lay on the east side of the island. In the morning the settlement was full of sun, and it was pleasant to sit at an outdoor café and have rolls and coffee with hot milk. Near us was a statue of Carlo Emmanuele of Savoy, who in 1737 had resettled a colony of Genoese people who had gone to North Africa to live but who had been threatened by hostile Arabs. Carlo Emmanuele had brought the people to San Pietro, where they had worked as tuna fishermen for ten generations.[17]

The town was attractive, with a waterfront esplanade, stone buildings with arched windows, and houses with balconies and ornamental ironwork.

Old men talking under the trees, Carlo Forte

We walked through narrow back streets, under archways, and up wide stone stairways to a central plaza where during the mornings old men sat on benches under wide leafy trees and told tall stories to one another. Later in the day the plaza was crowded with young people. A little nearby store sold the most wonderful Italian ice cream.

So far in the Mediterranean we had sailed 1,250 miles west from Cyprus. We still had 675 miles to go to Gibraltar. Our next destination was the Spanish port of Mahón on Menorca in the Baleares, about 190 miles away. Again we headed west in light winds. On the second night, however, the wind freshened from the north. At 2130 on July 24th we changed from the large genoa to the small genoa and tied one reef in the mainsail. Three hours later the wind was up to thirty knots, and we swapped the small genoa for the working jib. We plowed along to windward on the starboard tack at six to seven knots, bashing into the waves. We were close to the big island of Menorca and its port of Mahón on the southeast coast, where I thought we would find shelter from the storm.

At 0500, just before dawn, I identified the flashing light signal on Isla del Aire, on the southeast point of Menorca. The wind had increased to forty

knots from the northeast. There was a lot of water flying around, and we
had already filled the cockpit half a dozen times. We dropped the staysail
and continued with the small jib and single-reefed mainsail. We heeled a lot,
had some weather helm, and desperately needed a second reef. However,
Mahón was nearby, we were tearing along, and I reckoned we could hang
on for another hour. Certainly we would be in for breakfast. It was not to
be.

In a little while we could plainly see the black and white bands on the
tower of the Punta de San Carlos lighthouse at the southern entrance to
Mahón. We tacked once or twice because the current set up by the wind was
shoving us to leeward. Although we were on the east side of the island, heavy
seas from the north and northeast almost paralleled the coast. The seas had
a long fetch and heaved up big and lumpy before shattering into white streaks
of foam along the rocky shore. Some of these waves were reflected back to
sea at an oblique angle to the southeast. Other oncoming waves struck this
upset water and made a hellish sea. It was a lee shore at its worst. We should
have had a lee or partial lee from a headland north of Mahón that projected
eastward. In the storm, however, the whole entrance area was filled with
nasty-looking seas about to break.

Once north of the Punta de San Carlos lighthouse, we peered anxiously
to the west for the entrance to Puerto de Mahón. Where was it? The entrance
buoys were not visible in the seas that were running. During the night I had
laid out two courses on the chart based on suggested landmarks in the
Admiralty pilot book, but I did not recognize the prominent buildings and
points of land. Off to leeward were half a dozen tiny bays and fingers of
water reaching away from us. One was the harbor entrance to Mahón. Which
one? The flat light of the rising sun on the east-facing shore made it hard
to see well. It would have been foolhardy to have pressed on toward land.
Foolhardy? The right word was suicidal. I gybed about on the offshore tack
and headed back out to sea.

"This is all crazy," I said to Margaret. "We know exactly where we
are. We can see the entrance lighthouse. We have both small- and large-scale
charts and the Admiralty pilot book. Yet we can't see the way in to Mahón,
probably because we're at the wrong angle. In this glaring early light everything looks formless. Yet there is no way I'm going in any closer in these
seas."

Margaret went below to study the charts. "There's a lot of water
sloshing around down here," she cried. "Something's wrong!"

Margaret took the tiller while I went below. Water was indeed sloshing
around everywhere. The cabin sole was underwater. The logbook and pillows and half a dozen charts had fallen into the water and were sliding from
one side to the other. Yikes! Had we struck something? Was the hull holed?
Where was the water coming from? There was no time for speculation. It

was time to pump. Margaret cranked one pump while I worked the second. The water level went down.

During the trouble with the water in the cabin, we had eased off before the wind. Once we had pumped out the water, it did not come back. When we went back on the wind and heeled, we promptly filled the cockpit and had water below again. Was the water somehow leaking from the cockpit to the cabin? I decided to forget Mahón and head for the south coast where we could sort things out. With a fair wind we rushed past the southeast point of Menorca and reached along in smooth water with thirty-knot beam winds. I was surprised to see half a dozen sailing yachts, all rushing along with storm sails. I had never seen so many storm sails before.

We anchored off a beach just west of a place named Cabo de la Peñas. While Margaret surveyed the problems in the cabin I checked the cockpit drains, which seemed OK. I then looked at the cockpit bilge pump handle, which operated through a slot in the starboard cockpit seat. Where the handle went through the slot it was covered with a rubber seal and then a canvas boot. When I examined the seal and boot, they crumbled to pieces. The Red Sea sun had done its work. I lifted the starboard cockpit locker seat. Those rubber seals were also rotten and useless. When *Whisper* had been heeled with the cockpit and seats full of water, the sea must have poured through the cockpit locker top and the bilge pump handle slot. No wonder we had had water below!

We seemed to be washing out the inside of the yacht on a regular basis. First it was the freshwater tank leak. Then the flood from the faulty cockpit seals. We had coped with the first leak easily enough, but the second flooding was severe, and the salt water had made a mess inside. We needed a haven for a few days. The next morning the storm was over, so we sailed forty-two miles southwest from Menorca to the east coast of the big island of Mallorca to a place called Porto Cristo. We tied up at a small yacht club, where we had peace and quiet and the use of a freshwater hose. We spent the next five days hosing out, cleaning, and drying everything on board. I put new seals on the cockpit locker lids and double seals on the bilge pump handle slot.

We learned from newspapers and people in Porto Cristo that the storm had been the worst in living memory. Trees had been blown down, fishermen lost, and a festival canceled. No one had ever seen such a wind, it would never happen again, and so forth. We had heard such excuses all over the world for a long time. Nevertheless, weather was weather. Man was essentially helpless. Now, fortunately, the storm was gone and summer had come back. The drying out and re-stowing of *Whisper*'s gear and supplies had been a wretched job, and we had been fortunate to have found the pleasant settlement of Porto Cristo. On August 2nd, in light southerly winds, we sailed around the southern point of Mallorca to its capital of Palma.

Palma de Mallorca, with a population of 290,000, was a big city with hydrofoils, ferryboats, cargo ships, cruise ships, docks, and cranes. My eyes saw big hotels, high buildings, an enormous cathedral, tourist buses, streams of automobiles, motorbikes, and bicycles. The old sections of the city had balconies, sculptures, coats of arms, and intriguing inside courtyards. Before I arrived I was sure I would hate the place. Yet I liked Palma and had a great time. The local Spaniards were sympathetic to tourists and in general were calm, reasonable, slow-paced, and tolerant.

Palma's big harbor had a long waterfront roadway called Paseo Maritima. Tied up along this busy quayside roadway were hundreds of yachts, each held off with an anchor, and each side by side with her neighbors. We spotted two old friends, *Ho Hoq* and *Tortoise*—yachts similar to *Whisper*—and were soon moored near them and shaking hands with Ted and Jan de Villa and Joe and Bonnie Darlington.

The yachts along Paseo Maritima were large and small, new and old. Some were still under construction; others were rotten, rusting, dented, and falling apart. Some hadn't been paid for yet, and others had been abandoned. Some had one mast, some two masts, and some had no masts at all. Some yachts had sailed around the world; others looked as if they couldn't make it across the bay. We saw boat owners busy varnishing, hammering, sawing, painting, sewing sails, peeling potatoes, sleeping, cutting each other's hair, or just sitting drinking beer. We looked at flags from eighteen countries and heard the babble of strange languages. At dinnertime we smelled intriguing aromas from all over the world. Every day the lineup of yachts and spectators changed, and our daily walks along Paseo Maritima were fascinating.

Margaret took a bus to the dentist while I worked on the water tank problem. After some effort I got the big stainless steel tank loose from its forepeak fastenings and into the main saloon, where I was able to check it for leaks. By pumping a little air into the tank and using the old standby of soap and water, I soon found that the seams leaked through pinholes. The tank would have to go to a welder. When I tried to get the tank out of the main hatchway, however, I found that it was too big. The only thing to do was to cut the tank down. I was about to cut the tank in half when Ted de Villa stopped by for a cup of coffee.

"Why don't you take the hatch apart?" said Ted after looking at the tank and measuring the hatch. "You'll gain three inches and that may be enough."

I took the hatch to pieces, and we tried to slide the tank out. It started, caught, and all at once slipped out as smoothly as a suddenly unstuck drawer. Marvelous!

The local expert near Club Nautico welded two patches on the tank, but as fast as he fixed one place a new hole opened up. The truth was the gas-welded seams had rusted out. I needed a new tank. The welder offered to make a new tank of grade 316 stainless steel one millimeter thick. He would weld it electrically with an argon-shielded (TIG) technique, and then passivate the welds with acid both inside and out. However, he couldn't do it for a month.

"This is the high season," said the welder. "I have many important jobs for the big racing boats that are here for the regattas."

I shopped around elsewhere to have a new tank made but could find no one who seemed competent. I decided to do without the extra water tank and to carry five 10-liter jugs stowed where the old tank had been. This would give us a total of 50 liters plus 160 liters from the bilge tank or 210 liters total, versus the 320 liters of my old arrangement with the two permanent tanks. Since 2 liters of water per person per day is ample for all purposes, I thought we could manage with 210 liters, enough for two people for fifty-two days at sea.

For several days I played carpenter and rebuilt the forepeak area where the old water tank had been. There was a horror of broken woodwork and rusted fastenings, which I replaced with several small bulkheads and longitudinal-bearing pieces for the forepeak berth bottoms. When I took out the tank I found several cans of Campbell's soup that long before had slipped down along the sides of the tank. The cans had been battered into perfect octagonal shapes.

One day Margaret and I took a short train trip to Sóller on the northwest coast about twenty-five kilometers from Palma. The little train seemed more like a trolley car, and it was fun to ride through the countryside in the sunlight and fresh air with the local people who were out for a day of picnicking and sightseeing. We found Puerto Sóller a bit crowded and not so nice, but we enjoyed the town of Sóller. We had lunch in the central square, and spent the afternoon walking around the narrow streets looking at the old town houses and gardens before we took the train back to Palma.

Not only did Palma have yachts along the waterfront, it had marinas as well. We often walked to several near us to look at the really big yachts. Although there were a few large sailing vessels, most were giant power yachts fifty to seventy meters long with glistening paint, chrome, sloping windows, glass doors, hot tubs, a complex of antennas, and shoreside electric cables as thick as your wrist. Some carried helicopters and automobiles. All had large crews, often in smart uniforms. Most of these vessels seldom left the dock, and the crews always seemed to be waiting for someone. We noticed that when the owners or their guests were on board, each person seemed to have a glass in his hand. Margaret observed that not only were the owners alert to every kind of new boating gear, but they were also alert to every tax-saving flag of convenience, because we saw flags from Panama, the Cayman Islands, Guernsey, Vanuatu, and Liberia.

I thought a sixty-meter power yacht was big until I saw a seventy-meter yacht in the next slip. Some of the biggest power yachts had the green and white flag of Saudi Arabia. When I looked alongside on the dock I could scarcely believe my eyes when I saw the black Rolls-Royce with the custom brown top, uniformed men with machine guns, and guard dogs with handlers. The crew used a mere Mercedes-Benz to run errands.

In my eyes the best yacht by far was the 105-foot gaff schooner *America*. She was about fifteen years old and a Sparkman and Stephens replica of the original *America* that had begun the America's Cup competitions. We had last seen this yacht in Florida when she was rundown and shabby. Now this 144-ton vessel had a Spanish owner from Vigo who had spared no expense to put her in museum condition. She was low and sleek with a black hull, marked sheer, and sharply raked spars. The depth of her gleaming varnish, her paint work, and her shimmering brasswork were simply breathtaking. At the foot of her gangplank lay a beautiful hand-worked mat. One night we saw candles burning in special holders. *America* oozed class and distinction—a ship lover's dream—and in my judgment put all the power boats to shame. It was strange to see such a vessel jammed in with the high-sided chrome and plastic power yachts.

After looking at all the monstrous power yachts and the agglomeration of wealth and gadgetry and the phony dockside society, I was always glad to return to little ten-meter *Whisper* and to climb aboard my home. Life on board *Whisper* was sweet and satisfying. Was I guilty of sour grapes? Did I really envy all that money and ostentation? I certainly am not a fan of power yachts, but I would have liked to have had a meal and a sail aboard *America*.

On our last day in Palma we visited the enormous fifteenth-century Gothic cathedral, a place of pointed arches and great flying buttresses. Not only was the cathedral a religious center, it was a social center as well, and we saw hundreds of people milling about outside the church. The inside was dark and gloomy, and the ceiling seemed half a mile high. There was a religious service going on in a side chapel, but the place was so big that we could scarcely hear the priest's voice. We craned our necks at two giant circular stained glass windows that were patterned with reds and oranges and blues and violets of the most marvelous purity.

From Palma and the island of Mallorca we sailed west to Alicante on the Spanish mainland. Alicante has a splendid port, but the docks were empty. There were no ships, no trucks, no shouting stevedores, no containers, no piles of goods on the docks. Twenty-one of the twenty-two cranes stood tall and unused. What had happened to the shipping and commerce? Where were the ferries and the people standing by with their luggage? The hotels were empty too. When I went into a hotel to buy a newspaper, a dejected room clerk and a glum bellhop jumped to their feet and broke into smiles.

What I remember about Alicante is the impressive, partially restored castle on the hill north of town and the fixed-price cafés. A series of small restaurants had set meals whose content and price were displayed on outside blackboards. You looked over the various blackboards, picked a place, and went inside. The first course—already prepared—was brought instantly. There was no waiting, no stumbling over a menu, no order taking, and no interval while the chef did his act. When you finished the soup or whatever, the next course came immediately. You didn't have to hurry at all, but the time saved in meal selection and serving was surprising. Certainly it was simple for the restaurant because only large quantities of a few dishes needed to be prepared. Generally one waiter took care of the whole place and still had time to flag in a few customers from the street. The inexpensive price of the meal reflected all these savings. One day we had *carne;* the next day *pescado;* the third day *pollo.* It's a good scheme and could be followed elsewhere. The customers in these restaurants were ordinary Spaniards; foreigners were unusual, and the owner, waiter, or someone at the next table invariably asked us where we were from, which—with our rudimentary Spanish—launched us into amusing conversations. These little talks made us feel welcome and part of the scene.

From Alicante we sailed westward along the Spanish coast toward Gibraltar, still 575 miles away. The August weather was hot. We usually had our largest sails flying, and like the sailors of old we played the daily land and sea breezes to keep moving. In all we stopped at six small ports along the south coast.

The Spanish government has built a number of pleasure boat facilities. Some of these new ports are not close to a city or village, which means they have no supporting community. Typically we found no baker, no butcher, no tailor, no central market, no church. There was no heart and soul, no identity, no local *Spanish* society at all, only tourists. The cultural attractions were zero or worse, and these places had about as much charm as a piece of rusty chain.

Were we in Spain or Outer Mongolia? Instead of a hardware store where you could buy a few brass screws and a hacksaw blade, there was a French yacht broker. Instead of a mom and pop fruit store where you could get a head of lettuce and a bag of apples there was a fancy Italian dress shop with designer originals. Instead of a local fisherman with whom you bartered for a fish that was still flopping, a special yachtsman's store had frozen fish from Iceland. The absolute pits in this direction was a tourist port called José Banús. Among the Rolls-Royce Corniches and Lotus cars, we saw men with heavy gold chains around their necks and wrists out walking Great Dane dogs. A shop behind them featured such things as a large stuffed leather unicorn and a life-sized porcelain leopard (with spots). . . .

On the afternoon of September 3rd *Whisper* rolled along at two knots near Estepona on the Spanish coast. The wind was light and the temperature stifling. Though Gibraltar was only twenty miles away, I began to wonder about my navigation because the horizon was murky and gray and empty. Margaret handed up a cup of tea, and as I drank it I began to be aware of the bass hum of ship engines somewhere ahead. At 1500 the wind picked up to thirteen knots from the south, the temperature dropped, and we began to sail at six knots on the port tack. Suddenly the air cleared and the familiar black hump of Gibraltar hove into view. An hour later the wind rose to twenty knots. We tied one reef in the mainsail and dropped the staysail. The seas were quite modest, and as we approached Gibraltar's southern tip— Europa Point—we must have had a fair tidal stream because we made good time. At Europa Point the wind increased to twenty-five knots near the steep headland, but we were sailing well and the small genoa was pulling hard. We dodged several small oil tankers, slipped past the point, and eased into Gibraltar Bay.

Our sojourn in the Mediterranean was over.

CHAPTER TWENTY-FOUR

A Strait and a River

Gibraltar has three and a half square miles of land, a population of 30,000 people, and has been ruled by Great Britain since 1704. This tiny peninsula once guarded the entrance to the Mediterranean, but the time when thirty battleships anchored in the bay is long gone, and today there is more emphasis on hotels and taxicabs and airline schedules. Spain, feeling the pangs of nationalism, has persistently clamored for the return of Gibraltar and periodically closes the border while muttering darkly of "military action and other things." Nevertheless, Gibraltar's people are determined to remain British (a recent vote showed 12,138 for Britain, 44 for Spain). The reality is that Gibraltar is probably worth more to Spain as it is because of the trade and tourists it brings to the area.[18]

Margaret and I tied up *Whisper* at a reception dock where customs, immigration, and the police quickly cleared us. It was nice to experience the efficient British administration, and the uniformed officials were pleasant and agreeable. We then moved to a new marina near the airstrip. Unfortunately there was a lot of oil on the water from a tanker mishap in nearby Algeciras.

Like Tahiti, Gibraltar is one of the great meeting places of the sailing world, and sure enough, we saw Joe and Bonnie Darlington on *Tortoise,* and Emrys and Ingrid Thomas on *Naim.* We had met both yachts in Cyprus, we had all sailed west through the Mediterranean, and now the three of us were about to head across the Atlantic. We had great fun swapping tall stories while we ate together, and we helped one another with boat problems and advice.

Gibraltar is a good place to get British products and specialty items from distant places. I was able to buy some stainless steel fastenings, a supply of dry cell batteries, a coil of braided line, and a nautical almanac. We lugged aboard three or four boxes of food stores. Margaret and I rode up to the top of Gibraltar (426 meters) on a cable car. To the south across the deep blue of the Mediterranean we could see the brownish coastline of Morocco in Africa; to the northwest the hills of Andalucía receded into the summer haze. Below us was a maze of dockyards, apartment blocks, warehouses, and ships.

One day I met Ernest Chamberlain, an old friend from San Francisco. Ernest had been a broker for imported yachts, but after some business problems he had fled to the Far East.

"I sold my boatyard in Taiwan," he said, "and have just bought a small yard here in Gibraltar. It's over there," he pointed, "next to the airport and tucked behind the new marina. We have a small Travelift good for yachts up to thirty-eight feet and rails for larger vessels up to sixty-five feet."

Ernest looked almost the same as ten years before. Tall, lanky, a shy smile. His hair was now mostly gone except for a few white wisps.

"The last time we met was at a birthday party for you at your Hungarian girlfriend's ark in Sausalito," I said. "I bet you don't even remember her name."

"Go on," said Ernest. "You're a hard man."

"Her name?"

"Ah . . ."

We sailed for the Atlantic on September 9th at 0635. I was a bit nervous about the eight-mile-wide strait because there is a permanent east-setting current of two knots. Coupled to this, of course, is the normal six-hour reversing tidal stream. In the middle of the strait the west-going tidal stream does not overcome the current. This means that with a westerly headwind—common enough—a sailing vessel bound for the Atlantic has both the wind and tide against her. The current is less along the shore, where it *is* overcome by the westbound tidal stream. Unfortunately there are some unmarked rocks, notably La Perla (about five-eights of a mile off the north shore) on top of which lies a wreck covered at high water. With a fresh headwind the captain of a sailing vessel would be better off close-tacking along the shore; however, the problem of La Perla usually sends him to the middle of the strait where the east-going current and heavy shipping traffic combine to make life difficult.

We had had a letter from our Canadian sailing friends, Otto and Paulien Visser, that told how they had lost their yacht on the African side of the strait area because of unexpected current when the visibility was bad. I remembered reading that in 1962 it took Eric and Susan Hiscock on *Wanderer III* seven

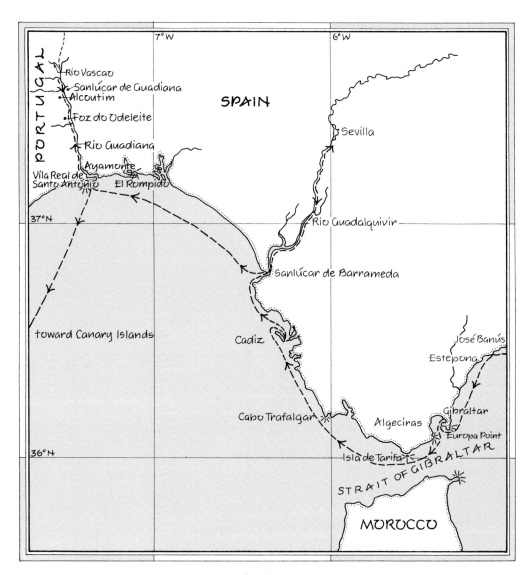

26. Gibraltar to Portugal

tries before they were able to breast the current and a foul wind. In the old days people on shore sometimes saw as many as one hundred sailing ships anchored near Algeciras waiting for a fair tidal stream and a favorable wind.[19]

Fortunately on *Whisper* we had a light northwest wind, which we combined with a favorable tide. I thought we would be able to keep track of our position and avoid La Perla by triangulation from the three big lighthouses we had in view, but we had to make several course changes to avoid small coastal ships, and we found it hard to take and plot the various compass bearings in the cross swell that was running. Nevertheless, we worked hard at the bearings from the lights and various objects on land, and by 0800 we were safely past La Perla. Two hours later we were abeam of Isla de Tarifa. The strait was behind us.

The wind switched to fifteen knots from the east, so we changed to the running rig and headed for Cabo Trafalgar, twenty-four miles to the northwest. The coastline was lovely and unspoiled, and we continued with a good wind that gradually veered throughout the day. As we passed Trafalgar I was surprised to see a large ship anchored on the offshore bank. Certainly the weather predictions must have been good. Margaret went to switch on a light below when she was looking for something in a locker and discovered that we had a general power failure. I put on my electrician's hat, and after poking around I discovered two broken hot wires at the starter solenoid on the engine. I heated a soldering iron on the Primus stove and soldered new terminals to the heavy wire ends. Once again we had power.

We were headed for the Río Guadalquivir and Sevilla on the Atlantic coast. However, we needed charts, so that evening we tied up inside the massive harbor works in the city of Cadiz (pronounced KAA-theeth), wilted from a long day of wind and sun. The next morning we took a bus to the naval station where we bought plans for the nearby coast and the Canary Islands.

The entrance to the three-hundred-mile-long Guadalquivir River was seventeen miles northwest of Cadiz. We hoped to do the forty-seven nautical miles upstream to Sevilla in one tide, so we studied the tidal tables carefully and arrived at the entrance on a Friday morning exactly at dawn. The recommendation was to begin the upstream trip at half flood. High water at Sevilla was four hours later than high water at the mouth of the river, so as we went upstream the time change favored us.

In the past we had had great fun sailing up and down rivers. We had gone up the Rio Calle Calle in Chile and had tried two small rivers in Uruguay. We had seen the Columbia River in Oregon, and sailed up four rivers in Maine. In all these rivers the navigation was generally easy because of good charts and ample buoys. Once across the entrance bar, the water was smooth, and strong tidal streams generally shot us along. Muddy bottoms and shores made anchoring easy; running aground was generally only an inconvenience. Best of all, we had often found reaching winds during much of the day, with upstream winds in the afternoons and downstream winds at night. We had learned that if we got confused or tired or headed by the wind, it was generally possible to anchor near shore out of the way of traffic.

The Guadalquivir was no different. We sailed between numbered red and green buoys, looked at the anchored Russian ship *Vladimir Favorskiy,* and hurried past the river mouth town of Sanlúcar de Barrameda. The stream was deep and wide, and some bends had been straightened and dredged. Here and there the banks had been crudely reinforced with sand bags and old tires because small and medium-sized ocean-going cargo ships went all the way to the industrial zone of Sevilla which even had shipyards. According to the pilot book, almost two thousand ships a year—with a maximum draft of 6.2 meters—went upstream to Sevilla.

Sometimes our wind fell light or was blocked by bluffs and we drifted; other times we had the rail down and sped along. We passed fishermen who used enormous dip nets that from a distance looked like white butterfly wings. At curves in the river, the trick was to time our tacks just before we touched bottom, but generally we had guidance from buoys. The landscape was a series of mostly dreary saltwater marshlands, except that on our port hand we saw large open grasslands where bulls were raised for fighting. Several times we saw these handsome black animals peering out at us like an image from a postage stamp or a sherry advertisement (I made a vow not to go aground on that side of the river).

After a few hours the river seemed like home; the sea was far away and forgotten. At noon a small tanker from Santander passed going downstream; an hour later the gray coasting ship *Cabo Formentor* overtook us, her river pilot's red and white flag bright in the sun, his wave reassuring. We began to see a few houses and settlements. People waved at us.

The pilot book spoke of a two-hundred-meter-long lock at the entrance to Sevilla. Could we get through under sail? Around a bend we saw a big squarish concrete structure across the river. The gate was open. We were going along at perhaps a knot and glided in. The water was perfectly calm. The walls of the lock rose vertically above us, we didn't see a soul, and there were no other vessels.

I glanced back. The gate was ominously closing behind us. We must have been seen. But by whom? The place was almost windless; nevertheless, we crept along with the last of the flood tide. We let *Whisper* continue for about half the lock length under the mainsail until I managed to stop the yacht by lassoing a piece of protruding ironwork with a heaving line. Margaret produced a cup of coffee while I wondered about our next move. I was thinking of a small anchor and speculating about the bottom of the lock when the upstream gate began to open. Ahead of us a horizontal image of more river and industrial Sevilla began to unfold. I cast off, and with the mainsail still hoisted we glided out as silently as we had entered. The lock tenders were certainly mystery men.

Now we were in industrial Sevilla with shipyards and mills and tall cranes. We heard hammering and saw the blue flashes of arc welding. The docks were piled high with minerals and lumber and containers ready for shipping. A smokestack from a chemical plant was spitting out some horrible-looking yellow fumes that I was sure would dissolve my lungs. In another half hour, however, the industrial maze was behind us and we were at the

Alfonso XIII Bridge. The crew of another yacht tied up along the shore told us that the bridge would open in fifteen minutes. We sailed back and forth in the wide river.

All at once we heard a great creaking and grinding. The giant bridge began to shake and tremble, cables squeaked, and we listened to what sounded like the death rattle of big machinery. The bridge staggered as it opened, and high above us an impatient policeman vigorously waved at us to hurry. Did we dare to go through? Would we be trapped forever if the bridge refused to open again? There was no time for speculation. We slipped past the rusty bridge, let go a stern anchor, and in a welter of collapsing canvas, heaving lines, and fenders, we tied up at the Sevilla yacht club with a dozen other foreign yachts. Our day had been full of fun, and it was the best sail ever. We were in the heart of Sevilla, one of the finest cities in Europe.

We stayed at the yacht club, which—like those in Argentina and Brazil—was an enormous social organization, rather than a group of sailing enthusiasts. The club had lovely grounds along the river with indoor and outdoor restaurants, three swimming pools, and courts for tennis, basketball, and Ping-Pong. A modest group of dinghies raced on the river, but it was clear that the restaurant menu had precedence over sailing trophies. On weekends the members brought their families. The women gossiped and sunned themselves, the children flocked to the pools, and the men talked while they dealt cards or stacked dominoes. As foreign sailors we were made welcome. We added a little color to the club, and the members were often down at the dock looking at *Whisper* and the other yachts from distant places.

We spent three weeks in Sevilla, a bustling city of three-quarters of a million people. We took a bus to the fifteenth-century cathedral—a colossus of carved stone, great archways, fluted columns, and sculptured doors. We walked past dazzling religious paintings and gazed up at glowing stained glass. We stopped at the tomb of Columbus, whose bier is borne on the stone shoulders of four mighty kings, resplendent in ornate vestments. We looked at religious figures covered with gold, and intricate carvings of wood and marble. We peered up at chapels with fantastic ceilings of interwoven triangles. The whole place was too rich, like an overlarge piece of Christmas cake. An hour of looking at one time was enough.

Next door we climbed up to the top of the Giralda, the old Arab tower that's the main focus of the skyline of Sevilla and rises some 118 meters into the sky. From on top, next to the bell tower, we could see out over Sevilla and look down on little streets and lanes and small cars and horse-drawn carriages.

One day on our way downtown we found the streets filled with people and no buses at all because of a big memorial parade for a favorite matador

Early Studebaker on tile painting, Sevilla

who had died from a goring in a recent bullfight. The whole city was shut down, and people were anxious to pay homage to their local hero. It was an important and serious occasion in Sevilla.

We had heard great things about a flamenco guitarist named Paco de Lucía. One Friday night Margaret and I went to see him in the Alcazar, a masterpiece of Moorish architecture that dated from the 1300s. We bought our tickets outside an ornamented gate, and with a mob of spectators we pushed through a long corridor lined with intricate tiles of blue and gold into the Patio de la Montería where the concert was to be held. We sat out-of-doors in a royal courtyard before a small stage in front of arched walkways and flowering plants. A full moon shone down from a quiet sky.

Paco de Lucía was slim man with a long thin face and large, nervous eyes. He walked to the stage clad in simple trousers and a white shirt. The young crowd was unruly and noisy until he struck the first chord; suddenly there was no one in the great patio except the guitarist.

The skill of the man was breathtaking. His guitar was a knife which he used with a furious slashing talent, and his notes cut into my heart. It was incredible how he could play a melody and the accompanying rhythm at the same moment with only one set of fingers. He ran up and down his ladder of notes like a sunbeam on a ripple of water.

In a twinkling the whole face of Spain was revealed. We heard lilting melodies, the strumming of minor chords, syncopated rhythms, flamenco clapping—all the accented life of Andalucía. We felt dark moods of despair; bright dances on the street; the flashing glint of passion. Sometimes the artist made his instrument laugh like a child or sigh like an old man. The audience was enthralled, and inhaled the music like perfume from a magical vial. Two hours of playing disappeared as quickly as a puff of smoke. Then Paco de Lucía was gone. The audience was almost too stunned to applaud. . . .

Our neighbor at the dock was the American yacht *Hornet,* a custom-built forty-three-foot fiberglass cutter from Kirkland, Washington. She was husky and well equipped with a big engine, an autopilot, various radios, a nice galley, and so forth. Aboard were Dale and Jeri Huber and their seventeen-year-old daughter Maureen. Dale was a retired doctor who was making a leisurely seven-year trip around the world. The hospitable Hubers stopped often and long, played a lot of bridge, took many side trips, and had a fairly big social life on their handsome vessel. Dale's daughter was a pretty young thing who dressed well, had a nice figure, and had a spark in her eye. All the young men on the dock had big eyes for Maureen and made ridiculous excuses to go aboard *Hornet.* Her father's dilemma was how to keep one of the young bucks from running off with her.

"I know my problem's nothing new," groaned Dale, "but she's got to grow up first."

Another yacht near us was *L'Artemis de Pytheas,* owned by Peter Tangvald whom I had met in Greece many years before. Since that time, Peter had built the sleek fifty-foot wooden vessel that he now sailed. The yacht was designed in the style of Francis Herreshoff with shoal draft and a centerboard, and built of exotic hardwoods (with twenty-four thousand copper fastenings) that Peter had fashioned with his own hands in French Guinea. Peter was tall and slender, a French-speaking Norwegian who was a U.S. citizen. Now he had a wife and two young children, and had had enough sailing adventures to fill three or four books. A consummate seaman, Peter sailed without an engine or electricity, with cotton or flax sails that he sewed by hand, and he was forever changing the rig on his vessel because he loved to experiment and try new things. Years before, Peter had written a book called *Sea Gypsy.* The name certainly fitted him. He was patient, determined, stubborn, and somewhat impractical, but he was bright, with a good brain, and regularly came up with original and clever ideas.

I couldn't help but compare Dale Huber on *Hornet* and Peter Tangvald on *L'Artemis de Pytheas.* Both were the same age, but their lives couldn't have been more different. Dr. Huber had worked hard all his life and had saved and invested his money. Now he was coasting in his senior years. Though he was a good seaman, his trip was mainly a voyage from port to port to visit different places. Sailing was a pleasant way to see the world.

Peter had sailed all his life because it was what he wanted. He had scraped out a living from boat designing, supervising yacht construction, writing, and doing odd jobs. His future seemed doubtful. Yet he was utterly fearless, and somehow he managed to continue. To him the ocean and the sailing were everything. The means were the ends.

I wondered which of my two sailing friends was happier. Or was that an unfair question? Each lived in such a different manner. What a diversity of life-styles we saw among the small-boat sailors.

In the mornings we worked on *Whisper*. I greased the windlass while Margaret sanded and oiled some interior woodwork. I removed two unwanted ventilators from the side decks and patched the holes; in the meantime Margaret painted two food storage boxes. I discovered a crack in the tiller head casting. I fitted the spare and took the broken part off to a welding shop which took a morning of hunting to find.

After lunch we often took long walks in Sevilla. A few blocks from the downtown shops and main street stores we could walk along narrow lanes with balconies overflowing with flowers. There were archways and patios decorated with heavily patterned tiles and fanciful wrought iron gates. We saw red tile roofs, pots with flowers, arabesque iron lamposts, and small fountains. We stopped in public gardens and squares, and sometimes had coffee or a glass of sherry in a little plaza or landscaped courtyard. The style of the old streets and houses was pleasing; unlike Siracusa in Sicily, which had a medieval feeling and was somewhat run down, Sevilla had a contemporary spirit, and things were kept more up to date. In Siracusa I had the feeling that I was looking at the past; in Sevilla it was the present.

Toward the end of our stay we discovered an area near the yacht club where there were small bars with two or three men who played the guitar and sang. These places had tiny dance floors, and we could watch the local people dance the Sevillana, a type of flamenco dance of the Andalucían gypsies. Generally four or five couples danced in turn while the rest of the people watched. Most of the dancers were expert and knew all the steps. A man and woman might come to a bar together, but they often danced with different partners who were chosen for their dancing ability. Everything was very jovial, and there was a lot of laughing and fun.

The Sevillana is an intense type of dance with a lot of eye contact, but no body contact at all. There are various forward and backward steps and some twirling. Once the music starts and two good dancers begin, there is a great deal of magic between them. When the music stops, however, the dance is over, the eye contact is lost, and the Sevillana is finished. The spectators in the bar watched each dancer's performance closely, and approved the various steps by smiling and applauding.

The *dancing* was the important thing. These brightly lighted bars were not places to meet people or to conduct high romance. Sex didn't seem to enter into the dancing at all, because two women often danced with one another. However, it was clear that the best dancing was between a tall slim man with glossy black hair and long sideburns, who was dressed in black with a waistcoat with silver buttons, and a pretty young woman with a yellow or bright blue patterned dress with a rustling, flaring skirt, high heels, and an elaborate hairdo.

The dancing had style and class and elegance. It was fun to watch and very pleasant. We loved it and went back again and again.

It was a bright Tuesday morning when we cast off our lines and pulled *Whisper* backward on the stern anchor we had left in the middle of the river. I hauled up the muddy fisherman anchor and coiled the warp while Margaret hoisted the mainsail and staysail. The wind was light from the east; the ebb tide had begun. We had told the keeper of the Alfonso XIII Bridge that we wanted to pass under at 0900. He had agreed, and promptly on the hour the rusty old girders began to shake and tremble. Would the decrepit machinery hold together for one more opening?

Cables shrieked, and the entire bridge shook as the bascule arms creaked upward. A policeman high up frantically waved at us. Margaret steered while I hauled up a light jib. We moved a little faster. Our friends at the yacht club who were watching our attempt to sail down the river ("Impossible," they said) waved goodbye. We eased through the opening in the bridge while bits of rust rained down on us from the unpainted girders. Suddenly we were underneath the iron curtain and through.

By 1030 we had passed the lock and were away downstream on the Guadalquivir. We continued until 1410 when the tide turned and the flood began to run against us. We anchored out of the main channel near buoy number thirty. We had a leisurely lunch and then a long sleep to catch up on the hours we had missed because of the Sevillana dancing. The river was deserted except for marsh birds and mosquitoes. The next morning at 0735 we resumed our downstream run with the ebb.

Near the mouth of the Guadalquivir River we again passed the little town of Sanlúcar de Barrameda. This was the seaport from which Magellan had sailed in September 1519 with five flag-bedecked ships, 265 cheering men, and a cargo of hope. Now, almost five hundred years later, on a sunny autumn morning, we looked at the same town and at the same wide sandy mariners' beach which lay golden and exposed at low tide on our port hand as we slowly headed downstream.

The beach in front of us was crowded with boats of all kinds: open pulling craft, high-bowed hand-liners, decrepit trawlers left to rot, local ferries, oared net-tenders, and bottom draggers used to collect edible shells. We saw a miscellany of small craft heaped with nets and poles and baskets and ropes. We passed a shipyard with six vessels neatly propped up with timbers. Two were steel trawlers resplendent in new paint; two were wooden trawlers on whose hulls men were tapping in white caulking with enormous mallets; two were new wooden boats whose shiny brown planks and smooth curves glowed warmly in the sun. Men hurried everywhere, climbing up ladders, passing up boxes of gear, new framing, metal parts. . . . A little group of workmen stood in a circle around a tall man in a hat who gestured while the others listened, their heads cocked to hear their boss's instructions.

As we slowly sailed along in *Whisper* on the last chuckle of the ebb, the water bubbled on the seaward side of the big green and red channel buoys. Farther along the shore we saw many people on the golden sand: couples walking slowly, old men (one drawing on the sand with his cane to explain something to his cronies), children skipping rope, men struggling with buckets and heavy boxes, and two Guardia Civil policemen in dark uniforms with revolver holsters that flapped on their right thighs as the men smoked and idly kicked the sand.

Along the great beach lay old hulls of all sizes moldering and collapsing. I wondered whether Magellan's *Victoria* had rotted away here after she returned from the first circumnavigation of the world. Of the five ships that started, only the *Victoria,* full of soft timbers and leaking, had limped back to Sanlúcar de Barrameda after her thirty-six-month voyage. Of the 265 sailors who had left with such enthusiasm, just eighteen half-starved veterans hobbled ashore to the church carrying votive candles and mumbling thanks to God. Had the voyage been a success? Yes, the earth was round. America was a continent separate from Asia, and there was a way through. For the first time man had become aware of the relative sizes of land and water masses on earth. The *Victoria*'s cargo of spices had paid for the entire expedition. But Magellan's bones lay in the Philippines. And what about the 247 sailors who didn't return?

As we sailed downstream I saw four kinds of hulks on the beach. Some hulls simply caved in at the middle, and the gentle curve of the hull collapsed like a punctured balloon. Some hulls twisted as they decayed, the timbers wringing and turning like a towel being wrung out. Some hulls simply broke away in place. The pieces were swept away by the river at high water, and the hull's freeboard was gradually cut down and down. Finally, some hulls lost their stems and sterns—their fronts and backs—and the bow and transom timbers and fastenings eroded away until only the midship section was left standing like a gull poised for flight.

Did the *Victoria,* I wondered, end up abandoned on this same beach, a skeleton of eroding timbers like all the rest? What was life anyway but a collection of new timbers, the seasoning and shaping into a useful hull, the long voyage, a gradual collapse, and the final rotting away? Man was a ship. Or was a ship a man? The metaphor was a circle. I was getting too philosophical again.

. . . .

CHAPTER TWENTY-FIVE

One More River

Now we felt the swell of the Atlantic again. We were set to go to the Canary Islands and then west, but first we thought we'd have a glance at Portugal and head up another river.

"You must see the Rio Guadiana before you cross the Atlantic," our friends in the Mediterranean had said. "It's the border river between Spain and Portugal. You'll find it peaceful and quiet."

After the social whirl of Sevilla, something pastoral was just what we needed. The distance was sixty miles to the northwest. The wind was light and from the southwest; the sun burned down from a cloudless sky. Red and yellow fishing boats worked in the distance, and when one of them pulled up a net we could see the glitter of white sea gull wings as the birds dived for scraps.

At 2134 Margaret identified the powerful Spanish light at El Rompido. An hour later we began to see the Portuguese light at Vila Real de Santo António at the mouth of the Guadiana River. Because of our slow trip down the Guadalquivir River and light winds on the ocean, we arrived off the mouth of the Guadiana River at midnight. I do not like night arrivals in strange places, but we had excellent charts and information. The sea was smooth, we had a fair, rising tidal stream, and the bar across the Guadiana

Whisper, Rio Guadiana, Portugal

was well marked with lighted buoys. To have entered in daylight we would
have had to wait twelve hours for a complete tidal change; in the meantime
an onshore wind might have appeared and stirred up the seas on the bar.

Everything seemed favorable. I had good feelings. Nevertheless, I bit
my lower lip with nervousness as we headed in. Margaret called out the
depths. I steered while I played with the sheets and tried to look nonchalant.
Whisper's keel needed one meter eighty centimeters, but a swell could easily
send a depth of three meters down to one meter fifty.

"Six meters twenty," she called. "Six meters ten. Five meters fifty. Four
twenty. Four thirty."

We had passed exactly between two of the entrance buoys, which were
flashing red and green.

"Four meters thirty. Three meters ninety. Three meters seventy. Three
meters sixty."

I was breathing deeply and twisting the main sheet into knots.

"Three meters sixty. Three meters sixty. Four fifty. Five meters fifty."

We had crossed the bar and were in the river! I rubbed the wrinkles
from my brow.

We passed between the flashing lights at the ends of the seawalls. The
big lighthouse and the town of Vila Real De Santo António were in front
of us. The river was quiet, and Margaret and I looked ahead at the dark water
which the great searching beam of the lighthouse swept every six and a half
seconds. In another thirty minutes we were abreast of the sleeping town. The
time was 0245. I dropped the anchor in an eight-meter patch while we sailed
along at two knots or so. We felt the anchor skid along the bottom, dig in,
and swing us around. We handed the sails and went to sleep.

The next morning we put the dinghy in the water. Margaret rowed me
ashore and returned to *Whisper* while I went off to see Portuguese customs.
A uniformed official said that I needed to check with the harbormaster first.
When I finally found the *capitania*'s office I was told that the harbormaster
had gone out. "Come back at 1100."

Vila Real De Santo António was a riverfront town of small houses and
shops, with a pretty park along the water. A scattering of Spanish tourists
who had crossed on the ferry from Ayamonte on the Spanish side strolled
up and down the main street. I changed a little money at the bank. Nearby
was a large and active fish market, and the produce market was booming too.
For the equivalent of seven U.S. dollars, I bought a load of fruit, vegetables,
meat, nuts, and bread that I could scarcely carry.

At 1115 I walked back to see the harbormaster, who was still gone. No
one knew when he would return. "Maybe never," shrugged a subofficial with
a grin. I said that I was sailing upriver and would check in with a *functionário*
upstream. At least I had made an effort.

Back on the yacht we lifted the dinghy aboard and hauled up the anchor and sails. As we headed upstream—north—we were surprised to see eight or nine yachts and a dozen husky fishing boats in a little harbor on the west bank just above Vila Real. With a fair wind and tide we skimmed along on smooth water and soon passed the little Spanish town of Ayamonte on our starboard hand. In Palma de Mallorca I had swapped a couple of books for a recreational boating guide to the Portuguese Algarve that included strip maps for the river. We had the maps on the cabin top in front of the helmsman, and we checked off each point as we sailed along. Every few miles there were customs houses on each side of the river. Portuguese on the west; Spanish to the east. The customs houses were deserted and in ruins, but they made good checkpoints.

The river was one-quarter to three-eights of a mile wide, clear of rocks, and meandered along between low hills partially covered with scrub trees. We found a least depth of three meters sixty centimeters at half tide. Once past the two towns at the river mouth and their fishing fleets, we saw little on the water except an occasional yacht.

The sailing was easy and pleasant, and the unspoiled river and country-side were beautiful. Unlike the Guadalquivir, which ran through marshy lowlands and had been deepened and straightened in places and had a some-what artificial look, the Guadiana was natural and untouched and ran through gentle rolling hills. We passed small vineyards, fig and olive trees, and fields of corn and melons. We saw farmers loading hay on patient donkeys, and men rolling hogsheads and smaller casks of dark wood down to the river where they were washed and soaked. Sometimes we heard the tinkling of bells around the necks of goats and sheep.

We continued upstream about thirteen nautical miles until the tide turned, and anchored at a hamlet called Foz do Odeleite. What could have been better? A perfectly sheltered anchorage, and peace and quiet. The only sounds were from kingfishers, magpies, and orioles.

The yacht was in reasonably good order and we had plenty of food aboard, so I decided to stay in the river for a few weeks and do some writing. While I worked at the saloon table, Margaret often went rowing up peaceful side creeks where she watched birds and collected wildflowers. Every day or two a yacht would appear—some going up, some down—and perhaps anchor near us. We exchanged gossip and information—what boats were upstream and down, new places for walks ashore, and farmers who had food for sale.

One afternoon we heard about a dance festival, so we sailed upstream another nine miles and anchored between the Spanish village of Sanlúcar de Guadiana on the east bank and the Portuguese hamlet of Alcoutim on the west bank. In Alcoutim a stage had been erected along the river and decorated with hundreds of small green and white flags that fluttered in the wind. As we anchored we heard music, so we hurried ashore.

The Portuguese dancers were dressed in traditional farmers' outfits, with the men in white shirts, dark trousers, leather vests, neck scarves, boots, and black felt hats. The women wore colorful blouses and peasant skirts overlaid with small white aprons, patterned white stockings, and short boots. A man and woman danced together with a lot of whirling and turning. Then a dozen couples danced in a circle with turns and bows and heavy foot stamping. The performance was pleasing, but it totally lacked the charm and sensuality of the Sevillana flamenco dancing in Seville. I was surprised that in going down one river and up a second—and merely stepping across a border—we'd slipped from a dancing style crowned with elegance and grace to a simple kind of rural folk dancing.

We sailed upstream another five miles to the confluence of the Rio Vascão. Along the banks of the Guadiana, among the willows and poplars and red-flowered oleanders, we saw trees with yellow-green fruit.

"I think they're lemons because the skins are wrinkly," said Margaret after studying the trees with the binoculars.

I thought they were wild apples. There were hundreds of the trees. Finally, when we were out rowing we picked some of the fruit, whose flesh was pulpy and coarse. Only later did we learn that we had picked unripe pomegranates.

On October 15th, I went shopping in Sanlúcar de Guadiana. The next day was Margaret's birthday so I went to the baker, ostensibly to buy two loaves of bread.

"Buenas dias, señora," I said to the baker's wife. "I want to buy a birthday cake for my wife. A surprise. Can you make me a nice cake?"

"Oh no, señor! It is not possible. We only make the humble bread. What you need is the especialista in the next village. He can make a cake that will bring the sparkle of love to your wife's eyes."

While this conversation went on, other members of the baker's family appeared. The baker wiping his hands on a towel. Silent children with enormous brown eyes. Assorted aunts in black. By now a few customers had dropped in. Soon everyone knew about Margaret's birthday and the cake. A modicum of gossip had begun.

I gave the baker's wife some coins and asked her to telephone the *especialista*. She went off to the village phone. How would I pay for the cake? The bus driver? Indeed, would I ever see the cake?

A little later when Margaret appeared outside the baker's shop, I quickly put my forefinger across my lips and winked at the baker's wife. She under-

Portuguese dancers, Alcoutim

stood, passed the word to the others, and looked sly and cunning when Margaret came in the shop. The aunts in black cackled with excitement.

The next afternoon I rowed ashore at the appointed hour and went to the baker. Sure enough, there was a box, and a white frosted cake with decorations. I showed the cake, and everyone looked and exclaimed, especially the baker's children with the big brown eyes. I paid and left the little shop after shaking hands with the baker, his wife, the children, the aunts in black, and the neighbors. My little transaction had been delightful. I had gotten the cake, and I had had a glimpse of life in a Spanish village.

That night Margaret and I had dinner with Hiller and Chris Masker on the American yacht *Terra*. The cake was a big success. I saved a big piece for the baker's children which I took ashore the next morning.

On our last trip down the river we stopped in the harbor at Vila Real to see the officials about clearance papers. We soon learned that when a herring boat came in from a successful night of seining, someone immediately set off a colossal siren to summon the fish buyers. It was obvious that the fish catch was much more important than the church or the time signal or the fire brigade.

I was fascinated by the Portuguese trains that ran near the harbor many times a day (and night). Each had a piercing whistle to warn people and cars at the road crossings. Vila Real was the last stop at the border, and the little green passenger cars were always empty when the trains arrived. When a train was ready to depart, going west on its outbound trip, the whistle shrieked and the brakeman signaled down the line. The engineer nodded and touched his levers, and all the little railroad cars rattled and jerked forward into motion. At that moment I wanted nothing more than to hop aboard with my suitcase and travel off to distant places. I guess travelers are not made, they're born.

. . . .

CHAPTER TWENTY-SIX

Halfway
Across the Atlantic

*W*e sailed across the bar of the Guadiana River on October 19th, bound for the Canary Islands, seven hundred miles to the southwest. The wind was brisk, on our nose, and the best we could do was a course a little east of south. We soon shortened down to the number three jib, put one reef in the mainsail, and dropped the staysail. We saw lots of Spanish and Portuguese fishing boats and a regular stream of big ship traffic to and from the Strait of Gibraltar.

The sea was rough. Rain poured down from low clouds. We didn't feel well. We were soft from life ashore and the weeks we had spent in the calm rivers. Not only were we sailing slightly east, but a strong tidal stream was pushing us east as well. If we weren't careful we would get shoved back into the Mediterranean. I surmised that a small east-going frontal system was passing north of us. The wind should veer; the tide would change; all we had to do was play for time. Since there was no point in sailing south-southeast toward the African coast, I hove-to on the port tack and slowly fore-reached toward the northwest.

Sure enough, a few hours later the wind began to swing clockwise, and the southwest wind went west, then northwest. Marvelous! We got going again, and soon were busy making more sail as the weather depression disappeared eastward and the sky cleared. Unfortunately, when I put up the staysail there were three big lumps of crude oil that had washed into the folds of the sail when it had been lashed on deck. I scrubbed the sail with detergent

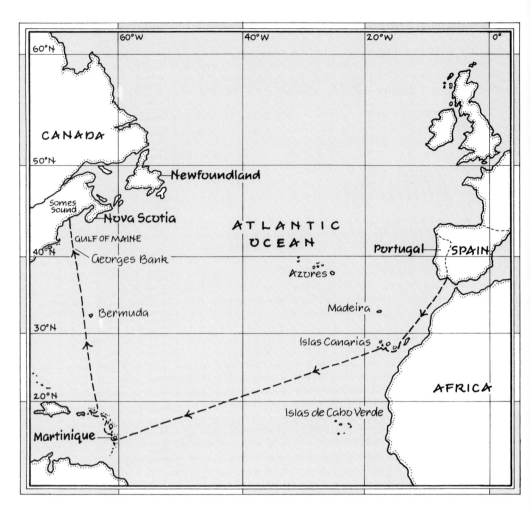

27. The Atlantic Ocean (Portugal to Maine)

and water, but the ugly oil marks did not come off. I cursed the ships and their oil dumping.

Just after midnight we had an enormous cruise ship and six other large vessels close around us. As I took compass bearings of the various vessels and considered evasive action, I realized that the seven ships were changing courses to avoid one another. Their moves made a sort of three-dimensional chess game. I kept a white flare in my hand and was ready to fire it to show my position, but little by little the ships edged away and soon the sea was clear.

On the second day we began to get our sea legs. The shipping traffic was less, the sea was smoother, and we had sailed away from the tidal influence of Gibraltar. For the next few days the wind continued to veer, and soon settled into the northeast. Had we found the trade wind? Certainly the sailing was better, although the wind was fresh and got up to twenty-six knots at times. With a number three jib poled out to starboard and a single-reefed mainsail eased to port, *Whisper* was overpowered. Her course was steadier and just as fast after a second reef.

On the fifth day I was routinely gybing the mainsail during a minor wind change when the Dacron reinforcement at the clew grommet for the second reef ripped off. This surprised me. I dropped the mainsail, set the trysail, and set to work to repair the sail. The clew tabling extended downward from the grommet twenty-three centimeters. It was obvious that the clew tabling should have extended *upward* for that distance as well. Once I started sewing, it was also obvious that the leech of the sail was very rotten. Though we had used a sail cover as much as possible, the tropical sun had done its cancerous work during the long sea passages.

On the evening of October 23rd we saw strange lights ahead, lights we could not figure out. Were the lights a tug with a tow? Warships of some kind? A bulk carrier? An oil rig? The mother ship of a big fishing operation? Or what? After two hours we finally got abeam of an ocean-going tug that was towing an enormous oil rig. Starting from the top down, the tug's mast carried a red, then a white, then a red light ("Unable to deviate from her course"); then three white lights ("Tow exceeds 200 meters"). Six lights in a vertical row.

The fresh northeast trade wind eased to ten knots during the next two days, and we glided along with full sail area on a lovely sea of deep blue. I was reading *The Last Lion,* a monumental account of Winston Churchill by William Manchester. Margaret was engrossed in *The Trail of the Fox,* a biography of Erwin Rommel by David Irving. I found it curious that both biographers had used animals to describe these World War II leaders. Were power and craftiness essential parts of leadership?

We were headed for Spain's Islas Canarias, a group of seven large volcanic islands 50 to 250 miles off the African coast at twenty-eight degrees north latitude. Our destination was the city of Las Palmas on the northeast coast of Gran Canaria, a circular-shaped island about 25 miles in diameter, which we reached on the morning of the sixth day from Portugal.

[From the log] October 23th. 1023. How pleasant it is to sail into a new port. I am rested after a good sleep, with a new island and a new harbor to unwrap. Ahead in the distance a white cruise ship turns across our course and heads east. To starboard a small oil tanker idles past, low in the sea like a water insect. In the distance I see the gray barrier of a long breakwater and white buildings marching up a hill. A little closer now a line of harbor cranes heaves into view. We pass a yellow and blue open fishing boat, its two occupants bent low over lines and hooks coiled in flat baskets. Now, as the white cruise ship shows us her stern, we see that she is a car ferry with a black squarish rectangle at her stern for unloading. I count five silvery oil tanks on the hill north of the city.

Close in, the skyline of Las Palmas was cut by docks, wharves, and the silhouettes of laid-up oil tankers. We soon heard the buzz of cars, and could see buses whizzing along expressways. We sailed into the harbor and tied up along a seawall with twenty French yachts, three U.S., two Swiss, two English, one German, and one Swedish. Another fifteen to twenty yachts were anchored nearby. One of the American yachts was *Tortoise;* Margaret and I were pleased to see Joe and Bonnie Darlington again.

Although there were big ships from various countries, more than half hailed from Russia. Downtown we noticed Russian sailors, and shops with signs in Russian Cyrillic script. Las Palmas was the first seaport I'd seen with billboards that advertised Japanese radios in Russian. I found an excellent hardware store (Alcorde) that had five floors of tools of every sort from many countries. The French and Spanish tools were first class. I bought a few metal files, two wood rasps, some offset screwdrivers, and an odd-sized metric wrench. My sailing friend Tom Zydler had recommended Las Palmas as a good place to buy a solar panel. After some hunting I found a shop where I purchased a forty-watt Japanese Kyocera panel.

Unfortunately the harbor had a slick of smelly oil. The trouble was that the oil operations were at the upwind (northeast) end of the harbor. When there was a spill of any sort, the oil drifted downwind and collected in the small-boat area, which had no downwind outlet to the sea. The authorities had erected a floating barrier for the oil at the entrance to the small-boat area, but it was only partially effective, and any oil that got past the barrier had no place to go. (Either the small-boat area should have been moved or a downwind drainage cut made to the sea.) The oil was a mess, its smell made me ill, and it drove us away.

We sailed to Tenerife, the next island west. It's a long, vaguely triangular-shaped island whose greatest dimension is forty-six miles. We had been told that Los Cristianos, a port in the south, was a good place for yachts. When we got there, however, we found the small harbor jammed to bursting.

The procedure for a ship entering an anchorage is to anchor in the same fashion as the vessels already there. If you find a fishing boat swinging on a single anchor, then you also drop a single anchor. If everyone uses both a bow and a stern anchor (to prevent swinging), then you do the same. When we entered Los Cristianos, however, we saw some yachts on one anchor and some on two. When the wind changed, the yachts on single anchors swung into the stationary yachts which caused much trouble.

Most of the anchored vessels were from France and their captains were on their first overseas voyages; the men were inexperienced and unsure of themselves. Los Cristianos was perhaps the first place they had ever used an anchor. Instead of changing their anchors or moving a bit, the captains threatened their neighbors. In this situation we moved quite close to the shore (away from the problem yachts), dropped a bow anchor, and took a stern

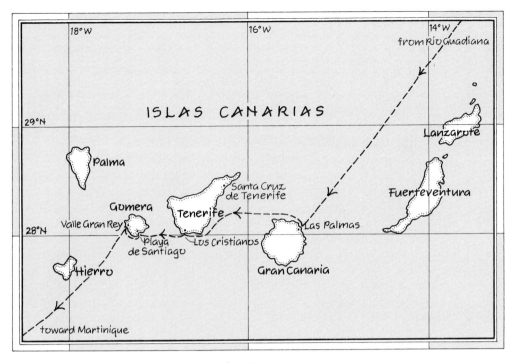

18°W · 16°W · 14°W
from Río Guadiana

ISLAS CANARIAS

29°N

Lanzarote

Palma

Santa Cruz
de Tenerife

Gomera

Tenerife

Fuerteventura

Valle Gran Rey

28°N

Las Palmas

Playa
de Santiago

Los Cristianos

Hierro

Gran Canaria

toward Martinique

28. Islas Canarias

anchor toward the beach. This way it was unlikely that anyone would swing into us, and no one could anchor between us and the beach.

I counted fifty-six yachts at anchor in Los Cristianos. In addition, one was on land and for sale. Eight were hauled out for bottom painting. One was at the fuel dock, and twenty-three French yachts—mostly small and home-built—were in a tiny inner harbor, known locally as the ghetto. Here there were many naked or seminaked women with tiny babies, much breast-feeding, and naked men pissing over the side. Many of the people were dirty and unkempt, and the yachts were generally run-down. The place seemed a breeding ground for ne'er-do-wells. On such a beautiful island where there was plenty of work for willing people, I found this collection of yachts and people inexcusable. One look filled me with disgust, and even the Spanish fishermen shook their heads when they walked past. I have no desire to say bad things about French sailors because I have many French friends who are expert sailors and wonderful people, but the scene in Los Cristianos was not good.

In spite of my grumbling, Margaret and I wanted to go ashore for a day and look around Tenerife. We rented a car and made a circuit of the island. It was only the second or third time on our world trip that we'd taken a car, and we had great fun speeding along a good road with the wind flying in our faces. We drove to Santa Cruz de Tenerife, the main city, and had a look at the parks and its new harbor seven kilometers north. We then drove to the central part of the island and gradually climbed through pine forests to the slopes of Pico de Teide, Tenerife's great solitary mountain, which sticks up 3,718 meters and is visible for fifty miles at sea. As we gained altitude we left the trees behind and soon were on the immense brown shoulder of the mountain. At the base of a cable car to the summit we saw a cluster of tourist buses and a pack of swarming ants. We didn't feel like waiting, so we drove on to the southwest coast.

We looked at various ports such as Los Gigantes, a new small-boat harbor in a resort-retirement town that wasn't even on our latest Spanish charts. The day was warm, dry, and sunny; the air was clear and sparkling. The hill above the harbor had hundreds of pretty villas facing the blue Atlantic below. The houses were new, with red tile roofs, and nicely designed. I particularly liked the red carnations and bracts of red and purple bougainvillea that tumbled over the white walls.

There was an incredible amount of resort housing going up along the southwest coast. The old banana plantations were disappearing under clouds of dust as great yellow earth-moving machines leveled building sites. Surveyors were laying out new access roads, and we sped past the steel skeletons of new high-rise hotels. Workmen in hard hats poured concrete into forms, and we heard the clang of hammers on metal as we passed. Men on scaffolding plastered outside walls, and we watched a crane juggling a giant window for a new hotel. Everyone seemed to be in a hurry, even the people on holiday and those presumably retired.

We passed a dozen real estate offices with signs in several languages. "Thirty percent down," "Creative financing," "Why freeze in Europe?" and so on. It looked to me as if the land speculators had found paradise. Real estate was booming, mostly for European customers, especially Germans, who were everywhere. In a coffee shop we heard German, not Spanish. The attendant in a gas station greeted me with: "Wie geht's?" Tenerife was a Spanish island, but I think the Germans had conquered it with money and attention. Hitler could have taken a few lessons from a panzer operation that was driven by deutsche marks instead of bullets.

Back at Los Cristianos among the anchored yachts we saw *Naim,* and our friends Emrys and Ingrid Thomas from Cyprus. Near us was *Half Pint,* a Swan 36 from Australia with Christopher Price and Sylvia Jamieson on board. Chris and Sylvia had chucked out a defective engine and had installed a new three-cylinder Yanmar diesel while at anchor, a prodigious undertaking.

Chris told us of a windward passage in *Half Pint* when both he and Sylvia were in the cockpit together. After some time one of them went below and was horrified to find large amounts of water. Everything was soaked.

What could have happened? Was the yacht sinking? Chris and Sylvia immediately set to work with the bilge pumps, but the water seemed no less. Only after a while did one of them discover that a forward portlight was closed, but not dogged down. Every foredeck wave let in half a dozen liters of seawater. Yet the portlight *looked* closed until someone actually saw water pouring through. It was a good lesson to remember.

From Tenerife we sailed to Gomera, where we stopped at Playa de Santiago on the south coast. Though the place was recommended and appeared to have shelter, a terrible surge crept into the tiny harbor from the east. There were six fishing boats on moorings, and half a dozen yachts with stern anchors out and their bows tied to an enormous seawall of stone blocks. Like the others, we laid out anchors and took lines ashore. However, as I watched, the surge increased to about two meters, and made great sucking noises as the water sluiced in and out. I remember so well motioning to a fisherman on shore that it looked doubtful. He motioned back that it was no good. I watched for another half hour and decided to clear out. I waved to the fisherman to cast off my bow lines, and I began to haul in the stern anchors. Because of the noise of the surging water, the fisherman and I communicated entirely by gestures. It was marvelous how we understood each other so well. He and I agreed that the place was definitely *malo*—bad—and that it would be a miracle if one or two of the small vessels were not matchwood before morning. I was certainly relieved to get out to the safety of the sea.

We sailed slowly up the mountainous west coast of Gomera, hove-to for part of the night, and the next morning went into the new harbor of Valle Gran Rey, another place that wasn't on our Spanish charts. We found a substantial new harbor with no oil, no crowding, no real estate speculators, and no surge.

Gomera's coastline was a series of high, dark cliffs with an occasional narrow valley. Here and there were tiny villages with steplike terraced fields that had been hacked out of the mountain slopes and farmed for centuries. The countryside was poor; the living primitive; the people proud. In Valle Gran Rey the locals were Spaniards who did a little fishing and farming and grew bananas.

Unlike the West Indies and other places where rainfall is adequate, the Gomera banana plants were drip-irrigated with a vast system of pipes, aqueducts, channels, gates, diversions, and so forth. Each field was sheltered by high masonry walls, and the stems of ripening bananas were enclosed in blue plastic bags to hasten ripening and to protect the fruit.

"The bananas are very labor intensive and require complicated watering and much care," said Richard Sanderson, a transplanted Englishman we met

A view of the mountain of Pico de Teide on Tenerife
from the northeast coast of Gomera

in Valle Gran Rey. Richard had a plantation with four thousand plants a
mile south of the harbor. Most of his bananas were sold in southern Spain,
but according to Richard, a grower got only one-third of the selling price
because various mafia-type middlemen took cuts. Richard was gradually
switching from bananas to mangoes because he thought the profit would be
better in the long run. However, a mango tree took about five years to bring
to production and required some difficult grafting.

We spent a few days getting *Whisper* ready for the Atlantic. On
November 12th our work was finished, so we put up our sails and slipped
away from Valle Gran Rey. Our goal was Fort-de-France, Martinique, 2,707
miles to the west. For starters we had winds from the north, so we headed
southwest to get clear of the islands. At sunset on the first evening we were
able to see Hierro, La Palma, Gomera, and Tenerife. Late that night I looked
out at the twinkling lights of Taibique and San Andres, two villages high
on the eastern slopes of Hierro. The little settlements looked so small and so
isolated, such tiny satellites of life.

We hoped for the northeast trade wind for the entire Atlantic crossing.
For the first few days the winds varied in strength between ten and twenty-six
knots, and we changed the mainsail area and the headsails accordingly. With

the running rig set and a headsail poled out, we rolled from side to side, generally more in light winds and less in strong. When the wind backed to the north we were able to haul in the mainsail, take down the headsail pole, and sheet the jib or genoa to leeward. Then as we speeded up and the apparent wind moved forward, we reached along with the fore-and-aft rig. We rolled less, and the motion was steadier.

The latitude of Gomera is twenty-eight degrees north. Martinique is fifteen degrees north, so we needed to get south for thirteen degrees or 780 miles. Since the trade wind is supposed to be more developed and stronger farther south, we shaped our course to work southwest until we reached thirty degrees west longitude. Our course would then be due west.

[From my journal] November 16th. Just before dawn I saw the most extraordinary sky. The eastern half was clear while the western half was layered with a sheet of thick, horizontal clouds. A bright moon shone down from the clear sky almost directly overhead, just ahead of the cloudbank. The light poured down from the moon, skimmed across the edges of the clouds, and opened their furrows and ridges into strange, ghostlike forms.

It seemed that I was looking up at the jagged edges of shattered glass. Or was I peering down into glacial crevasses and seeing new ice forms? Was it a backlighted snowbank cut by a knife and magnified a thousand times? A microscopic world of sugar crystals? Handfuls of sparkling mirrors?

I had the feeling that I was not looking at clouds at all but at the edge of the world. As I peered up and up I got a bit dizzy, and I leaned against *Whisper's* hatchway for support. Was I perched on the lip of a flat earth and about to topple over the edge? No wonder the sailors with Christopher Columbus had gotten excited at times and wanted to turn back to Spain.

However, as I watched, the moon slipped into the clouds. The searching light was gone. The door had closed.

I was jarred back to earth by noise in the cockpit. The tiller had worked loose from the tiller head. Although we used lock washers and double nuts on the bolts, the tiller fastenings needed tightening every few days. The steering vane lines pulled the tiller back and forth hundreds of times every twenty-four hours and somehow shook the bolts loose. I made a note to drill small holes through the bolts, to get castellated nuts, and to wire the three bolts together aircraft fashion.

Although our wind blew from some easterly direction, it was not steady, and we seemed to be forever juggling the sails. We had gotten south to twenty-three degrees north, and I began to see dozens of small puffy clouds, the cotton-ball indicators that usually meant a settled trade wind. Nevertheless, one night we were becalmed for eight hours.

By now we were well out in the Atlantic and had found our sea legs. Our appetites had returned. We had taken five dozen fresh eggs (which keep well if greased with Vaseline petroleum jelly). Sometimes for breakfast we had a four-egg omelet stuffed with sautéed onions and green peppers and ham (from a hundred-gram or four-ounce can). We had left with a good stock of fresh fruits and vegetables, and for lunch one day we had a large cauliflower with a cheese sauce and tomatoes.

For dinner I particularly liked *Whisper* beef stroganoff:

> 1 340-gram (12-ounce) can roast beef and gravy
> 1 small can (170 grams or 6 ounces) Nestlé Cream
> 1 small can (4 ounces or 113 grams) mushrooms (any type)
> 1 fresh medium-sized onion, chopped
> 1 tablespoon shortening (margarine, Crisco, or butter)
> A grating of nutmeg

Fry the onion lightly in the shortening. Break up the large pieces of roast beef with a fork and add them and the gravy to the onion. Drain the mushrooms (discard the water) and put them with the onion and beef. Heat over a medium flame for ten minutes. Just before serving, stir in half the can of cream. Heat through but do not boil. Grate the nutmeg on top, and serve over steamed rice. The beef stroganoff is tasty and a powerful meal for two.

By November 19th we were at thirty degrees west. We had worked south to twenty-two degrees north latitude, but we still had 420 miles to go to reach the parallel of Martinique. The sky seemed filled with squalls, and heavy rain drummed on the deck most of the day and night. The wind veered to the southeast, and Margaret and I ran the sails up and down as the squalls passed. In an effort to reduce chafe, I had been experimenting with a snap-shackle connection between the end of the spinnaker pole and the clew of a running headsail. In the late afternoon the snapshackle broke. Without a sheet, the headsail began to flog violently, and the pole banged against the headstay. I rushed forward and lowered the sail and pole, but the sheets got in the water and under the keel. It took a while to sort all this out, and I decided to go back to conventional bowlines instead of experimental hardware. At 1715 we had two reefs in the main, no headsail, and were doing six to seven knots. An hour later the sky was clear, all the sails were back up, porpoises were playing around the ship, and we were looking at a spectacular rainbow. The excitement was over. Or was it?

[From the log] November 22nd. 0903. For days we've had a terrible squeak that's been impossible to find, although we've hunted from one end of *Whisper* to the other. The squeak has been like a mysterious bird that always sings from somewhere else. Was it at the end of the spinnaker pole? No! Up the mast? I put my ear against the spar and listened carefully. No! I was sure the squeak came from a dry bearing in a block somewhere, so I oiled everything in sight. The squeak continued. Finally I went aft and watched the steering vane for a while. Suddenly the swinging vane quadrant let out a ferocious screech. Of course! The back of the vane mount had gotten slightly bent during the Bramble Cay episode, and the quadrant occasionally rubbed on it. One shot of Teflon spray ended the problem.

After thousands of hours of exposure to the sun and weather, the cloth in our sails had become thin and weak. We had new spare sails on board, but on this downwind crossing we preferred to use the old sails and to save our new sails for harder going. We often took down a sail that needed a few stitches or a patch. We had a roll of wide Dacron tape with super adhesive on the back that was good for rips and problem areas. We stuck a piece on each side, put in a few widely spaced stitches to be sure the patch would stay, and cranked up the sail again.

Sail mending

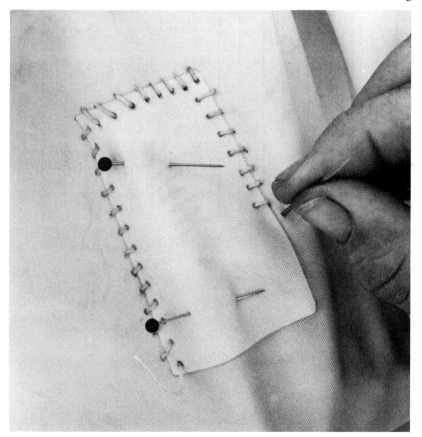

Just before noon on November 24th, I saw a sail four or five miles behind us on our port quarter. It was the first vessel we'd seen since the Canary Islands. The yacht appeared to be larger than *Whisper* and gradually got closer. I turned on a little portable VHF set we had acquired in Cyprus and spoke with Peter Mullins, who was from Guernsey in the Channel Islands. Peter was sailing from Tenerife to Antigua in a twenty-two-meter Joubert-designed ketch named *Chrisma of Sark* that had been built in France in 1978. He had sold his real estate business and was staking his future on the Caribbean charter business.

Because it's unusual for yachts to meet at sea, I asked Peter to take a photograph of *Whisper*. It's surprising how long it takes one vessel to overtake a second when the speed difference is only a knot or two. I dropped our genoa to let *Chrisma* come up with us before dark.

Peter had eight people on board, and when the sleek aluminum ketch pulled alongside us, I was amazed to see the captain steering while dressed in a tuxedo! Peter had decided to combine our meeting with a mid-ocean party. One woman wore only a fishnet, and everyone else was dressed formally or informally. When our little meeting was over, the crew eased *Chrisma*'s big main and mizzen, hoisted a genoa, and soon began to pull away into the setting sun. It was exciting to see the other yacht, and we all waved and shouted. The tuxedo was fun, but who will believe me?

. . . .

CHAPTER TWENTY-SEVEN

The Caribbean Atlantic and North

*T*he meeting with *Chrisma* somehow broke the Atlantic passage into two parts. Europe and Africa were behind us. America and the Caribbean seemed nearby.

[From my journal] November 27th. 0950. Fifteenth day from Gomera; 830 nautical miles to Martinique. We have been reaching along with a twelve-knot breeze from the southeast and going along splendidly—almost six knots on a reasonably smooth ocean. At times *Whisper* sails so beautifully that I can hardly believe it. I know that she goes better than she used to, and two changes have contributed a lot. The first is her folding propeller, lack of a propeller aperture, and a very streamlined rudder. The second reason is an extra hundred square feet of sail area.

A long passage at sea untroubled by any big problems is certainly a good time to get at peace with yourself. I feel mellow and relaxed.

The next night the wind got surprisingly strong. We deeply reefed the mainsail and sped through the night. At noon we showed 147 miles, our best run in the Atlantic so far. When I unreefed the mainsail in the afternoon I was horrified to discover two vertical rips below the clew for the deep reef. We sewed on more patches.

Every day I tuned in to the BBC for news and general interest programs for an hour or two. We thought the BBC was infinitely better than either the Voice of America or Radio Moscow, both of which droned on endlessly with dreary political stuff. One night I happened to tune to an English-language program on Radio Albania, a station I had never heard before. A woman—who spoke particularly well—thoroughly vilified England and the United States. The socialist movement was right, of course, and the trend of the future. A news synopsis followed, with every item slanted to fit the socialist mold. This was followed by a historical summary of the Albanian socialist movement since 1942. Interested listeners could write for copies. I couldn't wait to write.

On November 30th the wind blew from the southeast at sixteen knots. Martinique lay 430 miles to the west. A tropicbird with a bright orange bill and a high-pitched "kikikikikikiki" squawk flew around and around in the early afternoon and woke me from a deep sleep. Margaret was grumpy because she had tried a new recipe for Scottish oatmeal biscuits. They were a disaster, and when she threw them over the side they sank at once. In the evening we had a lovely view of Venus and Jupiter just above the new moon in the western sky. "In the new moon's upturned arms," said Margaret.

One day I climbed partway up the mast to check something. I happened to look down on the deck of *Whisper* from my high perch, and the thought went through my mind that the materials in my vessel were all new and had existed only a short time. When I started sailing about twenty-five years earlier, yachts were built of wood, cotton sails were going strong, and all the lines on board were made of manila, which was twisted from the leafstalks of a Philippine plant called the abaca. In just a quarter of a century, fiberglass hull construction had replaced wood, sails were made of Dacron, and Dacron and nylon lines had completely eclipsed manila. *Whisper*'s first two masts were made of spruce; the third was aluminum. Why? Because all these new materials are superior. Lighter, stronger, longer lasting, rot-resistant, tougher, and—in the long run—much cheaper.

I realize that a few purists still build wooden vessels, but time and the practical world are not on their side. The romantics still like varnished mahogany. I like it too. But I think the place for varnished hardwoods is for exterior trim and interior woodwork.

The revolution has not only been in materials. When I started sailing we carried a wind-up chronometer. Now Margaret and I had quartz crystal watches that required no daily winding and ran with incredible accuracy. We carried two sextants on board, but during the trip around the world we bought a satellite navigation device that made our sailing safer by giving us frequent fixes regardless of weather or time of day. We had a wind vane steering device that guided us across oceans day after day. When I had bought my first wind vane gear from inventor Blondie Hasler more than twenty years earlier, a crowd collected whenever we tied up the yacht at a dock. Now vane gear was commonplace. Another invention was a masthead navi-

gation light (publicized by Bernard Hayman) with a vertical filament bulb
that was visible for miles instead of pathetic kerosene running lights near deck
level.

As we sailed toward the Caribbean, I read about an interface scheme
between a loran C navigation device and an electric autopilot. This meant
that a sailor could find his position from radio beams and direct this information to a device that would steer his vessel. (The next step would be to radio
orders to the black boxes from land. Why go to sea at all?) Of course, the
loran and autopilot might break down. Therefore you would need two of
each. The electricity to run all this might be difficult, so you would require
a generator, plus a spare. The list could be extended and might include:

desalinizer	refrigerator
air-conditioning	bow thrusters
automatic radio direction finder	weatherfax receiver
satellite telephone system	radar
electric or hydraulic winches	radar alarm
sight reduction computer	omega navigation device
autopilot	depth sounder

In the end, what do these devices mean? Do they make for a happier
ship? Not necessarily. Do they make sailing easier and safer? Absolutely. By
keeping track of one's course, by steering, by helping with sail handling, by
securing weather information, and more, these inventions make life at sea
simpler and less dangerous. But wait! It takes human intelligence to evaluate
these systems. To decide when to use them and when not to, and what devices
to have. A sat-nav puts out dependable fixes, but it is well known that a
sat-nav occasionally shows a "fix OK" that is definitely "not OK." If one
keeps a dead reckoning plot, a bad fix can be discarded. A thinking human
can deal with an abnormality.

In Spain I was aboard a 9.8-meter double-ender that "had everything,"
including a whole rigging assembly of antennas. I thought back to the
simplicity and freedom of a similar double-ender I had seen in Buenos Aires.
The second yacht had no engine, no radios, no clutter of antennas, no gray
boxes filled with transistors and diodes, no auxiliary charging plants, no banks
of batteries, no switch panels, no thick bundles of wires, no pulsating dials,
no fire systems, no EPIRBs, no winking red lights.

One vessel was crammed with gear that had almost bankrupted the
owner and so cluttered up his sailing life with repairs and upkeep that he
scarcely went anywhere. The second yacht had nothing at all, which I suppose
is unwise today because some of the recent inventions are small, neat, and
wonderfully helpful at times. One needs to use a little judgment about how
much of this stuff to get. One also needs to remember that the virus of

acquisition is a troublesome plague because in distant places the electronic doctors are far away. Acquisition for acquisition's sake has no merit at all.

On December 2nd we logged 156 miles at noon and had only 130 miles to go. We were getting excited, and we kept peering ahead to the west although land was still far away and it was ridiculous to even look. During the last day the winds had ranged from sixteen to twenty-two knots from the northeast, and high cumulonimbus clouds towered around us. We generally had the running rig up, but the wind often backed a little to the north. This brought the apparent wind on the starboard beam. Then we changed to the fore-and-aft rig. This changing back and forth is the most troublesome aspect of the Bermudian rig, particularly out in the ocean when there is a sea running and the vessel is yawing back and forth somewhat. I have found it best to simply alter the course fifteen or twenty degrees so the poled-out jib for the running rig isn't backwinded, or the eased leeward jib for the fore-and-aft rig isn't made useless in the wind shadow of the mainsail. In other words, we stick to one sail setting or the other, and change course a bit to favor whichever rig we have up. Then when we change, we make it a significant course alteration.

That night we rushed along with two reefs in the main, the number three jib, and the staysail. Miraculously, the old genoa made by Franz Schattauer was still intact, although we had it spread out in the cabin for a few patches. We set our watches back another hour, which made three hours since we had left Gomera, forty-four degrees of longitude to the east.

[From the log] December 3rd. 0333. Lights from a northbound ship, the first we have seen since the Canary Islands. We are racing through the night at six to seven knots with only a small jib and the deeply reefed mainsail. The wind is twenty-four knots. The moon has set, and the only light is the glimmering bluish-red point of Canopus off to port. Ahead is a black void. This racing through the night toward land is a nervy business.

0400. The ship that I have been watching appears to be westbound and is perhaps headed where we are going. There may be a faint glow of white ahead to starboard. Or I may be dreaming.

0442. The ship has pulled ahead and we are following her. I see a definite loom of lights ahead to starboard.

0520. Pole down. Jibed to port tack. Running very hard under double reefed mainsail. Changed course from 270° to 230°.

0543. Red flashing light bears 276°. No characteristic yet.

0554. The flashing five-second red light is Isle Cabrit at the south end of Martinique. Seas three to four meters and very rough. An occasional wave is twice the height of the others.

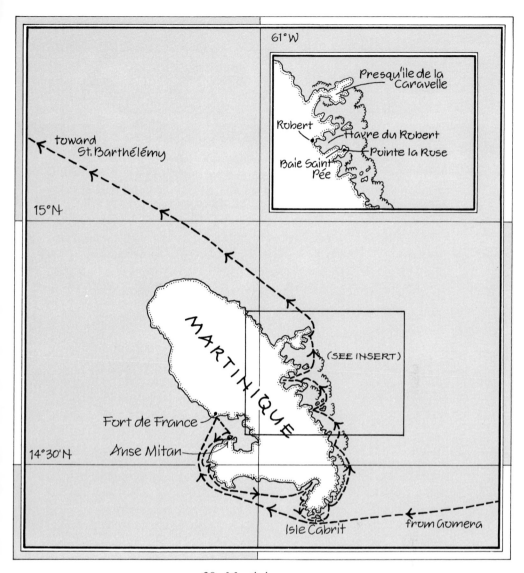

61°W

Presqu'île de la Caravelle

Robert

Havre du Robert

Pointe la Rose

Baie Saint Pée

toward St. Barthélémy

15°N

MARTINIQUE

(SEE INSERT)

Fort de France

Anse Mitan

14°30'N

Isle Cabrit

from Gomera

29. Martinique

By 0600 the dim outline of a large green island lay ahead on our starboard hand. Obviously we were in soundings because the surface water was feeling the shallow floor of the ocean. The west-going seas were upset and broken, and some of them swept across the cockpit and left flying fish behind. In a few hours, however, we were around to the western side of the island, and we raced along in smooth water. Now we saw fishermen and yachts and airplanes and villages. At 1130 we anchored off the capital of Fort-de-France between a white cruise ship and a cluster of yachts spread out along the waterfront of the big bay that was the main anchorage of the island. We had sailed 158 miles in a little less than twenty-four hours.

Martinique is a high, lush, mountainous island thirty-five miles long and twelve to fifteen miles wide. It's been a possession of France since 1635 and today has a population of 308,000. The people are mostly black and those of mixed race, with a few Arabs and East Indians. There are about 4,000 Békés—descendants of the French colonial settlers—and many French from metropolitan France. Josephine, the sultry mistress of Napoleon, came from Martinique, and a statue of her stands in one of the city parks. The island's main products are rum, sugar, and bananas; its main business is tourism, and visitors like the striking scenery, the lovely beaches, and the French atmosphere.

The city of Fort-de-France was a jumble of small stores and converted warehouses with roofs of red tile or corrugated iron that were accented here and there by dark slashes of greenery. We saw throngs of people, and the narrow streets often ran past old buildings with upper balconies and colorful balustrades. The traffic was horrendous, with small cars attacking from all angles. Even the incredibly green city parks were under siege by circling Renaults, Peugeots, and Citroëns.

Everything was jammed together, yet the town had a certain appeal, a nice sense of vitality, and the distinctive flavor of the West Indies. The young black girls were often slim and pretty; they dressed surprisingly well and always seemed to be in a hurry. We saw lots of uniformed French sailors and a variety of thin, fat, old, young, black, white, and brown-skinned people.

I wanted to see a doctor and Margaret needed new eyeglasses, so we stayed anchored along the waterfront with 60 other yachts. After a week we sailed across to Anse Mitan on the south side of Baie de Fort-de-France (there was a convenient ferry to the city), but we found 75 yachts anchored near the beaches. The weather was settled and the area was nice, but in case of a hurricane or a tropical storm, the nearby sheltering islands would have been hopelessly overcrowded with 135 or more small vessels. I preferred less populated places.

In some ways our trip around the world was finished when we returned to the Caribbean. True, we hadn't quite crossed our outbound track, but that point was at the island of St. Barthélémy, which was only 225 miles to the north-northwest. Somes Sound in Maine—where we had begun our adventure—was 1,900 miles farther north. However, it was only December; we wouldn't sail north until May because of winter storms.

We decided to stay in Martinique for a few months. I would continue my writing. But where to go? We had heard about isolated anchorages on the remote east coast. The anchorages were said to be coral-bound and dangerous. However, we knew something about coral pilotage, and we could be cautious because we were in no hurry. When we asked people about the east coast, all we got were blank stares. One highly touted guidebook was

Market, village of Robert, Martinique

superficial and dated, but we found a local guide by Jérôme Nouel (*A Cruising Guide to Martinique* with a dual text in French and English) that was excellent. The slim book was a thorough job by a patient sailor who had been to each place he discussed. Nouel didn't use secondhand information, he noted both the good and bad points, and he included a little information about the villages and countryside.

Off we went. We spent two weeks picking our way around the south and east coasts of Martinique past reefs, buoys, shoals, mangrove swamps, inlets, remote anchorages, and villages until we found ourselves in a small bay on the south side of Havre du Robert.

Baie Saint Pée was marvelously sheltered, and there were no other yachts anywhere near us. We were tucked behind two sets of reefs and the high land of Pointe la Rose. No tropical storm could touch us. The water was warm and clean, and it was easy to sail to the nearby village of Robert

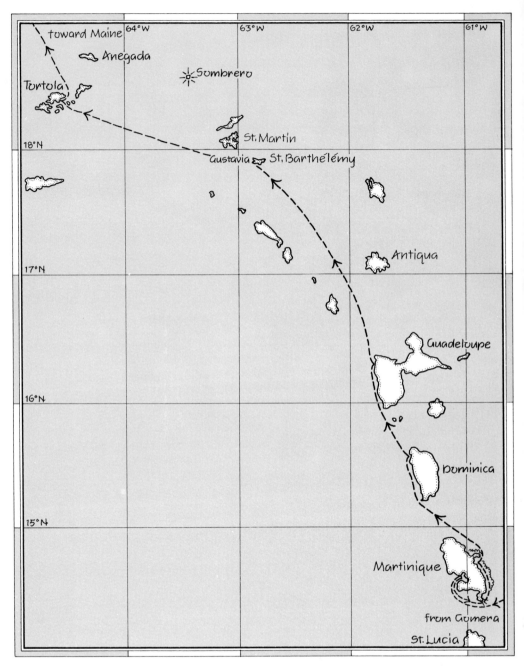

toward Maine
Anegada
Sombrero
Tortola
St. Martin
Gustavia St. Barthélémy
18°N
17°N
Antigua
Guadeloupe
16°N
Dominica
15°N
Martinique
from Gomera
St. Lucia

64°W 63°W 62°W 61°W

30. Martinique to the British Virgin Islands

every week or ten days for supplies. We were able to buy eggs from a local farmer, and we made friends with Jacques Lourd, a retired French textile engineer who lived at the head of the bay with his wife Gislaine and two small children, Gabriel and Martin. Young Martin, who was eighteen months old, was called Hurricane because his behavior was unpredictable, he was full of energy, and he smashed everything in sight.

Every morning I struggled to complete three pages of writing. Margaret did boat chores and went ashore to see her new friends. In the afternoon we swam in the turquoise water and went for walks. Sometimes we sailed to the nearby Caravelle nature reserve or visited the ruins of a sugar plantation. The months passed and my book grew. We were glad that we had gone to a well-sheltered area, because twice during the winter, tropical storms savaged the yachts and fishing boats on the western sides of the Caribbean islands. Many were wrecked and several people were drowned.

In March we sailed northward past Dominica and Guadeloupe, and on the first day of spring we slipped into the little port of Gustavia at the west end of St. Bartélémy. It was an exciting moment for us because we had just crossed the outbound track of our trip around the world. Our circumnavigation was complete!

We had written to our French friends Claude and Lisa Pittoors, who were day-chartering in their new aluminum cutter designed by Dominique Presles.

"You've tied the knot!" said Lisa when we put *Whisper* alongside the quay at Gustavia. She threw her arms around me and gave me a big kiss. I promptly pulled the cork from a bottle of Mumm's finest, and we all drank a toast to our good fortune and the delight of once again sharing a meal together.

A few days later we sailed north to Maya Cove on Tortola to visit our friend Stephen Becker, whose new novel *The Blue-Eyed Shan* was getting rave reviews. Then to Marina Key to see Fritz Seyfarth aboard *Tumbleweed*, and finally to Road Town, where we took *Whisper* out of the water for ten days to paint her topsides and bottom. We saw Joe and Bonnie Darlington, who had very capably sailed *Tortoise* across the Atlantic.

Conditions in the British Virgins had deteriorated during the three years we had been away. The roads were absolutely dreadful, we heard stories about corrupt ministers, and Tortola's public water systems were so bad that several of the yacht charter operations had set up small private desalinization units to supply their customers and shore staff.

Road Town, the capital, was the dreariest place on earth. One would think that a tiny independent country whose single industry was tourism would sweep up its trash and plant a few rows of flowering trees along the main streets and dress up the place a little with shoreside parks, benches, a museum, and reasonable restaurants. An architect, a city planner, and a

Friends from around the world—couples sailing to distant places (clockwise starting at top left): Pieter Boersma from Holland and Japanese-American Karen Toyohara on *Chenoa*; Emrys and Ingrid Thomas from Wales and Sweden on *Naim*; Joe and Bonnie Darlington from New York and Arkansas on *Tortoise*; Claude and Marie Louise Pittoors from France and St. Barthélémy on *Aveia*.

landscape expert could have done wonders. The officials should have been wearing smart uniforms, and the main harbor—wide open to southerly storms—desperately needed a breakwater and facilities for cruise ships and small vessels. The educational standards were pathetic. We heard people talk about becoming airline pilots and registered nurses when they could scarcely write their names. We met a woman in a store in Road Town who had been sold a computer so she could do "a complete cash flow analysis." However she didn't trust the computer and kept her money in a paper bag.

Toward the end of April we were almost ready to sail north. Our friend Russell Wheelock arranged for us to fill *Whisper*'s water tanks from a private catchment system, so we topped up with good water.

Russell managed one of the big yacht charter companies. He had recently been to France, where he had visited Bénéteau, a large-volume yacht builder. Russell spoke of the pressure that big builders put on suppliers like Goïot, for example, to cheapen their products. Goïot is a family concern that's been making the highest-quality hatches for a long time.

"If you put five hatches on each of four thousand yachts a year and can cut the costs by say $10 a hatch, you have made an extra $200,000," said Russell. "With business types running the plants, is there any doubt about the pressures on the suppliers? And if Goïot doesn't decrease its prices, the builder threatens to go elsewhere. It's the same for winches, masts, spinnaker poles, nuts and bolts—you name it. I find this a most discouraging trend—especially for someone like me who has to take care of these yachts on a long-term basis."

We sailed for Maine on May 1st. A few days earlier on a test sail near Great Camanoe Island, we had seen a lot of splashes in the water. "Whales!" I shouted. "Maybe a pod of small pilot whales." But when I looked again I saw that the splashes were from packages being dropped in the water from a light plane circling overhead. Each package was about two-thirds of a meter long and wrapped in brown paper and clear plastic sheeting. A high-speed motor boat appeared and began to pick up what I assumed was marijuana. We pretended not to see anything, but how can you not notice a plane dropping thirty or so small packages near you? And a boat circling to pick up the packages?

On the day we left Tortola for Maine we saw a large black whale surface three times, and hundreds of noddies and terns flitted and twisted and dived above schools of tiny fish. The birds were madly chirping, and my ears heard a thousand squeaky door hinges. For the first four days the wind above the tropical sea was from the east or southeast at twelve knots. We encountered masses of gulfweed, which promptly fouled our mileage log and made it useless. The gulfweed also collected around the wind vane water blade. Our biggest job was to push the weed away from the vane blade with the boat hook before the weight and drag of the weed tripped the blade.

[From the log] May 3rd. 1524. I have just sharpened all the galley knives and put water in the battery. I have checked around the horizon for sailors in life rafts, spouting whales, almost submerged cargo containers, and submarines. Nothing in sight.

After four days we had gone half the distance to Bermuda and were out of the trade wind and into the variables. The wind became light and fitful, the weather squally, and rain thundered down. The sailing was slow and poky. On May 6th we logged fifty-nine miles; the next day only forty, two poor days. One night I was taking down the spinnaker pole when the mast end lift line slipped out of the clam cleat. The pole suddenly fell, and I got a great crack on the head. This sailing was positively dangerous! What we needed was a positive line jammer or an endless line arrangement on a special winch.

Every day two or three tropicbirds circled us at their usual high speed while they chattered noisily. At night we saw satellites moving from south to north. When the sky was clear at night I tried to learn one or two new stars. The strangest star name was Zubenelgenubi (near Scorpius in Libra), a six-syllable mouthful that sounded more like an Italian dessert (zabaglione) than a navigational star. S-shaped Scorpio—in the southern sky—was wonderfully bright and clear with yellowish Antares in the middle and Shaula at the bottom.

On May 8th the sat-nav began to exhibit Chinese-type characters, so we got out a sextant and went back to celestial navigation. The next day we crossed thirty degrees north latitude and had 860 miles to go to Mt. Desert rock off the Maine coast. The weather was cooler, a pair of long trousers felt good, and stockings, long-sleeved shirts, and sweaters began to appear for the night watches.

On May 10th we passed the latitude of Bermuda. The winds were steady, mostly from the east, and at noon we showed 128 miles. The weather patterns are fairly predictable north of Bermuda, and we knew we would probably get a gale or two before we reached Maine. Weather systems from the Great Lakes region in the United States regularly move eastward. This means gale force winds from the southwest, west, north, and finally northeast as a low with a counterclockwise flow passes north of a ship. Since the Gulf Stream runs to the north or northeast at one or two knots or more, the seas get nasty when gale force winds blow against this river in the ocean.

Sure enough, on May 13th and 14th, the barometer dropped from 1022 to 1010 millibars. The winds went from southwest at eighteen knots to

31. Mt. Desert Rock to Somesville

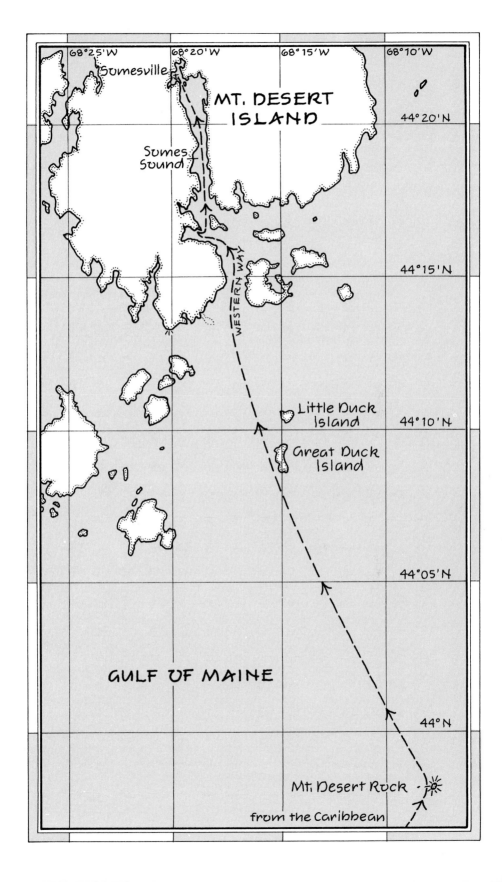

northeast at forty-two knots, and the winds across the Gulf Stream kicked up a hard sea. We went through the usual sail drill and finally stopped to wait. We knew we only had to play for time until the weather improved. "Hurry up, wind. Blow yourself out!" I shouted. "I'm tired of this."

While the wind blew its hardest, the barometer climbed steadily, and we hoped that the depression was moving to the east. By 0700 on May 15th the wind had veered to the east-northeast and dropped to twenty-two knots.

[From my journal] May 15th. 0637. Under way again after being hove-to since 1000 yesterday (twenty hours) in a nasty, forty-knot northeast gale with tough-looking seas. Although the motion was violent, I got a lot of sleep and feel quite rested. We had a scratch dinner of tinned chicken and the last of a loaf of bread plus lots of water. I am becoming a big water drinker and it's sip, sip, sip all day long. Our course now is north-northwest at six knots, not quite up to the mark but at least in the right direction toward Maine. The sky is clear and the sun bright.

We're obviously away from the warm Gulf Stream and into the Labrador current because the water is very cold. My hands got stiff and numb when I put up the jib at 0600. We hove-to yesterday under the backed staysail and deeply reefed main. It seems a miracle that these old sails stood up to yet another gale.

Now we crossed Georges Bank and saw fishing boats and later two big ships. I tried to get a shot of the moon for latitude, but it was only an overhead sliver that was hard to see with my eye, much less the sextant. For the first time in years we fired up the big oil stove and let it run. Its warmth was wonderful.

In the earliest hour of May 16th we were in the Gulf of Maine. Six fishing boats were around us. The sky was full of stars. "I may be dreaming," I wrote in the log at 0059, "but I think I can see the loom of lights— Boston?—very faintly to the west. Can we be approaching America? Is the end of the voyage in sight?"

At 0802 we heard the two sharp cracks of the sonic boom from the morning Concorde flight from London. Margaret rattled around in the galley, and soon the cabin was filled with the fine smell of bread baking. All day we ran before a steady southwest breeze of seventeen knots and watched fishing draggers at work. By early evening the barometer had begun to plunge, and by midnight it was down to 1007 millibars. Would we make it to the Maine coast before the next gale? By now both the radio direction finder and the sat-nav had stopped breathing.

At 0234 on May 19th (barometer 1005) I estimated that we were thirty-five miles from Mt. Desert Rock and were running toward a lee shore in poor visibility. However, I had a reasonable dead reckoning plot, and we had a good echo sounder whose readings we compared with our coastal charts. At 0815 on a dark and rainy morning I saw a light flashing every fifteen seconds at 340°, and I heard two powerful blasts of a fog signal every thirty seconds. Horray! We had found Mt. Desert Rock and the Maine coast.

By noon we had Great Duck Island abeam. Two hours later we slipped through Western Way Channel into the waters of Mt. Desert Island. The sky was clearing, and we headed north into Somes Sound. The air was cool and crisp, and the mountains of Mt. Desert Island rose on each side of us. The place looked lovely in its spring finery, and we admired the sleek spruce trees that crowded down to the water.

As we sailed along in light airs at low water we could smell the mussel beds on the shores and the aroma of iodine from the rocks. The resiny smell of the forest drifted out to us. Sailors call all these things the smell of the sea, but they really translate to the smell of the land, a friendly smell because it means home, a harbor, family, friends, and safe and familiar places.

We dropped *Whisper*'s anchor at the head of the sound at Somesville in the same spot we had left forty-six months and 30,786 miles earlier. We had visited twenty countries and anchored 269 times.

Now the long voyage was over. The music of five oceans was behind us. I took a cup of coffee on deck and sat in the cockpit and thought of our trip around the world. My mind reflected on all the people we had met and the high spots among the wonderful places we had seen:

> The tiny village on Raroïa in the Tuamotus
> Tahiti (the wonderful greenness, the friendly people, the music)
> Bali (the incredible rice fields and the tiny, graceful women)
> Keeling-Cocos (the beach at Direction Island)
> Coral pilotage during strong winds in the Red Sea
> The ancient anchorages in Turkey (those wonderful Greek walls at Loryma)
> Seville (the dancing and the guitar playing)
> The pleasant Rio Guadiana in Portugal

I thought of the different anchorages, the meals with friends, the parties, the jokes, the walks along the water on so many seafronts, the ocean birds, the dolphins. I thought of our relief at getting off the terrible reef at Bramble Cay. I thought of our blessed arrival at Suez after the heat and headwinds of the Red Sea. I thought of my struggles with the languages. I thought of the officials (the Australians and their paperwork, the duplicity of the Turkish customs men). I thought of the Egyptians who were so gross in their human dealings to be almost comical. I thought of the wonderful sea passages across the Pacific and Indian oceans, the clouds, the blazing sunsets, the stars at night.

The people and experiences and sea passages all tumbled together into a mélange of living at the peak. It was a miraculous adventure that could never be taken from us.

Notes

. . . .

1. Clements R. Markham, *The Sea Fathers* (London: Cassell, 1884), pp. 173–174.

2. Harry Pigeon, *"Islander* Does It Again," *Yachting* (December 1938): 50.

3. Bent Danielsson, *The Happy Island* (London: Allen and Unwin, 1952). A charming book about life and problems on a remote atoll in the Tuamotus.

4. Harry Pigeon, *Around the World Singlehanded* (London: Rupert Hart-Davis, 1960), pp. 121–122.

5. Douglas Lockwood, *I, the Aboriginal* (Sydney: Seal Books, Rigby, 1962). An enthralling, well-written look into the mind, customs, and culture of the aborigine. If you think aborigines are simply wild savages who are stupid and dumb, you should read this book.

6. William Dampier, *A New Voyage Around the World* (New York: Dover, 1968), p. 317.

7. Eric Hiscock, "Christmas, Cocos, and Mauritius," *Yachting World* (June 1975): 76–79.

8. Peter Tangvald, "Safe and Unsafe Cruising Areas," *The Spray* (July-December 1979): 62–63. *The Spray* is published by the Slocum Society, whose address is Box 176, Port Townsend, Washington 98368.

9. Jean-Pierre Greenlaw, *The Coral Buildings of Suakin* (London: Oriel Press, 1976). Suakin must have been an intriguing place in its heyday, as this sympathetic book suggests. "It takes more than putting building materials together to create architecture, but no one can explain exactly what that more is, except that architecture has a spirit and building has not." The drawing of old Suakin on page 000 is from this book and is used by courtesy of Associated Book Publishers (U.K.) Ltd.

10. H. M. Denham, *Southern Turkey, the Levant, and Cyprus* (New York: Norton, 1973), p. 38. Captain Denham's guides are somewhat dated, but authoritative, concise, and nicely illustrated and printed.

11. A good account of Phaselis is in Gören Schildt, *The Sea of Icarus* (London: Staples Press, 1959), pp. 197–207. Also see G. Peabody Gardner, *Turkish Delight* (Salem: Peabody Museum, 1964), an account of a gentleman's sailing trip along the Turkish coast.

12. George F. Bass, *Archaeology Beneath the Sea* (New York: Walker, 1975), and *A History of Seafaring* (New York: Walker, 1972), pp. 23–24.

13. W. E. Benyon-Tinker, *Dust Upon the Sea* (London: Hodder and Stoughton, 1947); Schildt, *The Sea of Icarus*, pp. 175–176; Denham, *Southern Turkey*, pp. 22–23; Lawrence Durrell, *The Greek Islands* (New York: Viking, 1978), pp. 146–148; Adrian Seligman, *No Stars to*

Guide (London: Hodder and Stoughton, 1947). The confused events between the Italians, Germans, Greeks, and English in the Dodecanese Islands during World War II are extremely hard to sort out. Even the Russians ran a few small convoys from the Dardanelles to Syria. I have been unable to find a summary account. Poor Kastellorizon seems to have gotten the worst from all sides, although the place declined steadily after 1912. There are persistent stories on the island that the British were guilty of looting during World War II (goods from the old captains' houses were said to have been sold in Nicosia, Beirut, and Alexandria), but these reports need verification and sorting out. A modern history of the island including what happened in the Dodecanese during World War II would be a good project for a patient researcher.

14. Schildt, *The Sea of Icarus,* pp. 163–164.

15. A useful but starchy guide to the islands is Stuart Rossiter, *Blue Guide Greece* (New York: Norton, 1981), p. 663 and elsewhere. For a quick general background, see Alexander Eliot, *Greece* (New York: Time, 1963). For general small-boat pilotage, see H. M. Denham, *The Aegean* (London: John Murray, 1983). When Captain Denham warns about tourists and crowding, take heed and go somewhere else!

16. S. W. C. Pack, *The Battle of Matapan* (London: B.T. Batsford, 1961); Henri Michel, *The Second World War* (New York: Praeger, 1968), 1:182–194. A superb, clear-headed, two-book set about all aspects of World War II, with particularly good summaries and writing.

17. H. M. Denham, *The Tyrrhenian Sea* (New York: Norton, 1969), pp. 92–93.

18. G. T. Garratt, *Gibraltar and the Mediterranean* (New York: Coward-McCann, 1939), p. 174.

19. Eric Hiscock, *Beyond the West Horizon* (New York: Oxford University Press, 1963), pp. 181–183.

Index